Notes from Woketopia

James Macpherson

Connor Court Publishing

Published in 2021 by Connor Court Publishing Pty Ltd

Copyright © James Macpherson

All rights reserved. No part of this book may be reproduced or transmitted in any form or by any means, electronic or mechanical, including photo copying, recording or by any information storage and retrieval system, without prior permission in writing from the publisher.

Connor Court Publishing Pty Ltd
PO Box 7257
Redland Bay QLD 4165
sales@connorcourt.com
www.connorcourt.com
Phone 0497-900-685

Printed in Australia

ISBN: 9781922449863

Front cover design: Ian James

For my father

Colin F. Gibbons

You are my hero. I owe you a great deal.

(The term "great deal" is figurative and does not relate to any royalties from the sale of this book)

CONTENTS

	INTRODUCTION	7
1	FAITH AND POLITICS IN WOKETOPIA	11
2	LGBTQI'S WOKE DICTUMS	51
3	FREEDOM OF SPEECH IN WOKETOPIA	91
4	WOKETARDS EVERYWHERE	107
5	EVERYTHING IS RACIST IN WOKETOPIA	155
6	LIFE IS CHEAP IN WOKETOPIA	209
7	CELEBRITIY WOKETARDS	221
8	ISLAM AND ITS WOKE ALLIES	243
9	GENDER EQUALITY IN WOKETOPIA	251
10	WOKE GOES THE ENVIRONMENT	269
11	POLITICIANS BEHAVING WOKELY	289

INTRODUCTION

In June 2021, a female patron of Korea Town's Wi Spa in Los Angeles was shocked to find a naked man in the changeroom.

She promptly complained to staff but was told the man had a right to be there because he identified as a woman.

In a video of the altercation that went viral, the female customer can be heard protesting: "I see a dick! It lets me know he's a man! He is a man. He is not a female!"

Her argument is well thought-out and eloquently presented. Allow me to summarise it for you:

> *Men have dicks.*
> *A person in the female change room has a dick.*
> *Therefore, there is a man in the female change room.*

But staff at the Wi Spa were unimpressed and unmoved. They continued to insist that they could not ask the person with the dick to leave the female locker room since that would be discrimination and therefore, unlawful.

The offended woman continued arguing: "It's OK for a man to go into the women's section, show his penis around the other women – young little girls, underage? ... Wi Spa condones that – is that what you're saying?"

The video shows a male patron of the spa approaching the woman and asking if she was talking about a transgendered person.

"There's no such thing as transgender. He has a dick," she retorted.

The Christian Post reported this incident as "highlighting the brewing tension between single-sex spaces and gender identity non-discrimination policies".

They should consider renaming their publication The Christian sit on the fence Post.

The incident in the Wi Spa does not "highlight tension between single-sex spaces and gender identity non-discrimination policies".

Rather, it highlights the brewing tension between sanity and insanity; between normal people trying to go about their lives and the weirdly abnormal people who have turned the whole world into a woke spa where the only thing being massaged is your brain.

Normal people understand that a man walking around with his penis hanging out is a man.

Normal people also understand that even though a man might wish to be a woman, his wishes do not change the physical reality of his situation, which is that he is a man … with his penis hanging out … in the women's change room.

So why did a video of a woman doing nothing more than observing reality – and reacting as a normal person would react – go viral? Why did so many people find it fascinating to watch?

Could it be that we have now reached a point in Western culture where simply being normal is seen as an act of bravery, even heroism?

Have we now arrived at a stage in history where courage is required simply to say what normal people would say and to react the way normal people would react in any given situation?

It should not require courage to explain that men have a penis. But so many normal people have gone quiet – hiding their common sense and keeping their normality to themselves – that normal people are now regarded as a curiosity.

Where once history was decided by a clash of religions or by a clash of political ideologies, the history of our age has come down to a clash between the normal and the abnormal; the sane and the insane.

This collection of essays – based on news items during 2020 and 2021 – lays bare the insanity of woke culture and the sheer absurdity of identity politics.

The only way to prevent Australia being transformed into a dangerous Woketopia is for normal people to point out the obvious, to laugh at the ridiculous and to speak the truth.

All that is required is courage, and a keen sense of humor.

1

FAITH AND POLITICS IN WOKETOPIA

WHAT ON EARTH IS WRONG WITH HAVING A CHRISTIAN IN THE LODGE?

From the moment Pentecostal church-going Scott Morrison became Prime Minister his Christian faith has been the subject of hot debate.

His expectation-defying re-election 12 months ago only intensified matters.

Commentators on the ABC's *The Drum* wondered if Morrison might try to turn Australia into a theocracy, forcing everybody to memorize the Bible and speak in tongues.

Twitter lit up with people worried that Australia's most famous church, Hillsong, might suddenly control the whole country, swamping the nation with positivity and catchy tunes.

That the church Scott Morrison and his family attend is not part of Hillsong was completely missed on social media where the comfort of opinion is rarely, if ever, disrupted by the discomfort of thought.

Radio National said that Morrison attended a "US-style church" though neither Horizon Church nor the Australian Christian Churches – a group of more than 1000 Pentecostal churches throughout Australia with which it is affiliated – has any connection to America.

At the *Guardian*, social commentator Van Badham, warned ominously that our new Prime Minister's church believed that God wants people to prosper. She failed to explain how a PM who believed that *poverty* was God's intent for people might improve the nation.

Comedians on the ABC mocked the Prime Minister for being tough on border control when Jesus had encouraged us to "imagine there's no countries".

Or was that John Lennon?

Whatever.

The ABC will no doubt call Morrison a hypocrite if he doesn't "welcome the stranger" like Jesus taught and, in the next breath, they will call him a hater if he defines marriage like Jesus did.

The ABC like their Christians as they like their gays, indigenous people and women – strictly left-leaning.

So long as you believe that Jesus was a kind of pot-smoking vegan, more concerned about renewable energy than heaven and hell; more interested in interfaith dialogue than in objective truth; more committed to preaching social justice than to advocating personal responsibility, then your Christian faith is to be lauded.

But if the mainstream media suspect that you believe Jesus was God in the flesh dying for the sins of mankind, your Christian faith is to be loathed.

This aversion towards religious people who actually believe their religion – as opposed to those whose faith is really just secularism under a cloak of respectable spirituality – began the moment Islamic jihadists crashed passenger jets into the World Trade Centre. Suddenly religion was seen as the greatest threat to social cohesion.

Such a view is not without merit. Religion encourages adherents to believe their view of the world is right and, by implication, that all opposing views are wrong.

Such exclusive claims make it easy to disparage the "other". If others are wrong about the big issues of life, then it makes sense to separate yourself from them. And once we have separated ourselves from the "other", it is easy to stereotype them and then to oppress them and ultimately to commit violence against them.

What makes religion particularly dangerous is that we may do all of this with a sense of self-righteousness. If we are on the side of God, then who are *they* to tell me I ought not oppress them? Who are they at all?

For a while we believed the problem of religion would fade as economic prosperity and technological advancement made belief in God redundant. Who needs God when Google is the source of all knowledge and a meeting of bureaucrats in Paris can decide global temperatures?

But the world is becoming more religious, not less. Even in the Western world, where the number of professing Christians is declining, we are importing religion via our immigration programs.

Unable to stamp out religion, we have decided to neuter it by insisting that, whilst people can believe whatever they want, they must leave their religious beliefs in their church. This is why we now hear politicians advocating "freedom of worship" rather than "freedom of religion" – a subtle but profound shift.

If we can reduce religion to an hour-long ceremony held once a week in a dedicated building, then we can quarantine it. Our preferred secular utopia will be free to advance without challenge, so the thinking goes.

But religion properly understood is much more than a ceremony; it is a set of answers to the big questions of life. A person's religion tells them who they are (identity); why they are here (meaning); how they may discern right from wrong (morality) and their ultimate fate (destiny).

Everyone – whether we spend our weekend worshipping in church or swiping right on Tinder – has a view about identity, meaning, purpose and destiny. The insistence that "religion must be kept out of the public square" is really just a polite way of saying "keep your antiquated, traditional worldview to yourself whilst we impose our modern, enlightened worldview on you".

This was illustrated perfectly when Australian rugby player Israel Folau was condemned for saying homosexuals would go to hell unless they asked God's forgiveness.

Folau was told his views on the afterlife were wrong and that he ought not to have voiced them. But, in opposing Folau, his opponents were themselves making definitive statements about what is true and what is moral.

To pretend that only 'religious' people make exclusive truth claims is disingenuous. Every person, consciously or not, operates by a worldview that they believe to be true. Folau's crime was not to have expressed a religious view but to have expressed a different view to his progressive betters.

It is foolish to insist that people must not make exclusive truth claims since the very insistence itself is an exclusive truth claim. Those wanting to banish religion from the public square because religion encourages exclusive views are guilty of the very thing they deplore and are every bit as dangerous.

Since we all hold worldviews we believe to be true, the question is not how do we get rid of those who claim to be the holders of truth but, rather, which set of exclusive truth claims are most likely to create a harmonious society?

History shows that the exclusive claims of Christianity, now being pushed from the public square, are actually those most suited to creating the inclusive society we desire.

A 2018 report by independent human rights watchdog Freedom House rated nations according to the individual liberties citizens enjoyed. Of the 20 freest nations, 19 had or continued to enjoy Christian majorities.

This is not an accident. Nor is it an accident that the cry for inclusivity is rising, not from Islamic or Eastern nations, but from the West which grew out of a Christian tradition. The point being missed in the debate about inclusivity is that Christianity's claims are not the obstacle to inclusion but the instigator of it.

Christianity's foremost claim is that Jesus Christ alone is divine. We might expect this view to make Christians dangerous. The idea that their founder – unlike Muhammad, or Buddha or Krishna – is God, could lead to arrogance and the oppression of those who think differently. But if Jesus is God in flesh, what does the ultimate human look like?

The ultimate person, according to the Christian faith, looks like a man who blesses those who curse him, forgives those who injure him and lays down his life for those who oppose him.

The claim that Jesus is God should produce, in all who believe, a love for and willingness to serve all who do not.

The second bold claim of Christianity is that men cannot earn God's favour; they must instead receive forgiveness as a gift.

This should produce a humility in believers that leads them to expect those who do not believe as they do may well in fact be better people than they are. If the only prerequisite for becoming a Christian is admitting you are not a good person, there is no room for moral vanity or virtue signalling.

The problem of religion is not solved by eradicating religion since that only serves to replace one set of exclusive beliefs with another. And if the twentieth century taught us anything, it was that godless regimes are even more oppressive than the religious ones they replace.

What is exclusive about Christianity makes it the idea most likely to produce an inclusive society.

Having a practising Christian in the Lodge might actually be cause for hope rather than fear.

POLITICIANS MUST BE PROTECTED FROM JESUS' WORDS

THE Greens are right to demand that the long-standing tradition of opening each day of Federal Parliament with The Lord's Prayer be abolished.

The words of Jesus are dangerous, and politicians must be protected from hearing them lest they startle the entire country by governing with wisdom and humility.

For those unfamiliar with the prayer that Greens' senators describe as "insulting" and "jarring", let me explain the 10 nation-destabilising ideas from which our leaders must be insulated.

"Our Father Who art in heaven ..." is a shocking acknowledgment that the highest office bearers in the land might not actually be the highest office bearers in the universe. Should politicians realise this, they may start acting with humility and become completely unrecognisable to their own electorates.

"Hallowed be Thy name ..." is the dangerous admission that we must live for something bigger than our own name or self-aggrandisement. This could inadvertently lead to politicians no longer naming pet policies after themselves. A highly undesirable outcome.

"Thy Kingdom come, Thy will be done on earth as it is in heaven ..." could cause politicians to consider if perhaps they ought act according to noble convictions rather than simple convenience. This would throw the public service into total confusion.

"Give us this day our daily bread..." is just plain offensive. If there is a God, He (or she) has not been distributing the bread according to the Greens' favourite slogans – "equality" & "fairness". If He (or she) was fair, the Greens would have more bread than the people the Greens don't like, such as those actually making the bread.

"Forgives us our sins ..." is a self-esteem sapping admission that none of us is perfect. Even senators are beset by the flaws of human nature and are therefore prone to mistakes. This is a dangerous idea that

our MPs should never, ever, under any circumstances be allowed to contemplate lest they stop thinking of themselves as our betters.

"As we forgive those who sin against us ..." is a devilish promise to respect the common humanity of those with whom we disagree rather than simply demonising them. The Greens are right to insist MPs must never hear this, lest civility break out in Parliament and those sitting in the public gallery think they are in the wrong building.

"Lead us not into temptation ..." is the unflattering idea that we are all prone to wander off on tangents. Were politicians to think about this they might start acting with caution rather than haste. And then we wouldn't have Pink Batts or Cash for Clunkers or the NBN.

"But deliver us from evil..." is the foolishly outdated idea that evil actually exists when, in fact, we know the problem is really structural issues that can be fixed by constant Government interference in the affairs of free men.

"For Thine is the kingdom, the power and the glory ..." is an insidious idea that may lead politicians to wonder if perhaps building monuments to themselves is mere vanity. We don't want MPs thinking there is a cause greater than their own name or political stripe, lest they begin to work together for a greater good; and then where would we be?

"Forever and ever, Amen..." is the lie that we will soon be gone but that the decisions we make will echo on in the lives of our children's children. Should MPs have to hear such words they might start thinking beyond the 24-hour news cycle.

God, er, Greens forbid!

THE GREENS DON'T HAVE A PRAYER OF GETTING AWAY WITH THEIR HYPOCRISY ON CHURCH NUMBERS

NOTHING makes Leftist heads explode like Christian leaders who venture an opinion outside the four walls of the church.

So when Hillsong Pastor Brian Houston dared to question government restrictions on church services, NSW Greens MP David Shoebridge was immediately triggered.

"Brian Houston from Hillsong is once again trying to pressure the Liberal Party to deliver for his church. This time by easing coronavirus restrictions to allow hundreds to repeatedly mingle together in his churches. Let's hope science trumps faith," the self-described social justice activist tweeted.

This is the same Greens MP who ignored health advice and marched through the streets of Sydney with 20,000 Black Lives Matter protesters in June.

This is the same Greens MP who ignored health advice and visited a remote indigenous community just two days after the BLM march, much to the dismay of indigenous leaders who claimed he was putting lives in danger.

And this is the same Greens MP who said not a word when, in July, the Auburn Gallipoli Mosque in Sydney's west was given permission to host 400 worshippers.

But when the leader of Australia's largest Christian Church suggested health restrictions might be eased for churches, the Greens MP was suddenly more concerned about public health than Florence Nightingale.

"Let's hope science trumps faith," he tweeted, to the delight of his followers who loved that he had created a false dichotomy between science and faith whilst managing to get "trump" in there as an added bonus.

But Mr Shoebridge didn't explain the "science" that says it is safe from December 1 for 300 guests to attend a wedding but not a church service.

Mr Shoebridge didn't explain the "science" that says it is safe for Hillsong's 4000 seat auditorium to have 100 people but not 200 or 500 or 1500 people.

Nor did he explain the "science" behind rules in NSW that allow entertainment venues, including theatres and concert halls, to have a capacity of 50% while churches must have no more than 100 people no matter the size of the building.

Mr Shoebridge didn't explain the science because he couldn't. There is no science behind these arbitrary rules.

At best, Christian churches have been forgotten by politicians seeking to ease Covid-19 restrictions. At worst, Christian churches are being discriminated against.

And Mr Shoebridge's assertion that churches wanting to open were acting unreasonably because, you know, "faith", was nothing but a cheap caricature of the Christian community.

Pastor Houston said on Monday: "Churches can be trusted to abide by the rules, as we have done every step of the way. We are all committed to keeping people safe, but it seems churches are not even being considered for steadily relaxing restrictions."

Unlike the BLM protests that Mr Shoebridge supported, Pastor Houston said he was committed to obeying the law.

And unlike the Auburn Gallipoli Mosque that Mr Shoebridge supported, Hillsong was not asking for any special exemption from restrictions.

Pastor Houston was simply asking to be held to the same standard as other venues that host gatherings.

This wasn't about "faith" so much as fairness; fairness that the Greens love to go on and on about – unless it's got to do with the church.

Anglican Archbishop of Sydney Glen Davies said yesterday he had discussed "inconsistencies" in Covid-19 rules with the NSW Health Minister and expected the government to announce revised guidelines for churches today.

But Mr Shoebridge complained "Brian Houston from Hillsong is once again trying to pressure the Liberal Party to deliver for his church", as if a citizen asking his elected representatives for help was somehow sinister.

Perhaps Mr Shoebridge considers Christians to be second class citizens.

Or maybe Mr Shoebridge is just miffed that a bunch of happy clappers in Sydney's west attract twice as many people every Sunday as the Greens have members nationally.

IT'S HELL FOR EVERYBODY WHEN POLITICIANS PLAY THEOLOGIANS

A STRANGE thing happened at the last Federal election. Labor politicians demanded to know whether or not the PM believed gays would go to hell.

Israel Folau, a deeply religious and outspoken footballer, had posted on Instagram that homosexuals (among others) would go to hell unless they repented. Labor wanted to know if our deeply religious Prime Minister agreed.

But Labor did not go far enough. It is all very well for the political class to establish that gays are safe from eternal damnation, but what about the rest of us? We, too, need our political leaders to provide assurances about the afterlife.

That Prime Minister Scott Morrison was forced to clarify that he does not think homosexuals would end up in hell must have come as a relief to millions of Australians who believe Canberra has the power to control not only the climate, but eternal life.

There is no need to worry about missing out on heaven if you are homosexual because politicians on both sides of the House agreed at the last election, you are heaven-bound, and so that settles it.

No need for Saint Peter to stand at the Pearly Gates checking the Book of Life for your name – just mention that Sco-Mo and Bill Shorten agreed you're okay, and you'll be waved straight into Paradise.

But while gays are resting easy, secure in the knowledge that they are going up rather than going down, the rest of us are trapped in a kind of political purgatory.

Consider how Israel Folau must now be feeling.

If those running for Pope, er, Prime Minister, have decreed that gays do not go to hell, what of people like Folau, who disagree with homosexuality? Surely they are now in danger of hell themselves? Or do they just lose multi-million-dollar contracts in this life? It would be helpful if Labor, or even the Australian Rugby Union, could provide some theological advice here.

The then Deputy Opposition leader Tanya Plibersek insisted that the question of whether or not gays would go to hell was really a question of whether or not politicians supported "equality".

But this only served to add to the confusion surrounding Labor policy on eternal damnation. Did the Deputy Leader mean that Labor supported equality of opportunity or equality of outcome?

Would a Labor Government encourage a merit-based entry system or were they advocating quotas for heaven, to ensure that Paradise is representative of the general population?

Senior Labor frontbencher, now Deputy Leader, Richard Marles hinted at more detail when he told Sky News that: "This is a question about whether public figures ... go out there and make the point that a group of law-abiding Australians are going to go to hell."

Keen political observers noted that, according to the senior Labor MP, it seemed law-abiding Australians would not suffer the flames of eternal torment. But others argued more policy work was needed.

If "law abiding citizens" were not destined for hell, what of law-breaking citizens? Suddenly mums and dads who had received traffic infringements were desperate to know whether or not, under a Labor Government, their political betters would believe them headed for hell.

MPs were asked to clarify whether exceeding the speed limit would cost you just a few points in this life, or all of your points in the next. And if, Canberra-forbid, it was the latter, was there a suspension period that could be served before being reinstated to the Good Place?

For less well behaving Australians, Mr Marles musings on who would and would not go to hell raised serious questions that have still not been answered.

If one breaks the law, but serves time in the Australian prison system, does that punishment cancel out any eternal consequence? Surely it would be unfair to be punished twice for the same crime. Could Labor give assurances this will not be the case?

Mr Marles Sky interview hinted there might be another get-out-of-jail-free card that, should Labor ever ascend on high, we can play in the afterlife. He was adamant that gays would not go to hell because they were law-abiding "Australians".

It is a relief to know that Australian citizenship is recognised in heaven and that an Australian passport gets you more than just free entry into New Zealand.

But what of other nationals? Do non-Australian passport holders automatically qualify for celestial citizenship? Would Labor support a turn-back policy for those who jump the queue and try to enter heaven without the appropriate visa?

Whilst Mr Marles would not be drawn on such questions, he said that the Prime Minister's views were "out of kilter" with most Australians. This raised the awful prospect that Labor might push for a plebiscite to decide, by popular vote, who was and who was not fit for heaven.

Better that our politicians remain focused on this life and leave the next one to be debated by theologians.

AMENSTY'S STRANGE IDEA OF FAIRNESS

AMNESTY International insists that Christian schools should be stripped of their right to prefer staff who practice Christianity because this is discrimination, and discrimination is not fair.

At present, religious schools are allowed to preference job applicants who subscribe to their religious values. But Amnesty argues that this is not fair to applicants with different values.

If people with values contrary to Christianity are unable to work at Christian schools then they will be left with no alternative but to seek work at one of several thousand public schools where their views are uncontroversial, and this would not be fair.

The bigger problem, though, is that if Christian schools only employ staff who agree with Christian values then they will be easily able to retain their Christian character.

This means Christian parents may enroll their children at Christian schools while non-Christian parents will typically choose to enroll their children elsewhere. And this, for reasons unknown, is not fair.

In order to create fairness, Amnesty insists that the Government should force Christian schools to employ people who don't agree with their Christian ethos. In this way, the school's entire rationale for existence is undermined and parents won't see any point enrolling their children at all.

Religious schools will close down leaving only non-religious schools. And then things will be fair.

But Amnesty has yet other ways of enforcing 'fairness'.

Advocacy program manager Ms Emma Bull said public funding from a secular government should not be used to "contribute to discrimination", because discrimination is not fair.

To eliminate discrimination, which is not fair, Ms Bull called on the Government to actively discriminate against religious schools so that funding could be distributed fairly.

If Christian schools insisted on employing only Christian staff - which is not fair because it is discrimination – then parents at those schools should receive nothing in return for their taxes. And this will make things fair.

Advocates of religious freedom, such as Professor of Law at Sydney University, Patrick Parkinson, insist that what Amnesty disparage as "freedom to discriminate" is really the "freedom to select".

He argues that religious groups should have the freedom to select the staff they want, rather than being dictated to by Government.

This would create a situation in which religious schools could maintain their religious charter and live or die based on how many people wanted their services.

While this idea seems to have merit, it robs unelected, unrepresentative Left-leaning groups like Amnesty of the chance to dictate how free people conduct themselves.

In order to stop Christian schools discriminating in the name of Christian values, Amnesty propose to discriminate in the name of secular values. And this, apparently, is fair.

HEAVEN HELP US IF AOC IS THE FUTURE OF THE CHURCH

PRO abortion, pro gay marriage, pro trans ideology Congresswoman Alexandria Ocasio-Cortez is the future of the Catholic Church, according to America's national Catholic newspaper, because "kind".

The *National Catholic Reporter* made the claim this week after AOC gave a speech calling for politicians to treat each other with dignity and respect.

The speech was a rebuke to Republican Congressman Ted Yoho who had allegedly called her a "f-ing bitch". Congressman Yoho denied he said that.

AOC told Congress it was time to treat "women with dignity, respect and civility".

Under a headline "AOC is the Future of the Catholic Church" NCR executive editor Heidi Schlumpf wrote: "Rep Alexandria Ocasio-Cortez repeatedly railed against the 'dehumanizing' of others and instead called for treating people with dignity and respect. These are themes often repeated by Pope Francis.

"If there is to be a future for the Catholic Church in the United States – it must resemble Ocasio-Cortez in her passion for justice and human dignity, and in her courage and integrity, even in the face of vulgar attacks."

The National Catholic Reporter apparently doesn't mind that AOC supports abortion, which is contrary to the Bible's teaching on the sanctity of human life, because "kind".

The National Catholic Reporter doesn't seem to care that AOC supports homosexual marriage, which is contrary to the Bible's teaching on marriage, because "kind".

The National Catholic Reporter doesn't worry that AOC supports trans gender ideology, which is contrary to the Bible's teaching on human sexuality, because "kind".

The National Catholic Reporter doesn't raise an eyebrow at AOC's Marxist leanings, which always result in some form of oppression of the church, because "kind".

I'm going to go out on a limb here and bet that 99% of the world's population believe others should be treated with dignity and respect. So maybe we are all the future of the Catholic Church!

If Jesus arrived in New York today, rather than in Bethlehem 2000 years ago, the *National Catholic Reporter (NCR)* would insist he turn up as a non-binary bishop driving around in a hybrid Toyota Prius with a "Coexist" sticker on His way to an interfaith dialogue with a Wiccan and a couple of imams where he would tell everyone "Don't mind me, I'm just here to cheer for you as you discover your truth".

The NCR have reduced Christianity to "be kind" which sounds noble and makes for a great Hallmark greeting card. But jettisoning all doctrine in exchange for a mushy "just love everyone" harms rather than helps, as G.K. Chesterton pointed out in his book *Orthodoxy*.

"The modern world is not evil; in some ways the modern world is far too good. It is full of wild and wasted virtues," Chesterton wrote.

> When a religious scheme is shattered (as Christianity was shattered at the Reformation), it is not merely the vices that are let loose. The vices are, indeed, let loose, and they wander and do damage.
>
> But the virtues are let loose also; and the virtues wander more wildly, and the virtues do more terrible damage.
>
> The modern world is full of the old Christian virtues gone mad. The virtues have gone mad because they have been isolated from each other and are wandering alone. Thus some scientists care for truth; and their truth is pitiless. Thus some humanitarians only care for pity; and their pity (I am sorry to say) is often untruthful.

This is exactly the trap the NCR seem to have fallen into. While the

Bible says that "God is love", our secular societies have reversed that statement and declared that love is god. It's a clever sleight of hand that allows one to crucify God whilst simultaneously claiming the higher ground.

It is true that Jesus said we must love our neighbour. But it must not be forgotten that He said this was the *second* most important duty of man. The first duty of a man was to love God. And there is good reason for this.

If people are made in the likeness of God, as the Bible teaches, then we cannot properly know each other unless we first know God.

It's in understanding God that we rightly understand one another so as to be able to love our neighbour well.

Replacing the absolutes of Scripture with a cover-all call to "be kind" does not produce the promised river of love but a bog of sentimentality.

A church that can't preach truth because it might come across as unkind to those not wanting to hear it is a church with nothing to say and nothing to offer beyond "arms are for hugging".

The National Catholic Reporter would neuter the church with kindness and "love everybody" to death – which is neither kind nor loving.

As for Alexandria Ocasio-Cortez's call to treat others with dignity and respect, when one of her colleagues last year called the President a "mother-f#$er", AOC dismissed the resulting upset as "faux outrage" and said she backed her colleague.

So, if indeed AOC is the future of the church, at least critics of the church will be pleased that she seems to have hypocrisy down pat.

THE GOSPEL ACCORDING TO DAN

Those who accuse the Victorian Government of trying to remove religion from the public square with their so-called gay conversion bill are wrong.

It is the eradication of traditional religion and the instalment of another, rigorously enforced orthodoxy that is the goal.

This was made clear in comments from outgoing Victorian human rights commissioner Kristen Hilton, published at the weekend in *The Age* newspaper.

We were told that the Change or Suppression (Conversion) Practices Prohibition Bill, passed by the Victorian government last month, was to stop archaic practices like electric shock therapy being used on gay people.

Now, no one was arguing that electroshock therapy could transform gay people into heterosexuals, and no churches were practising it.

But if the Victorian government wanted to make doubly sure parishioners were not being electrocuted by clergy, no-one was going to object. The government might have banned lobotomies, floggings and tearing people limb from limb while they were at it.

Oh, and there was the suggestion (explicit in the Bill but played down by proponents of the legislation whenever they were asked about it) that it would be appreciated – on threat of a fine, or worse – if Christians didn't oblige gay people who wanted prayer to resist their sexual urges.

Many argued that this was a step too far. But their protests were ignored and a government that specialises in locking its citizens down won the right to dictate what its citizenry may or may not ask of their God.

When it comes to exercising power, the Victorian government is nothing if not inclusive – in that their powers include more and more and still more.

As if this wasn't enough, Hilton told *The Age* newspaper on Sunday that her office would "educate faith leaders and the broader community about the harm caused to LGBTI people by suggesting there is something wrong with homosexuality".

Wait! What?

Government bureaucrats are going to "educate" faith leaders concerning what they should and should not say about God's blueprint for human sexuality?

That's right. Public servants, ordained in progressive ideology, will school church leaders in what constitutes acceptable religion according to Saint Dan and the holy orders of the Church of Spring Street.

But Christian leaders ought not worry. Hilton told *The Age* that her office would "only use their powers as a last resort if education and outreach failed".

Their "powers" include the ability to compel people to appear at hearings and to comply with orders such as attending compulsory re-education programs.

So, in a classic case of "we can do this the easy way, or we can do this the hard way", the Victorian Equal Opportunity and Human Rights Commission will only compel church leaders to be re-educated concerning their theology of human sexuality should they fail to change their views after being asked nicely.

Christians have always believed that sex was created by God as a gift to be enjoyed within the confines of marriage, and that marriage is between a man and a woman.

Any sex outside of that – whether pre-marital, extra-marital or gay sex – is less than God's ideal and therefore a sin.

Understandably many people don't like the Bible's teaching on sexuality and so make their own arrangements apart from God.

Others don't like the teaching but decide they want to follow Jesus even more than they want to follow their sexual urges, and so they willingly submit their behaviour to God's laws, asking Him for the grace to do so.

The Victorian human rights enforcers don't like God's precepts either. But instead of walking away from God or submitting to God, they intend to "educate" God.

They will not expel God from the public square. They will reimagine Him in their own image, reflecting their own sensibilities with legally enforceable creeds that seem right in their own eyes.

And so they have arrogantly set themselves on a collision course with their own citizens. And with God.

"THAT PERSON" WHO MUST NOT BE NAMED

Australia's greatest tennis player turned Christian minister is vilified every January for daring to hold a traditional view of marriage and biology.

Like clockwork, at this time every year, the high-priests of diversity condemn the 78-year-old grandmother for the unforgivable sin of holding views divergent to their own.

These preachers of tolerance and love summon every derogatory term they can conjure to demonise the sporting great for daring to believe – as Christians always have – that two men don't make a marriage and that imagining you are a woman doesn't make it so.

Normally the baying mob demand that her name be erased from the tennis arena named in her honour.

This hunting season they are demanding that she does not receive the nation's highest award for her services to sport.

But the venom directed at the winner of 24 singles grand slam titles is especially toxic this year, even by the Left's own pernicious standards.

Victoria Premier Daniel Andrews spoke at length about her but, pointedly, refused to use her name.

"I'm quite sick of talking about *that* person every summer," he told journalists yesterday, emphasising the word "that".

The irony of refusing to use the name of a person you disagree with because you are against dehumanising fellow citizens was lost on the media pack and no doubt never even occurred to the righteously indignant Premier.

Andrews said "*that* person" who ought not be named held views that were "disgraceful, hurtful and cost lives".

How it was that Dan Andrews could remember the views of a senior citizen on the other side of the country, while having no recollection of how the most important decisions of his government's hotel quarantine program were made, is a mystery.

And how many lives would be lost because of *that* person's views he did not say.

Would it be more or less than the 800 lives lost, not because of "views" but because of actions his own inept government took in response to the pandemic?

"I think it's worth saying again: Grand Slam wins don't give you some right to spew hatred and create division," Andrews said.

Someone needs to tell the Premier that having different views is not creating division; but demanding someone not be honored for sporting achievements because they do not hold state-approved views most certainly does create division – and is nothing if not a manifestation of hatred for those with whom you disagree.

Oh, and "*that* person" has a name. She is Margaret Court.

She's far more a lady than Daniel Andrews will ever be a gentleman.

WHAT SAINT VALENTINE AND MARGRET COURT HAVE IN COMMON

The same people who revile Margaret Court will today celebrate Valentine's Day, without even a hint of irony.

Few will realise that today is the anniversary of Saint Valentine's 'cancellation' at the hands of the Roman state for his views on sex and marriage.

The priest, like Australia's greatest tennis champion, found his Christian views suddenly out of step with the times in which he lived.

And like the 24 grand slam singles titles winner, Valentine insisted he could not change with the times since his views were beyond the times.

Emperor Claudius II was, just like the Wokerati right before the Australian Open tennis tournament every January, immediately triggered.

He had Valentine thrown into prison on threat of death if he did not bring his views into line with the third century.

Of course, Margaret Court has not been jailed for refusing to bring her views into line with the twenty-first century. Not yet anyway. But the threats she has received are, nevertheless, waypoints on the continuum.

Recant your Christian views, or your tennis achievements will be memory holed.

Give up your Christian faith, or be shamed by the media.

Change your definition of marriage, or the mob will make your latter years hell.

As if Pastor Margaret Court is motivated by sporting awards, or the applause of the media, or comfort, any more than Valentine was motivated by promises of freedom.

And besides, who would give five cents for the religion of a man or a woman of God whose convictions could so easily be bought?

Valentine would not deny Christ. Instead, he would infuriate the State further by attempting to convert even more people to Christianity.

For this, Valentine was beaten to death and – for good measure – his head was removed from his shoulders.

(A little like being beaten up in the media and – for good measure – having your name removed from the tennis arena).

The date was February 14, 270AD.

Legend has it that, before his death, Valentine prayed for his jailer's daughter to receive her sight and she was miraculously healed. He sent her a note signed "from your Valentine" and it is this note which is said to have inspired today's romantic missives.

Today in Perth another minister will be praying for her critics to receive their sight and, who knows, miracles do happen.

But the real inspiration of Saint Valentine is his fidelity to Christian teaching on sex and marriage in the face of unimaginable pressure to compromise.

And so, to Margaret Court I say, happy Valentine's Day. After all the brickbats you've received, you deserve a bouquet.

HILLSONG CHURCH IS TO BLAME FOR ABSOLUTELY EVERYTHING

Forget coronavirus, the Chinese Communist Party and climate change: the greatest threat to Australia is Hillsong Church.

If you believe what you read on Twitter – which would require the faith of Saint Paul and Pastor Brian Houston combined – more than half of the Federal Cabinet are Hillsong members.

This, of course, is not true.

But imagine for a moment that it is. This would mean the country is being run by a group of people who believe that every Australian is made in the image of God and therefore has intrinsic value and worth.

Cue scary music.

Gather your loved ones and escape to someplace where such dangerous views have not yet infected the political system – like China. Or North Korea.

Rumours of a happy clapper religious coup began when someone anonymously tweeted this week:

> *Australia's population. 25.5 million. Hillsong has 43,000 members in Australia. 0.0019% of the population. Federal Cabinet has 22 members. 13 are Hillsong posse. 59.09% of the cabinet. Not concerned? You should be. Digest the numbers.*

The numbers should not be digested. They should be spat out because they are patently false.

My family attend Hillsong and don't know of a single Cabinet member who is part of the church. I checked with a friend who is in leadership at Hillsong, and he didn't know of any either.

But as the Bible says, gossip tastes sweet – and so thousands of people not only swallowed the anonymously-posted lie but retweeted it so that the baying online mob could accuse Australia's largest Christian church of malfeasance.

Let me give you just a sample of the thousands of tweets that followed:

> "ASIO needs to look at the Hillsong cult seeping into our Government and governance."
>
> "Is being a Hillsong member mandatory for LNP MPs as Nazi party membership was in 1930s Germany?"
>
> "It is clear that these Hillsongers have a plan ... and that is to dominate our politics by all and any corrupt means."

We could go on, but you get the idea. Mums and dads who attend

Hillsong are Nazi cult members, nefariously working to overturn secular democracy.

Let's not call it a war on Christianity, but it does seem like Christians are the only group that can be derided, criticized, and accused of conspiracy without those voicing the criticisms being shouted down as bigoted or intolerant.

And in case you are tempted to dismiss this Hillsong-derangement syndrome as affecting only a bunch of crazy nameless trolls, former senior public servant and policymaker Paul Barratt retweeted the smear and added: "Given the low number of Hillsongers in the population, the numbers gaining pre-selection and the numbers appointed to Ministerial office seem wildly improbable statistically – there has to be co-ordination of effort."

Former *Courier-Mail* senior journalist Terry Sweetman threw chum into the social media water, tweeting: "Remember when Tony Abbott's cabinet had at least eight Catholics out of 19 members, far in excess of the 22.6 percent of Catholics in the general population. Must be Hillsong's turn."

He was duly rewarded with, at last count, 108 retweets and more than 400 'likes'.

Barrister David Ewart tweeted: "More people follow Collingwood than Hillsong how would you like it if they made policy?"

Now it's tempting to imagine how much money might be diverted to dental care if Collingwood members were setting government policy, but I digress.

Mr Ewart didn't mention which government policy Hillsong was setting. He also neglected to mention that Collingwood has more members than both the ALP and the Liberal Party.

But hey, it's all fun and games, isn't it?

Well, only if you don't know your history.

This week it's Pentecostals.

Next week it will be an even less fashionable religious minority that is attacked by the baying mob.

And eventually you'll end up with enough people agreeing that "We need to out who in Cabinet and Parliament are Hillsong/Pentecostalists", as one woman – getting that 'round 'em up' vibe going – tweeted enthusiastically.

Replace "Hillsong/Pentecostal" from the aforementioned tweet with the word "gay" or "trans" or "blacks" (or any other identity for that matter) and tell me if you'd be allowed to get away with it.

MASTERCHEF WIN LEAVES A BAD TASTE IN THE MOUTHS OF THE HATERS

First Hillsong won Australian Idol. Then, they won the Federal election. Last night they won Masterchef.

It was all too much for the godless hordes on Twitter, who were busy convincing themselves that the result of a cooking show proved they were being held, against their will, in a theocracy.

Last night's Masterchef grand final was spoiled for many viewers by the realisation that surprise winner, the affable Justin Narayan, was a former Hillsong youth pastor.

"I can't believe a Hillsong youth pastor won Masterchef! What the F#^k," said a typical Tweet.

"I just found out Justin is a pastor at Hillsong and now my night is ruined. I just wish so bad he wasn't a Hillsong pastor," cried another hysterical viewer.

So many people Tweeted similar sentiments (by which I mean hate) that Hillsong, rather than Masterchef, began trending on social media.

You could have been forgiven for thinking people had been watching Pastorchef.

Social media was abuzz with conspiracy theories, suggesting that Pentecostals had used their mysterious powers to influence the show's result.

And why not?

If you believe social media, it was Hillsong that caused Guy Sebastian to win Australian Idol in 2003 – even though Sebastian attended what was then Paradise Church in Adelaide.

And it was Hillsong that caused Scott Morrison to win the 2019 Federal election – even though Morrison attended Horizon Church in Sutherland.

It really is quite amazing how the same people who insist that Christians worship a "magic sky fairy" also believe those same Christians wield supernatural influence over everything from national elections to singing competitions and now cook-offs.

"Does anyone know if the judges or management of Masterchef are Hillsongers?" tweeted one.

"Has Masterchef been infiltrated by Hillsong as has the Liberal Party?" tweeted another.

"I did wonder if he (Narayan) was Hillsong. It's probably rigged. Like they rigged (Australian) Idol," Tweeted a third person who forgot to mention that Hillsong were also responsible for coronavirus, global warming and bindis growing on your front lawn.

Oh yes. If you believe Twitter, there are Hillsong people lurking behind every tree, dominating every federal cabinet meeting and now, manipulating even the taste buds of Masterchef judges. They are busier than Kevin Rudd.

Many viewers were desperately concerned that Narayan would tithe to his church from the $250,000 prize money.

If he celebrated his victory by spending 10 per cent of his money on a wild night out, no one would care. But, as one viewer warned, "His winnings better not go to Hillsong."

"So this p@#k is a Hillsonger? F#$k him! I hope it's a poison chalice. The less this bloke makes out of this, the less the Hillsong cult get from tithes," said another viewer, as others warned ominously that money given to the church would be used to promote homophobia.

Well, we wouldn't want anyone promoting hate against others now, would we?

THEIR ABC'S DIVINE COMEDY

ABC viewers have complained that the public broadcaster showed footage of Hillsong easter services rather than focusing on "mainstream churches".

"Why have ABC News included footage on Hillsong in its segment on Good Friday church services? They are not a mainstream church," insisted a tweet that was liked and shared thousands of times.

You can hardly blame ABC viewers for being confused about what constitutes mainstream Christianity.

If you get your religious news from the ABC you would be quite convinced that a mainstream church is one led by a transgendered minister preaching to wooden pews barely populated by a Mardi Gras of "allies" about how Jesus was actually a socialist revolutionary who – regardless of whether or not He actually existed – serves as a useful example to support whatever woke fad is being pushed from the pulpit this week.

Now if you think I'm exaggerating for comedic effect, you're wrong. My satire skills are no match for actual ABC news reporting.

The Drum aired a story over the Easter weekend celebrating "the first trans person to be inducted into an Australian mainstream church".

You might imagine that a mainstream church ceases to be mainstream when it appoints a transgendered minister. But such thoughts do not occur to journalists at our public broadcaster.

The ABC reported that the Uniting Church minister, who came out as trans in 2017, embodied Christianity's call for "transformation".

Well indeed. But I'm not sure that the Apostle Paul had gender transitioning in mind when he told the Corinthians, "If anyone is in Christ he is a new creation, the old has gone, the new has come."

Last time I checked, Holy Communion did not include puberty blockers.

Nevertheless, the transgendered reverend was shown walking into a church, the front door of which was adorned, not with a cross, but with a sign that said: "Act on Climate!"

Well of course. As the Good Book says: "For God so loved mother earth that He gave carbon credits so that whosoever reduces his emissions might not die from fossil fuels but have everlasting solar power."

Can I get an 'Amen'?

Inside the church, the ABC reporter referenced Biblical teaching that God created humans as male and female. This was dismissed by the transgendered minister as "an incredibly ideological statement that ignores the experience of people like me".

Now 'people like me' are perfectly free to pursue a religion that makes a god of their individual experience. But they are not entitled to call it mainstream Christianity. Actually, don't even call it Christianity.

The central message of Christianity is that Jesus is God. And if Jesus is God, guess who is not?

That's why a lot of people reject Christianity. It's an afront to the human ego. And it's hard to give up being the god of your own universe when you've been playing at it all your life.

Yet the ABC would have viewers believe, right before the holiest day on the Christian calendar, that a mainstream church is one in which we remake God in our own image. That might be a mainstream secular club, but it's not a Christian church.

A member of the transgendered minister's church told The Drum's reporter: "This church endears me greatly because it is open and receptive to people of all walks of life no matter what."

Which is a bit like saying 'I like this church because it's not a church at all'. And that rather undermines the whole point, doesn't it?

All of which might explain the inverse relationship between the increasing number of stories the ABC does on woke elements within the Uniting Church and the decreasing number of people actually attending the Uniting Church.

Hillsong, by comparison, is booming. Thousands attended Easter services at their Sydney Norwest location. Tens of thousands more gathered at sites across the rest of the country and still more watched online.

Sure, they've had their share of scandals. But that is to be expected in the Christian church, whatever the brand, where the only requirement for entry is to admit that you are not good enough for entry.

But when the ABC dared to show footage from Australia's largest church in their easter news package, viewers were angrier than a mob at a crucifixion.

People demanded to know why "mainstream" churches weren't featured, by which they presumably meant churches where anyone's "lived experience" overrides anything the Bible says; and where saving the planet is more important than saving souls since people's souls are perfectly fine the way they are.

You can knock Hillsong for being big and bold and brash if you prefer your religion to be small and apologetic and timid.

And you can criticise Hillsong for bringing in too much money and for having too many large auditoriums if you prefer your church to be penniless and to meet under a tree.

But just because you don't like their style doesn't mean they are not mainstream.

In terms of what they believe and teach (which let's face it, is the essence of Christianity) they are as mainstream as Christianity gets. So mainstream that they turned the Apostle's creed – the core beliefs of Jesus' disciples – into one of their most popular songs.

It goes like this:

> *I believe in God our Father*
> *I believe in Christ the Son*
> *I believe in the Holy Spirit*
> *Our God is three in one*
> *I believe in the resurrection*
> *That we will rise again*
> *For I believe in the name of Jesus*
> *I believe in life eternal*
> *I believe in the virgin birth*
> *I believe in the saints' communion*
> *And in Your holy Church*
> *I believe in the resurrection*
> *When Jesus comes again*
> *For I believe, in the name of Jesus*

That's mainstream Christianity in rhyme.

Meanwhile, churches the media would have you believe represent the mainstream may well be inoffensive in style, but are completely freewheeling in doctrine.

Resembling nothing like traditional Christianity they are more likely to sing:

> *I believe in Mother Nature*
> *I believe in Wind and Sun*
> *I believe in the spirit of Gaia*
> *The coal industry is done*
> *I believe in decarbonisation*

Mother Earth will rise again
For I believe, environmentalist Jesus
I don't believe there is life pre-natal
I don't believe sex is assigned at birth
I don't believe there are only two genders
I don't believe you even need the church
I believe in gender transition
Socialism must be tried again
For I believe, in social justice Jesus

Churches traditional in style and freewheeling in doctrine are cancelling themselves. Their old-fashioned style is unengaging, and you can hear the same wokey doctrine in a dozen other progressivist forums without the need to disrupt your Sunday.

The prize for being considered mainstream Christianity by the ABC is to be loved by people who will never darken your doors on a Sunday.

Meanwhile, actual mainstream churches that deliver the timeless Christian message in a timely style are packing them in, even as the Twitter mob shouts: "Crucify them".

A CHRISTIAN BELIEVES HE IS DOING GOD'S WORK. STOP THE PRESSES AND HOLD THE FRONT PAGE!

Two things happened last Tuesday involving religion. See if you can guess which one caused Leftists' heads to explode.

Last Tuesday the Islamic Republic of Iran was appointed to the UN's peak women's rights body. Also, Australia's Prime Minister addressed a group of Christians on the Gold Coast.

Now if you imagined that having a misogynistic regime – one that jails women for not wearing a hijab, bans them from singing and prevents them from travelling abroad without their husband's permission – appointed to the Commission on the Status of Women caused even a peep of protest from the Left, you'd be mistaken.

No. The Left's fury was reserved entirely for the PM who dared to say that he believed he was doing God's work.

"Scott Morrison tells Christian Conference he was called to do God's work as Prime Minister," wailed the headline in The Guardian, provoking readers to vent their outrage on social media.

Far from outraged, I was trying to work out how this was even news.

A Christian believes he is doing God's work? Well stop the presses and hold the front page!

The media might as well have reported that the Pope is Catholic.

If a Christian PM said he *didn't* believe he was doing God's work, then that would be news.

And if the PM said he believed he was doing the *devil's* work, well then that would definitely be news. And likely cheered by the Left. Which would not be news.

Speaking of the devil, Scott Morrison told pastors at the Australian Christian Churches National Conference that while social media has its uses, it "can also be used by the evil one".

Every parent who has ever worried about the influence of social media on their children – by which I mean every parent – said "Amen. Preach it PM!"

But the Left, who view humanity as a virus destroying the environment and so have given up on having children, were left with nothing to do but mock the PM for referencing the devil.

The Left are funny like that.

Design "Satan Shoes" containing a drop of human blood in the sole, as rapper Lil Nas X did, and you're an edgy artist. But mention Satan to Christians at a Christian conference, as Scott Morrison did, and you're, well, the devil.

The Left are scared of the devil because he represents the

personification of evil – a force which they do not and cannot believe in. If evil exists then some problems are beyond the State's power to fix. And that makes the State's continual quest for unlimited, god-like power to fix every human ill look, well, evil. But I digress.

Just as he'd talk tech-talk at a conference of supercomputer developers and weather and crop prices while out on the land, Morrison talked God-talk to the pastors.

The PM went on to tell the conference that when visiting disaster zones he sometimes says a silent prayer for people as he hugs them. He called it "laying hands on people" which, to the uninitiated sounds strange, but to Christians is a well-known term that simply means to place your hand on the person you are praying for.

Now a sane person would prefer to know that when the PM is hugging them he is thinking "God bless" rather than thinking "God, not another loser who wants a hug. I hope there's a vote in this".

But the insane Left reacted by accusing the PM of praying for people without their consent.

That's how unhinged the Left are. They demand that you get people's consent before you are allowed to even think good thoughts about them!

And if the soulless Left don't believe in the power of prayer, what do they suppose happens when someone prays?

Nothing, obviously.

So the Left were upset at the PM for thinking a prayer they didn't know about and that had no effect on a person they'd never met.

Lord, help them. (Consent was neither sought nor given in the praying of that prayer. Sue me.)

FEAR AND LOATHING REACH NEW HEIGHTS AS LYLE SHELTON REACHES THE SENATE

For an "irrelevant blow-in", Lyle Shelton sure has wokey Leftists all in a tizz.

News that the former Australian Christian Lobby director will replace Fred Nile in the NSW Senate sent the unhinged Left into apoplexy yesterday.

Chief proponent of diversity and inclusion and tolerance and love, the independent member for Sydney Alex Greenwich, warned that Shelton would feel "completely out of place" in the NSW Parliament.

"NSW and our Parliament values and celebrates the LGBTI community," he said.

You have to love it when the same people who insist that Shelton doesn't speak for Christians insist that they, on the other hand, speak for the entire State of New South Wales.

Greens MP Abigail Boyd, who detests mean-spirited people, reacted to news of Shelton's arrival by tweeting: "Just when we thought the NSW Parliament couldn't get any worse" which, naturally, was very mean-spirited.

NSW Labor MP Rose Jackson replied simply: "Oh no" – though it was unclear whether she was commenting on Shelton or just realising that she followed Abigail Boyd on twitter.

In response, Mr Shelton tweeted:

"Looking forward to having a coffee with future colleagues. I don't bite."

Which is exactly what you would expect a hateful bigot – by which we mean a Christian – to say.

Alister Lawrie, a policy manager at the Public Interest Advocacy Centre, tweeted:

"Lyle Shelton to replace Fred Nile in NSW Parliament, from November 2021. That is a truly chilling sentence, especially for the LGBTI people of this state. The stuff of nightmares for anyone who is not a cisgender, endosex, heterosexual man."

So Shelton is an "irrelevant blow in" and, at the exact same time, "the stuff of nightmares for anyone who is not a huh? what? er? man".

Surely you are irrelevant. Or you are a nightmare. You can't be both.

Jane Caro replied: "Awful news for women too" which, if you think about it, was a pretty funny reply.

Political journalist Malcolm Farr pointed out that Shelton had previously stood for the Nationals, Bernardi's Conservatives and, more recently, had attempted to join the LNP.

"Lots of attempts, lot of knock backs," he wrote.

In other words, Shelton has a demonstrated ability to bounce back from defeat and a determination unmatched by many others. It was hardly the blistering putdown Farr had imagined.

Political editor of *The New Daily* Josh Butler tried to make Shelton look like a failure and a fraud.

"Lyle Shelton (currently based in Brisbane) is being parachuted into the NSW upper house to replace Fred Nile" he wrote.

> "Comes after an unsuccessful 2019 Senate run in Cory Bernardi's Conservatives party plus a recent stint with QLD LNP. 3 parties in 2 years, and finally into political office."

You'd almost think Shelton was the first politician on earth to taste defeat before enjoying success; Not to mention the first person in history to be parachuted into political office. You know, apart from Victoria Greens Senator Lydia Thorpe. And NSW Greens Senator Mehreen Faruqi. And Federal Labor Senator Kristina Keneally ... you get the idea.

Alex Greenwich, who led the same-sex marriage "Yes" campaign and who has opposed Fred Nile on just about every issue, tweeted:

> "Letting a politically irrelevant blow-in fill your vacated shoes is a sad legacy to leave after 40 years in Parliament."

I'm sure Fred Nile would have taken that on board if only he had been able to stop laughing at the notion that Alex Greenwich cared two hoots about his legacy.

Other tweeters variously described Shelton as "disgusting", an "irrelevant zealot", a "fascist", a "complete knucklehead", a "vile sh*tweasel", "pond scum rising to the top" and "a political whore, prostituting himself out to parties, seeing who will leave the money on the side table" which sounded suspiciously like that particular tweeter knew a lot more about whoring than he did about Shelton.

Others warned that "this country is cooked", "democracy is a myth" and that "you don't have to be elected by the people under Morriscum's Pentecostal Government". That last one would have been retweeted 10,000 times if only the author had remembered to insert the word "Hillsong" in there.

In summary, reaction to news of Shelton's impending arrival in the NSW Senate was, to steal a line from Macbeth, tweeted by idiots, full of sound and fury and signifying something – that they are indeed worried by an articulate, principled man who will stand for conservative Christian values.

Why else react with such venom?

Shelton should be encouraged.

NYC WOULD RATHER PEOPLE WERE SICK THAN TREATED BY CHRISTIANS

WE are continually warned that doctors who believe in traditional marriage might deny medical treatment to gay patients.

Amazingly, the New York City Council has turned this on its head and decided to deny gay patients to doctors who believe in traditional marriage. That'll teach the bigots!

New York City Council Speaker Corey Johnson announced at the weekend that it was "time for Samaritan's Purse to leave NYC".

He tweeted: "Their continued presence here is an affront to our values of inclusion, and is painful for all New Yorkers who care deeply about the LGBTQ community."

Samaritan's Purse, a Christian charity, set up a 68-bed respiratory care unit in Central Park after the Federal Emergency Management Agency asked them to assist local hospitals overwhelmed with Covid-19 patients.

The problem though, explained Mr Johnson, was that while the doctors supplied correct care they did so with incorrect opinions.

"Samaritan's Purse," he revealed, "requires its volunteers to agree to a written affirmation 'that marriage is exclusively the union of one genetic male and one genetic female.' Hate has no place in our beautiful city."

If Samaritan's Purse is filled with hate then they are doing a terrible job of showing it. Over the past four weeks the Christian charity's 72-member disaster response team has provided free medical care to hundreds of New Yorkers, and all without first checking if patients were gay.

But this did not deter Mr Johnson, a gay man who had a long history of LGBT activism before being elected to the New York City Council in 2013.

The second most powerful elected figure in America's largest city continued: "I'm aware that our battle against COVID-19 is still ongoing, and that our health care system still needs support. But as a city that values diversity and compassion for all, we can't continue allowing a group with their track record to remain here when we're past the point they're needed."

In other words, as tolerant people we must run these people with different beliefs out of town.

Well, nothing proves your commitment to "inclusion" and "diversity" and "health care" like denying medical aid for the sick because the medics providing that aid happen to hold views about the definition of marriage that don't conform to the State approved narrative.

Mr Johnson tweeted that "this group, led by the notoriously bigoted, hate-spewing Franklin Graham, came at a time when our city couldn't in good conscience turn away any offer of help" by which he presumably meant "this group, led by a Christian, answered our city's call to help residents of all races, religions, genders & orientations at great personal risk when New York City medical infrastructure had failed them".

It's quite a way to say thank you.

2

LGBTQI'S WOKE DICTUMS

"CERTAIN GENDERS"

THE UK Health Department announced yesterday via Twitter that Coronavirus was having a disproportionate impact on "certain genders".

A few people – specifically, those who had completed junior school biology – immediately wondered what chance the Health Department had of containing a world-wide pandemic when they hadn't yet worked out there were only two genders.

A ninth grader told news media: "When the Department says certain genders are more likely to contract Coronavirus, they need to be more specific about which ones.

"And if they are pushed for time, maybe they could just pick one of two available genders that actually exist."

He added: "The Health Department's tweet is as embarrassing as it is unscientific. The middle of a pandemic isn't the time for cringeworthy pandering. The Government shouldn't ask us to trust them and 'follow the science' when they can't even say male or female."

Meanwhile, others demanded to know how many genders the Health Department was aware of, and whether any of them had accidentally escaped form a Wuhan laboratory.

Carly Woke, a reporter at the BBC, which last year produced an educational film claiming there were more than 100 genders (that part is true), worried that a pandemic meant pangender people would be particular vulnerable since both words started with "pan".

"The modelling is terrifying," she told viewers from a safe space in the broadcaster's London studios.

Skye Cadet, head of Gender Studies at Oxford, told the BBC that the Health Department should immediately advise which of the 100 genders was least susceptible to Covid-19 so that everyone could identify as that one.

"This is a huge breakthrough," they (her preferred pronoun) said.

"If we all stop identifying according to our violently assigned at birth gender and instead identify as, say, non-binary pansexual two-spirit genderqueer women, then we can beat this virus."

When asked how it was that Covid-19 was able to recognise which socially constructed bias & stereotypes a person was conforming to before infecting them, they insisted: "We just have to trust the science."

At the time of writing the Health Department had been unable to confirm reports that the virus was only affecting males and females.

Experts pointed out that, if the reports were true, it would mean all other genders imagined by the UK Health Department would seem to have totally immunity.

INDIVIDUALS WITH A CERVIX

CANCER is a serious disease and nobody - least of all me - wants to get cancer.

So when CNN urged "individuals with a cervix" to get tested, I immediately wondered how to find out if I was one of those individuals?

The July 31 tweet read: *"Individuals with a cervix are now recommended to start cervical cancers screening at 25 and continue through age 65, with HPV testing every five years as the preferred method of testing, according to a new guideline released by the American Cancer Society"*

Individuals with a cervix.

Did they mean, like, in a jar?

Is a cervix like a mole? I have a couple of those. My dad has a few too so it's probably hereditary. Should I ask my dad if he has a cervix?

I dialled dad's number but hung up the phone before he could answer. No point stressing out the old man about possibly having cancer of the cervix. He might not even *have* a cervix. Who could know!

While on hold trying to book an MRI to find out if I had a cervix - and if so, whether my cervix was cancerous - I googled "cervix" and learned that a cervix is a cylinder-shaped neck of tissue that connects the vagina and uterus.

"That's odd," I thought. "I don't actually have a vagina. Or a uterus."

And then I realised, "individuals with a cervix" are women.

You cannot imagine my relief. I don't have cancer of the cervix. I *can't* have cancer of the cervix. I'm a man!

Even so, you can't trust everything you read on the internet. So I checked with my wife.

"Babe, do you mind making me a coffee? And how do I know if I have a cervix?"

She gave me that same weird look she gave me last week when, having read a CNN piece on transgender rights, I started to fear I might menstruate.

"Only females have a cervix," she replied. And then she patiently explained: "Juvenile human females are called girls. Adult human females are called women. Since the beginning of time, individuals with a cervix have been referred to as women."

And as an individual with a prostate, I tend to agree with her.

Why CNN would say "individuals with a cervix" rather than use the more succinct term, "women", is a mystery. But I suspect they would really love to have said "Comrades with a cervix".

CNN claimed that using the term "individuals with a cervix" rather than "women" was their way of being inclusive.

Well, using the term "idiots" rather than "journalists" when referring to CNN staff is my way of being inclusive.

When CNN deny a group of people who actually exist – like women – for a fantastical one they have imagined – like men with a cervix – they've lost me.

CNN should stop erasing women and pretending that they are being progressive.

Anyway, thanks to CNN I now understand that scene from the Titanic where Kate Winslet's character, Rose, says: "Jack, I want you to draw me like one of your French individuals with a Cervix"

I only now realise she meant a French *girl*!

And Michael Bolton crooning "When a maaaan loves an individual with a cervix" also makes sense now. He loved a *woman*!

But honestly, when you're singing about individuals with a cervix, it's hard to go past the late great Roy Orbison's 1964 classic "Oh, Pretty Individual with a Cervix".

Individual with a cervix, walking down the street
Individual with a cervix, the kind I'd like to meet
Would be a woman ...
CNN I don't believe you, you're not the truth
No one could be as woke as you
Mercy!

Individual with a cervix, won't you pardon me?
Individual with a cervix, I couldn't help but see
You're a woman ...
Not a man like you claim to be
That's why you get a pap smear, unlike me
growl

Individuals with a cerebral cortex might want to completely ignore CNN.

THE FAKE TRANS WOMAN IS THE MAN WHO ASSAULTED YOU

A TRANS WOMAN who assaults a woman was never a real trans woman, according to British Liberal Democrat and former equalities minister Lynne Featherstone.

Ms Featherstone was responding to concerns that allowing men to self-identify and be legally recognised as women, without any medical diagnosis, would endanger women.

Proposed changes to the Gender Recognition Act, currently being debated by UK politicians, have created fears that men could use the law to access female change rooms and assault women.

But Ms Featherstone told Pink News on July 9 that such concerns were "unkind".

"Any man pretending to be a woman to do that is a male criminal not a trans woman," she said.

Featherstone evidently believes transwomen are ideologically incapable of harming women.

In her brave new gender fluid world, a trans woman is trans until she assaults a woman, at which point she proves she was simply a man in a dress.

I'm not sure it will be much consolation to the victim of a sexual assault to later learn that her assailant was a fake trans woman rather than a real trans woman.

The obvious problem with self-identification is that there is no test by which to determine honestly trans women (whatever that means) from dishonestly trans women, by which I mean a heterosexual male predator who thinks popping on a frock is more than worth it to get into the ladies' room.

But since self-identification is to be believed uncritically, how do you distinguish between the two? Will one be evilly twirling a moustache? And if so, which one?

Any woman protesting that a man was in the ladies' bathroom would be in danger of prosecution for a thought crime.

So the only way to know whether the trans woman in the bathroom should really be in the bathroom is to wait and see whether or not he sexually assaults you!

But don't worry. If you are raped, authorities will retroactively redefine the perpetrator in order to continue claiming no members of the preferred group have ever committed such a crime and therefore you were perfectly safe throughout the entire assault.

Let's say we agree with Featherstone that the trans woman assaulting your daughter in the bathroom is not a trans woman but a male criminal – what measures do we take to protect against male criminals? How about not legally recognising them as trans by virtue of self-declaration? Is that just too simple a solution?

It's "unkind", says the former equalities minister, who employs the term "kind" and "unkind" to provoke the suppression of opposing views. This cynical manipulation of most people's desire to do good is absolutely monstrous.

NO PENISES IN THE POOL. PUH-LEASE!

For almost one hundred years, Sydney women have been able to bathe at Coogee's ladies-only pool, free from the prying eyes of pervy men.

But much has changed since the McIver's Ladies Baths – reserved for the exclusive use of women and small children – opened in 1922.

Back in those days, England had a king, Australia had a Labor Prime Minister and women doing laps of the historic ocean pool had vaginas.

Fast forward to 2021.

England has had a queen for the longest time. The Liberal in the Lodge is unassailable. And women tucking penises in their swimsuits have bomb-dived all the other bathers looking for privacy at Coogee pool.

The gals at the Randwick and Coogee Ladies Swimming Association aren't against a bit of gender freestyling – they're swimming laps in the twenty-first century, after all.

So they decided that trans women should be able to dip their toe in the women-only pool; provided that their trans sisters had fully transitioned, meaning their toe was the only thing being dipped in the water.

"Only transgender women who've undergone a gender reassignment surgery are allowed entry," the Swimming Association's website stated.

Cue outrage.

This was a clear case of ladies with vaginas discriminating against ladies with penises.

Members of the University of NSW Student Representative Council released a statement describing the Association's "outdated" definition of women as "disgusting".

"Anyone who identifies as a woman ... should have access to this space," the statement said. "To our community, students, and staff at

UNSW – your gender identity needs no validation from anyone but yourself."

The students did not explain how a women-only pool remains a women-only pool if women are only what the guy in the bikini says they are.

"Trans women are women," the students insisted, in what now passes for debate on university campuses; the aggressive repetition of mindless slogans as if they were reasoned argument.

"Any statement to the contrary lacks empathy, understanding and scientific rigour and is based in bigotry."

There was zero empathy or understanding for the woman who wrote on the Baths' Facebook page: "Please don't give in to the trans bullies. Muslim women rely on places like this. Trans identifying men can go everywhere; Muslim women cannot."

She received a curt response.

"Muslim women need to take the opportunity to learn that having the biological parts does not make you a man"

Right. Because, you know, "scientific rigour".

But the gender-fluid cheerleaders at the Student Representative Council were just warming up.

They went on to warn that a policy stating only trans women who opted for full emersion would be considered to be female swimmers was itself a form of violence "and will only increase community violence toward transwomen".

This cynical manipulation of people's goodwill – 'let us swim or you will be responsible for violence against us' – worked a treat, as it usually does.

Within 24 hours of the complaint, the historic women-only pool had become the progressive women-are-only-an-idea pool.

The pool's website now says: "Yes. Transgender women are welcome to the McIver's Ladies Baths, our definition for transgender is as per the NSW Discrimination Act."

The NSW Discrimination Act defines transgendered women as someone "who identifies as a member of the opposite sex by living, or seeking to live, as a member of the opposite sex".

So, there you have it.

If you identify as a member of the opposite sex; and would like to swim as a member of the opposite sex among members of the opposite sex who have been trying to avoid members of the opposite sex for the past hundred years, well now you can. And barely a ripple of protest.

SO NOW WE CAN'T EVEN TALK TRANSGENDER ISSUES?

Question: How many trans activists does it take to change a lightbulb?

Answer: The same number that it takes to have an article questioning trans ideology erased from a major newspaper – one.

The Melbourne Age ran an opinion piece on its website Sunday in which a mum expressed reservations about her daughter's desire for a sex change.

But less than an hour after trans activist and La Trobe University lecturer Yves Rees complained that the paper was "peddling transphobic nonsense" – by which she meant a parent's sincere concerns for her child – the paper issued a public apology and promised to delete the piece.

Age editor Gay Alcorn wrote: "I apologise Yves ... given the sensitivity in Melbourne due to the recent death of a young trans woman, I am having it removed from our site."

And just like that, *The Age* newspaper, aping Pravda, disappeared the viewpoint of a caring parent for ideological reasons.

One wonders if *The Age* will now submit all its content to the LGBTQ crowd for approval before publication.

What is the point of a free press if it makes itself subservient to the heckler's veto?

The "transphobic nonsense" that Yves Rees found so offensive was a mum expressing concern that health professionals seemed too ready to affirm her teenager's claim to be transgendered.

The mum, who had consented to testosterone treatment for her daughter, wrote that she worried about "a relentless motion towards permanent medical changes" when it was unclear to her whether the child might change her mind about changing her sex.

A posse of hysterical rainbow bullies took to Twitter to deride the mum as being nasty, vindictive, hateful and harmful. Her article was "crappy writing by a crappy parent," they said, outraged that she had referred to her daughter as "she".

"Anyone who misgenders their own child should have them removed from their care," thundered one activist.

Well if a parent can't express doubt about their child embarking on a series of body-altering treatments that are in many cases irreversible, when in all other areas that same child is not granted the capability to consent, then children may as well be wards of the state.

ABC radio presenter Patricia Karvelas called the article a "truly bewildering piece".

"My god ... I imagine this is what parents were writing about gay kids once," she said, forgetting that if your "gay kid" later decides he is not gay, no harm done. But if your trans kid later decides he is not trans, well good luck unscrambling that egg.

Alcorn's decision to vanish a woman's honest account of her experience trying to find appropriate treatment for her daughter's dysphoria did not save her from the mad ravings of the sex-change-happy Twitter mob.

They insisted that such articles might lead trans people to commit suicide. They were outraged that it had been published so soon after the body of a missing trans woman was found in bushland in East Kew. Police have said they were not treating her death as suspicious.

"Cancelling my subscription to *The Age*. Absolutely vile to publish this hateful crap at any time, let alone today," tweeted one unhappy reader.

"It's repugnant opinion like this that drives trans people to kill themselves," warned another.

"The recent passing of this human being can, in part, be attributed to irresponsible 'journalism' like this. Never ever post transphobic shit again, blood is on your hands."

All of which begged the question, if the risk of trans people committing suicide is increased by the publication of a mum's concern that her teenager might have misdiagnosed herself as trans, isn't that evidence of deeper issues being experienced by those at risk?

Or is it a manipulative cry-bully tactic aimed at silencing any dissent from the 'gender is fluid', 'trans women are women' and 'gender is a social construct' narrative?

Surely a recent High Court ruling in the UK which found that puberty blocker drugs given to stop the natural development of transgender identifying children were "experimental" and weak on evidence proves confused teenagers and their parents need discussion, not censorship from journalists who are terrified by ideas and determined to play to the sensibilities of micro-groups.

Hysterical outrage from activists claiming that an op-ed is "dangerous and harmful" ignores the fact that medical interventions involving children can likewise be "dangerous and harmful."

The article published in and then quickly removed from *The Age* was fair comment on an important issue of national interest. It's a conversation that should be had. All sides deserve to be heard.

Children's lives are at stake.

TIM SMITH'S GENDER CONFUSION

Politicians are finding it hard to think straight when it comes to gay conversion laws.

Take Victorian Liberal MP Tim Smith who today insisted that attempts to change or to suppress a person's sexual orientation – even through prayer – must be criminalised because "you are what you are".

"This is pretty cut and dry," the outspoken MP declared. "You are what you are. I read reports about people praying, or some such to stop people from being gay or some rubbish. I mean this is nonsense.

"You know I prayed 20 years ago that I'd be six foot four, well I'm five ten. This is actually quite insane. It's demented. You are what you are. We are all made in the image of God. Can I make that point as a very, very bad Anglican."

God will judge whether Mr Smith is a very, very bad Anglican. I think we can all judge that Mr Smith is a very, very bad thinker.

Mr Smith believes it should be illegal to pray for a gay man to go straight since "you are what you are". He believes homosexuality, like height, is a biological constant that cannot be changed.

Well okay, leaving aside the fact that science is yet to find a gay gene, let's indulge Mr Smith and imagine he is right about homosexuality being as genetic as one's height, or the shape of one's nose, or the colour of one's eyes or the type of one's genitals ...

Wait. Did someone just say genitals?

The same Mr Smith who insists it should be illegal to pray for a person to stop being gay because "biology", also insists it should be illegal to counsel someone out of a sex change because "feelings".

It would be fascinating to hear Mr Smith explain how it is that same-sex attraction is an immutable biological fact while one's gender is a feeling, completely disconnected from chromosomes or from genitalia.

Mr Smith is a politician who enjoys the comfort of opinion without the discomfort of thought.

And he's a politician who enjoys the luxury of speaking "as an Anglican" without the inconvenience of believing like an Anglican.

He's the sort of person who could do with your prayers. But praying for Mr Smith would be "demented" and "quite insane". He is what he is.

MEN HAVE A PENIS AND WOMEN HAVE A VAGINA. OH WAIT …

Men have a penis and women have a vagina – but only a crazy brave person would say so.

Perth Lord Mayor and Channel 7 host and sportscaster Basil Zempilas was crazy brave on Wednesday.

Showing a reckless disregard for his own well-being, the newly elected mayor said publicly that biology determines gender.

He might as well have run naked through a minefield screaming "Yippee ki-ya".

Zempilas was hosting a radio show when his co-host, talking about transgender issues, said: "That's the new era Basil, get into it. If I subscribe to being a girl, I am a girl."

A careless Zempilas replied: "No you don't. No. No. Wrong. Wrong."

And then he said what has been unsayable since Bruce Jenner appeared as Caitlyn on the cover of *Vanity Fair* back in 2015.

"If you've got a penis, mate, you're a bloke. If you've got a vagina, you're a woman. Game over."

Most people listening knew that it was true. But *everyone* listening thought it was a crazy brave thing to actually say.

Social media was suddenly angrier than a lesbian tennis player drawn to play on the Margaret Court Arena.

"He's transphobic. Does he realise it is the 21st century not the 1960s?" tweeted one LGBTQI ally as if announcing the date was all that was necessary to damn Mr Zempilas.

"I hope strong action is taken and he is forced to resign (as Lord Mayor)," demanded another because, presumably, if Mr Zempilas was not removed from City Hall he might next insist that there were two rather than 71 genders, creating a tear in the space-time continuum and sucking all of Perth into another dimension called reality.

Mr Zempilas was variously described as "repugnant", "unhinged", "an utter embarrassment", "a nasty piece of work" and "a true enemy of intellect & decency" for the crime of stating a biological fact.

The TransFolk of WA chairperson, Hunter Gurevich, said the Lord Mayor's comments "fundamentally deny contemporary science" which said a lot more about contemporary science than it did about the Lord Mayor's comments.

"Perhaps the Honourable Mr Zempilas would consider consulting experts in the field before providing comment, as would befit a public figure," he said.

You can get away with almost anything in public life these days. But insisting that a quick check between your legs will provide reliable proof of gender is *not* one of them.

Mr Zempilas should have known that telling the difference between boys and girls was now a "field" best left to "experts".

But the Lord Mayor was nothing if not a quick un-learner.

So just 24-hours after suggesting genitals were a good indicator of gender, Mr Zempilas was telling anyone who would listen that they were not.

"They're not my views. They are not in keeping with my values and that is not how I think," he told journalists.

Mr Zempilas did not say what he now thought about gender but whatever it was, it certainly had nothing to do with penises or vaginas.

And as for values, well he very much valued his job. And who could blame him? It's not like he was the author of Harry Potter and therefore independently wealthy enough to survive being cancelled for daring to point out anatomical realities.

He was clearly hoping that both his thinking and his values had devolved sufficiently for the regressive Left to call off the mob.

And he was repentant. So repentant.

"It was bad broadcasting. It was a moment of stupid broadcasting and I regret that moment," he said in an act of dramatic verbal self-flagellation.

"I am very sorry for the comments that I made. They were inappropriate. I wish that I hadn't made them. And I understand the error of my ways."

Finally, he begged not just for forgiveness but for the chance to be rehabilitated as the Lord Woke of Perth.

"I made a mistake, and it's my mistake to accept. I have to do better, and I will do better. It's my job to be better than that and it won't happen again," he promised, adding that he would invite people from the transgender and non-binary communities to meet with him and educate him.

Surely this was evidence he had won the victory over himself. He loved Big Brother.

He was not crazy brave at all. He was just crazy.

MEN NOW MAKE MORE BEAUTIFUL WOMEN THAN WOMEN. THIS IS PROGRESS?

A transgender woman has been crowned Miss Intercontinental New Zealand. But it's 2020, so you just know there will be a twist to this story.

And, of course, there is. The beauty pageant winner is Filipino. All of which means that this year's Miss Intercontinental New Zealand is a foreign-born, biological male.

Could there be a more fitting result in a post-truth world where nothing is ever as it seems?

The mandated response, as we all know, is to applaud and to tell each other how lucky we are to live in a world where people are so open-minded and accepting that literally anyone can be the most beautiful woman in the room, even a man.

But how are we to live with such absurdity?

We have resolved the contradiction by agreeing that if we all say in unison that a biological man who believes himself to be a woman is in fact a woman, then he is. Or rather, she is.

(As you can see, it takes practice. But with the help of woke media and LGBTQ+ activists who threaten to punish those who stray from the narrative, you can get the hang of it quickly enough).

And hey presto! Faster than a beauty queen can say "world peace", the contradictions dissolve.

Women can have a penis. Men can be pregnant. And 26-year-old transgendered woman Arielle Keil can be named Miss Intercontinental New Zealand, less than 12 months after reportedly paying surgeons $15,000 to create her breasts and vagina.

Author Stephen King tweeted in July: "I believe trans women are women. I do not believe that hate speech and shaming speech are acceptable. Those things are the enemy of rational discourse. Treat even those with whom you disagree with the dignity you expect yourself."

Putting aside the fact that King wrote "trans women are women" and "rational discourse" in the same tweet; and ignoring King's claim that stating biological facts now constitutes hate speech, the fiction writer's aim is laudable.

Decent people wish only happiness for transgendered people such as Arielle Keil who, reportedly, has led a difficult life.

Arielle, who was born as a boy named Andrew, claims to have been bullied throughout childhood and thrown out of home when he told his parents he wanted to become a woman.

He says he battled depression and that he had often wanted to take his own life.

Thank God he did not. Keil has now reconciled with his father and is studying fashion design in Auckland. He presents as a thoughtful and intelligent person.

But redefining reality in order to make people feel better about themselves is neither kind nor sustainable.

Tell a plump woman that she does not look fat in that dress and no harm is done. But tell a man that if he believes himself to be a woman then he is, and you create all sorts of unintended consequences.

Insisting that biological men can become women by changing their pronoun is certainly not kind to women who are stripped of their dignity in the verbal sleight of hand.

Such play-acting reduces women to a mere costume – a thought in a man's head.

Surely this – not glancing at one's watch while a woman speaks, as former prime minister Tony Abbott once did – is real misogyny.

Trans activists complain that to deny trans women are real women is to cruelly deny their existence as people. This is silly. To say Arielle

Keil is not a woman does not deny her existence any more than saying Rachel Dolezal is not African American denies that Rachel Dolezal exists.

But it should seem rather obvious that to say trans women are women risks disappearing women – or, as CNN like to call them so as to be more trans-inclusive, "people with a cervix".

See what I mean?

And spare a thought for the Miss Intercontinental New Zealand runner up.

If she had spent thousands of dollars on plastic surgery in an effort to look more womanly, she would have been derided as "fake". But when a biological man like Arielle Keil spends thousands of dollars on plastic surgery so as to look more womanly, he is said to be beautiful.

And if you disagree, you're a bigot. That's peak male privilege right there.

Life is hard and some people struggle greatly, for reasons the rest of us find difficult to comprehend.

We owe it to each other to be as kind and as compassionate as we possibly can.

But raging against reality to create a world in which charity for our fellow man (or woman) completely overwhelms clarity about who men (or women) actually are is not the way to do it.

HOW THE WOKE SNAKE SWALLOWS ITS OWN TAIL

THE woke tower's foundation of sand is on view for all to see now that lesbians have been told they will be breaking the law if they exclude men identifying as women from their gatherings.

In a case of Woke v Woke, Tasmanian Anti-Discrimination commissioner Sarah Bolt has ruled biological men who are attracted to women while imagining themselves to be women are just as lesbiany as lesbians.

The ruling, reported in *The Australian*, has outraged actual lesbians who insist that transgendered women can't be lesbians because they are not real women and therefore cannot be same sex attracted, except to men. Which would make them gay, rather than lesbian.

LGBTQ activists, shocked to learn that they are subject to the same anti-discrimination laws they have been subjecting the rest of the community to, announced they would appeal the decision.

A Gay and Bisexual Alliance spokeswoman told *The Australian* "I want to exclude people with penises", which did not make her sound like a very inclusive lesbian.

She continued: "There are many events that cater for the trans community in Tasmania. This event was going to be just for lesbians who are same-sex attracted."

Wait. The LGBTQ community isn't actually focused on inclusion? Colour me astounded.

Evidently, inclusivity means including only those you want to include.

> "What do we want?"
> "Diversity!"
> "When do we want it?"
> "When it suits!"

Funny, I don't remember the LGBTQ community using *those* lines during the same-sex marriage debate.

And speaking of 'LGBTQ community' – that fantastical pride parade of authentic selves harmoniously fighting oppression – it seems they have now decided that the feather boas are the constrictors.

The so-called LGBTQ community is more akin to warring Afghan tribes that only come together when they have a common enemy (by which I mean Christians) to fight. The rest of the time they revert to the same old prejudices.

A spokeswoman told *The Australian*: "Many lesbians feel uncomfortable having transgenders in their spaces, because they are not female; they are biological males.

"We are forced to have them in our groups but none of us want to date them ... I feel discriminated against on the basis of being a lesbian same-sex attracted (woman)."

So, like a woke snake swallowing its own tail, the prestige minorities are now consuming each other in pursuit of becoming the ultimate exclusive minority.

They risk spinning in such ever-tightening circles that they will end up disappearing completely.

I will admit that it does seem ridiculous that lesbians must include people in their lesbian groups who, from a biological standpoint, are actually heterosexual men.

But then again, it was the LGBTQ circus that championed gender alchemy.

If female athletes must include biological men in their Olympic events, and if female bathers must include biological men at their female-only pools, then why should lesbians get to be transphobes?

Unable to discriminate on the basis of sex, and prohibited from discriminating on the basis of sexual orientation, the only alternative was to argue that gender was biologically determined after all. Which is exactly what the Gay and Bisexual Alliance is now saying.

When ideology meets reality at the Launceston lesbian bingo night, the rubbery woke speak is quickly ditched for chants of "follow the science".

Like I said. "Bingo!"

Perhaps this is the beginning of the end for the crazy, twisted gender knot that western society has tied itself in.

Can we finally admit the idea that individuals can change biological sex is a pretend belief that people mostly hold to look good in front of others?

And can we also admit that most people will quickly drop the idea if enough of those others start publicly challenging it, or if biological men in frocks line up to croon k.d. lang oldies at lesbian karaoke night – whichever comes first.

The real problem though, is not discrimination against lesbians trapped in men's bodies but something far more sinister - the power of an unelected, unrepresentative public servant like Sarah Bolt to define who you can and cannot associate with.

While it's enormous fun watching progressives eat their own - aided and abetted by publicly-funded 'experts' – we dare not be silent or indifferent since we can be sure our autonomy will be up for grabs next.

As Martin Niemoller famously said, first they came for the Launceston Lesbian Trivia Night, and I did not speak out because I was not a lesbian, at least not in the traditional sense. So then they came for the rest of us and by the time I realised my country had turned into a quagmire of identity politics and discrimination laws it was too late, because there was no-one allowed to speak the truth and bring the nightmare to an end.

GAY CROSSWALKS

West Vancouver Police appealed for public assistance last week to help identify a driver accused of 'defacing' a recently installed LGBTQ Pride crosswalk with a tyre mark.

The police department's twitter feed announced they would be "investigating a mischief to property, after someone defaced the department's new Pride crosswalk."

"On July 7, 2020 at 4:04pm staff inside the police station heard a loud and sustained tyre squealing outside. When officers took a closer look, they discovered that someone had just left tyre marks across a portion of the crosswalk."

"This is very upsetting," Cst. Kevin Goodmurphy said. "For whatever reason, this person has chosen to leave a gesture of hate on a crosswalk that stands for the exact opposite."

So in Wokier than Woke Canada, a crosswalk now *stands for something* ... other than just, you know, where to safely cross the road.

The problem, of course, is that when you turn a section of road into a political message you're unsure whether a subsequent tyre mark on that same section of road is also a political message.

And so it was that when Vancouver Police discovered a tyre mark on their rainbow coloured crosswalk last Tuesday, they suspected it was a *homophobic* tyre mark.

In Vancouver, if you leave a tyre mark on a regular crosswalk it's called driving. If you leave a tyre mark on an LGBTQ Pride crosswalk, it's called a hate crime.

So congratulations to the West Vancouver police for making a mockery of police work. It's tough to argue against defunding the police when police resources are being used to protect pro-gay crosswalks from anti-gay Bridgestones.

If you can be arrested for driving over a crosswalk in a disrespectful manner, you wouldn't want to walk across it with muddy shoes. Perhaps it's just safer to only use West Vancouver's LGBTQ Pride crosswalk if you're gay.

Police investigating tyre marks on a crossing is funny because it's ridiculous. But it's worse than ridiculous; it's wrong. When you politicise crosswalks and then prosecute someone for driving on it, you are forcing political views on the population via their environment.

In defence of the West Vancouver police, the photo they tweeted of the offending tyre mark did seem to indicate that the driver of the car was making a right turn, which everyone knows is more hateful than a left turn.

LONDON MAYOR CELEBRATES NON-BINARY DAY

LONDON Mayor Sadiq Khan yesterday took time out from doing nothing to stop acid attacks in order to promote International Non-Binary Day.

"All gender identities are valid," the mayor tweeted as he encouraged Londoners who have not yet been stabbed or disfigured by an acid attack to become allies of non-binary people.

It remains to be seen whether being an ally means the Muslim mayor will take a couple of two-spirited gender queer transsexuals down to his local mosque for prayers on Friday.

Actually, since most of London's two-spirited gender queer transsexuals are employed full-time by the BBC and therefore not free on a Friday, the Mayor will have to settle for escorting a couple of boring old run-of-the-mill non-binary types to the mosque.

This raises the awkward question of which entrance they will use; the males only entrance or the inferior female's entrance? Or is there a non-binary entrance? If all gender identities are valid, as the mayor insists, surely he has planned ahead.

But the better question is why Sadiq Khan is fixated on how everyone else identifies rather than concentrating his own efforts on identifying as a mayor with correct priorities - bins, buses, trains, police ...

Instead, he comes across as an overexcited Maoist Young Guard chanting thought-terminating cliches, but waving a little pink & blue rather than red book.

This is not the first time the London Mayor has used his position to promote the anti-science nonsense that there are more than two genders.

Back in February of this year he tweeted:

> "Trans women are women.
> Trans men are men.
> Non-binary people are non-binary.
> All gender identities are valid."

If transwomen are women ... doesn't that logically mean then that women are transwomen? And if transmen are men, then aren't men transmen?

And, of course, sea horses are horses and horses are sea horses.

ALL ABOARD THE GAY TRAIN

The UK's first fully decorated Pride Train made its inaugural journey last month, staffed entirely by an LGBTQ crew.

The biggest gay flag reportedly ever seen in the UK was painted on the side of the 11-carriage train which travelled from London to Manchester.

The inside of the train was filled with gay posters and gay literature for passengers.

The fabulously gay train conductor used the sparkly intercom to give passengers regular gay related facts and information as well as announcing which glittering station the gay train was sauntering into next.

And if all of that is not queer enough for you, passengers were required to jump to their feet and dance to Kylie Minogue's "The Loco-Motion" every ten minutes.

Admittedly I made that last bit up. Then again, I don't know that they didn't do that. It might have been YMCA. Or it might have been nothing at all. Who knows?

Launched by Avanti West Coast, who run routes from London to Birmingham, Manchester, Liverpool, Wales and Scotland, the gay train was unveiled two months after the end of Pride Month which just goes to show that not even gay trains can run on time.

The woke mobile's inaugural journey reportedly ran without incident though some passengers complained that a gay train shouldn't have to run on straight tracks.

A spokesperson for Avanti West Coast said the gay train was "a sign of the steps we are taking toward a more inclusive, diverse and equal society".

Right. Because nothing says inclusion like a gay train staffed entirely by homosexuals.

One wonders how they ensured the crew were fully LGBT+ compliant. How could anyone be sure that the guard was really a transexual or that the customer service woman was really a lesbian? What sort of risk assessment did they do?

But what better way to demonstrate that one's sexuality is no longer something that should keep you from certain jobs than by demanding applicants declare their sexual preference in order to know whether they qualify for the job.

Police are already gearing up for when the train is tagged. Graffiti on the gay train will, of course, be denounced as a hate crime. The train crew will probably all become sick with PTSD and activists will insist that, as a result, all trains should be painted with rainbows.

The stupidity of a gay train should be clear for everyone to see. When the bosses at Avanti West Coast realise that gay people have always been able to travel on normal trains, they are going to feel incredibly silly for wasting so much time and effort creating a gay train.

Of course, Avanti West Coast's Pride Train has nothing to do with equality or diversity or inclusion but is rather a corporate orgy of intersectionality that makes fun of the very people it proports to represent.

The gay community have spent 50 years fighting to be perceived as just like everybody else, only for a bunch of social justice worriers to come chugging along and turn them into a 5-star cringe circus train.

Avanti West Coast are not bringing inclusion. They are treating gays as if they are freaks that need everybody to throw rainbows at them and tell them how special they are just to get a train.

MELBOURNE UNIVERSITY'S ATTACK ON WOMEN, ON FREEDOM – ON ITSELF

Melbourne University has warned staff teaching a course on feminism they must not say anything that could cause harm to transgendered students.

One imagines the university's geography faculty will now rewrite their course so as not to harm flat earthers.

And staff teaching evolutionary biology will reconfigure lectures in order to avoid harming creationists.

What is certain is that the whole silly episode will, itself, one day form the basis of a social studies course investigating mass stupidity.

Melbourne University vice-chancellor Duncan Maskell gave the warning after the hurty feelings brigade – also known as the University of Melbourne Student Union Queer Political Action Collective –

insisted a second-year philosophy subject on feminism was harmful to transgendered students.

They complained the subject was taught by a lecturer who had dared to ask women to detail how their experience of female bathrooms had been impacted by the inclusion of trans women.

The lecturer, Dr Holly Lawford-Smith, said "philosophy is all about asking questions".

But, according to newspaper reports, the woke-chancellor told staff this week that "the academic freedom to pursue questions concerning transgender identity" had to be balanced with "the damage and harm that our transgender colleagues experience from those questions being pursued".

Maskell didn't say what damage and harm women might experience from those questions *not* being pursued.

Nor did he say what damage and harm his university might experience when prospective students realised intellectual curiosity had been cancelled and so there was little point enrolling there.

When pursuit of truth must be balanced by feelings, you're no longer fit to run a university.

The vice-chancellor did say that respect when discussing trans issues was important because "transgender people are first and foremost people".

If he had sat in one of Dr Holly Lawford-Smith's classes he might have learned that women are also people – provided, of course, that idea doesn't harm someone in the student union.

Melbourne University is now considering a "gender affirmation policy" that would ban academics saying anything that has the potential to harm transgender staff and students.

This means the only person who would be unsafe when a question is asked about trans issues is the person asking the question.

The draft policy says: "Where the university determines that an activity or event poses an unacceptable risk of harm to [transgender and gender-diverse] members of the university community, it may determine not to conduct or host the activity or event on those grounds."

What constitutes "harm" is not clear which, of course, is part of the evil genius of such policies. The woolly nature of the offence is deliberate so that people, who cannot possibly know if they are likely to be in violation of the policy, will self-censor.

But essentially, the university's policy prohibits any ideas that aren't the student union's.

It is an attack on freedom, an attack on women and an attack on itself.

The University of Melbourne is now a dangerous place, not just for women but for anyone with an inquiring mind.

They should seek to study and work at competitor universities more interested in seeking truth than supplying emotional bubble wrap and where they are more concerned about stopping actual harm rather than preventing hurty feelings.

HOW SINGER SAM SMITH CANCELLED HIMSELF

In a classic case of unintended consequences, non-binary singer Sam Smith will find himself neither here nor there when awards for best male and female performers are announced at this year's Brit Awards.

Smith – who told the world in 2019 that "I'm not male or female, I think I flow somewhere in between" – is now complaining that he is excluded from the best vocalist award which is decided along gender lines.

His album Love Goes, which has been in the British Top 40 for five months, is eligible for British album of the year when the awards are announced in May. But Smith has inadvertently cancelled himself from the best male artist category.

Smith told his 15 million Instagram followers: "I look forward to a time where awards shows can be reflective of the society we live in."

The good news for Smith is that they already are. Ninety-nine per cent of Brits identify as either a man or a woman.

But this is not enough for Smith who insists on using pronouns they/them.

He wants the awards to reflect "society" – by which he means a minuscule minority.

It is telling that he did not ask for the awards to reflect reality.

Organisers of the Brit Awards have, as you would expect, reacted wokely.

They issued a statement last Friday promising to "evolve the show to be as inclusive and relevant as possible" by which we presume to mean they will ignore science to be as ridiculous and as irrelevant as possible.

"The gendered categories are very much under review," the Academy said. "We need to consult more widely before changes are made to make sure we get it right."

Well of course.

The Brit Awards only have male and female gendered categories at present because organisers have only had the chance to consult biology.

But after organisers consult more widely, by which they mean read Twitter, big changes are expected.

One imagines that the 2022 awards will feature hundreds of categories ranging from best male and best female vocalist to best polygender and best gender apathetic (yes, that's a thing) vocalist.

But surely the most progressive thing to do would be to simply lump anyone who doesn't identify as male into the female category. They're already doing it in sport.

They could give awards to the Best British Male Solo Artist and to the Best British Non-Male Solo Artist. Problem solved.

Sure some ladies will complain, but only because they are trans exclusionary bigots.

If this is unacceptable then perhaps the Brit Awards should keep the male and female categories but add a third – Best British Seeking Attention by Any Means Solo Artist.

Sam Smith would clean up.

CAN A $50 NOTE IDENTITY AS A $100 NOTE?

If you were to believe everything you read in the mainstream press, the greatest threat we face is from the intolerant.

But as with most things you read in the mainstream press, the opposite is in fact the case. We are most endangered, not by the intolerant, but by the tolerant.

We are not in danger of being overwhelmed by bigots who reject everything as much as we are in danger from open-minded fools who accept everything.

'Bigot' has come to mean anyone who can make up his mind in an organised fashion, while tolerant and open-minded are terms now typically associated with people who cannot seem to make up their mind about anything at all.

A bigot insists that marriage is between a man and a woman. The tolerant agree that marriage is whatever you want it to be.

And only a bigot insists that there are just two genders. The tolerant understand that there are dozens of genders. Or, if you prefer, there are no genders at all. Whatever. No judgement here.

On and on we could go. Our minds are so flattened by broadmindedness that they are in danger of losing all depth.

Like the foolish carpenter who discarded his ruler since its measurements seemed far too arbitrary, we have abandoned objective truth – with its ugly habit of excluding other options – and we are now busy constructing a rickety new world using the ideas of the moment as our only reference point.

Tellingly, we have not abandoned objective truth altogether.

If I use a $50 note to pay the LGBTIQA+ activist for a $100 item, they will not accept my explanation that the $50 note has recently started identifying as $100.

Yet other fixed points such as right and wrong, good and evil, normal and abnormal have all but disappeared. Anyone who appeals to them is said to be a bigot.

In the face of this maddening broadmindedness, what the world needs most right now is intolerance.

Some people will be immediately triggered by this suggestion because our culture has led them to believe that intolerance is always wrong. These same simple minds believe that tolerance is always right.

But a moment's thought show's that tolerance is not always good and intolerance is not always bad.

Tolerance is an attitude of reasoned patience toward that which we do not like. Tolerance restrains us from showing anger or inflicting punishment when we don't agree.

But more important than its definition is its area of application. Tolerance applies only to people, never to bad ideas. Intolerance applies only to bad ideas, never to people.

Digest this and you will immediately see that our problem in the West is not so much intolerance, which is bigotry, as our problem is tolerance which is indifference to truth and error and a philosophical casualness that is applauded as enlightened and broadminded.

I'm not saying we don't need more tolerance. What is Jesus' command to "love your enemies" but a call for greater tolerance?

But tolerance must only go so far, and no further. Jesus commanded us "love your enemies" not "love your enemy's ideas".

We must be gentle with the erring but violent with the error.

Sadly, we have muddled the two. We are more likely to love ideas we should hate and to hate people we should love, all in the name of broadmindedness.

Charity is for people, never for bad ideas.

Concerning wrong ideas, we must be intolerant. And it is in this area that we must snap out of our penchant for sentimental gushing that currently welcomes every crazy idea because, well, "who are we to judge?". And we must stop destroying every person with whom we disagree because, well, "bigot!".

An engineer must be intolerant of bad maths or the bridge he builds risks collapse. The police officer must be intolerant of drivers running red lights or people will die. The doctor must be intolerant of bad hygiene or patients become even sicker. And all of us must be intolerant of the broadminded and good-natured tax man who adds seven and three and tells us we owe fifteen.

Our culture is like the mathematician who, afraid of being called a bigot but very concerned with being seen to be progressive, encourages squares to discard one of their sides and so only too late discovers he has lost all his squares.

Right is right, even if nobody is right. And wrong is wrong, even if the whole world is wrong.

We don't need people to be right when everyone is right. But we desperately need more people who are brave enough to be right when the whole world is wrong, or we will discover only too late that we are standing with feet firmly planted in mid-air.

HOW LGBGTI DOES A MEMBER OF THE LGBTQI COMMUNITY NEED TO BE?

How LGBTQI does a member of the LBGTQI community need to be?

Packed to the Rafters star Hugh Sheridan will be asking himself that question after his lead role in a Sydney Festival production was cancelled this week.

The Adelaide-born actor was to star in Hedwig and the Angry Inch – a musical about a gay man who has a sex change so he can legally marry another man.

The show was due to open at the Enmore Theatre in January. But it has been postponed after transgender activists complained that Sheridan was "cis-gendered", which means he is a man who is not wondering if he might be one of 71 other genders.

It mattered little that Sheridan had spent October promoting the musical by explaining to journalists that he was a very well credentialled member of the LGBTQI community, having had relationships with men (gay) and with women (bi), and having refused to label himself or his sexuality (questioning).

Sheridan was missing a 'T' in his LGBQI where 'T', of course, stands for 'Trans' – not for tolerance – and so Sheridan had to go.

So much for the inclusive LGBTQI community we constantly hear about.

"I'm still single, and everyone is on the smorgasbord!" Sheridan had told *The Daily Mail* in October.

If that wasn't a commitment to diversity, I don't know what is!

So, apart from thinking about changing his gender, it's hard to imagine what more the four-time Logie award winner could possibly have done to be included in the inclusive rainbow pride 'love is love' family.

But The Queer Arts Alliance were having none of it.

They complained to the Hedwig producers that "the choice to cast a cisgender male as a transgender character is offensive and damaging to the trans community".

That Hedwig was a work of fiction about a fictional character did not matter. The lead actor needed to be transgendered in order to pretend to be transgendered.

Hedwig producers caved in to the criticism and announced on Tuesday that they would postpone the show in order to find a replacement for the not quite LGBTQI-enough Hugh Sheridan.

In the musical the lead character's sex change goes horribly wrong, leaving him with a dysfunctional one-inch lump of flesh between his legs. So one presumes the lead role can only go to a transgendered actress who is able to provide evidence of a botched sex change operation. That ought to narrow the search considerably.

The show's producers said of the original casting process, "we auditioned a wide, diverse range of performers and no one from any background was excluded from this process".

Presumably, they will now look to recast Hedwig with auditions from a narrow, uniform range of performers and everyone from all backgrounds except one very specific background will be excluded from the process.

All this to prove their commitment to inclusion.

A spokesperson for the Sydney Festival said: "The values of equality and inclusivity have long guided the work of Sydney Festival. With these values in mind, the festival supports the producer's decision to postpone the January season of 'Hedwig and the Angry Inch.'"

All of which meant they were committed to excluding Sheridan because of their commitment to inclusion.

But yesterday, in a final twist, American Stephen Trask, who wrote the musical back in 2001, told the Sydney Morning Herald that the play's main character was never transgendered.

Hedwig, he said, was a gay man who was bullied into a sex change by his boyfriend.

Hugh Sheridan might not know what it's like to be a transgendered woman but he certainly now has lived experience of what it is like to be a gay man, bullied by sex change happy activists.

So without realising it, the LBGTQI enforcers have made Sheridan perfect for the very role they insisted he should not have.

MOURNING THE NON-EXISTENT TRANSEXUAL MURDER EPIDEMIC

Imagine a funeral where mourners stand grieving around an empty coffin.

Those gathered for the service are inconsolable. That there is no corpse is entirely beside the point.

They have a funeral at this time every year, whether anyone has actually died or not.

Welcome to Sydney's Transgender Day of Remembrance, an annual vigil to highlight what we are told is an epidemic of violence toward trans people by the intolerant among us.

The problem with the event, according to an ABC News report, was that organisers had struggled to find victims to remember.

The Transgender Murder Monitor, an international register of transgender homicides, has recorded 3317 deaths around the world in the past 10 years, only two of which occurred in Australia.

You could be forgiven for thinking this was good news. Two murders in 10 years is not an epidemic; it's not even a pattern. In fact, two names barely make a list.

But organisers of Sydney's Transgender Day of Remembrance saw this as a problem rather than as a cause for celebration.

Dr Eloise Brook from the NSW Gender Centre told the ABC: "After we've had our memorial, I've always wondered at the lack of names of our own community that we included.

"It began to seem to me that we were memorialising an empty coffin and it just didn't quite seem right."

Instead of celebrating the live-and-let-live attitude of tolerant Australians, Brook set out to find Australians who were killed for being trans so that they could be added to the very short list of names to be read on Remembrance Day.

It was a bit like mourners at a funeral who, upon hearing that there was no need for a memorial since no-one had actually died, insisting, "There's got to be a body around here somewhere".

Brook told the ABC that six months of research failed to turn up even one person killed for being transgendered.

This was good news, right? Evidence that Australia is one of the most accepting, not to mention safe places, on earth. Cancel the funeral and get the party started!

But no. This was evidence of "death by bureaucracy", according to Brooks.

Authorities must have misgendered the dead. Or perhaps trans murders had been incorrectly recorded as death by suicide or by misadventure.

Brook said she finally "hit gold", finding around 10 names of people in a Melbourne University Archive who might have been murdered for being transgendered back in the seventies and early eighties.

She said their names would be added to the existing two to be read on Remembrance Day.

Brook's struggle to find evidence of trans homicides in Australia comes in the wake of American studies showing little evidence that transgender Americans are killed at an unusually high rate, despite media claims of just such an epidemic.

Wilfred Reilly, an Associate Professor of Political Science at Kentucky State University who is an expert on empirically testing political claims, examined data from the Human Rights Campaign and found that trans people were killed at *much lower* numbers than the average American and seldom for actually being trans.

His findings were published last December.

Similarly, Chad Green, who identifies with the LGBT community and is a senior contributor at The Federalist, reviewed 118 trans murders recorded by the HRC since 2015 and found that "four appear to have been directly anti-trans motivated".

These findings fly in the face of the narrative we have been led to believe – that there is so much hatred toward trans people, to even question trans ideology is to risk setting off waves of violence against them.

Earlier this year Democrat Presidential nominee Joe Biden describe violence against trans people as "an epidemic that requires national leadership". He accused President Trump of fanning "the flames of transphobia".

Back in Australia, Dr Andy Kaladelfos, a UNSW Criminologist who specialises in crimes against the LGBTI community, told the ABC: "It doesn't seem to make sense that there would only be two recorded violent deaths of transgender people."

And it doesn't make sense. Unless, of course, transgendered people are not being murdered for being trans as we have been led to believe.

And if that's the case, then activists are needlessly creating fear amongst trans people who already suffer high levels of stress and anxiety.

Moreover, claims that people who voice concerns about – or disagreement with – transgender ideology are feeding an epidemic of violent hatred towards trans people would turn out to be false.

It would suggest that Australians are mature enough to disagree with trans ideology without hating trans people and stoking supposed "flames of transphobia".

THE UN DECREES THERE IS NO WRONG WAY TO BE A WOMAN

It's not for nothing that the United Nations entity for women is called UN Women. They do, after all, spend most of their time UNwomaning women.

Last year UN Women tweeted "Trans women are women at the end of the day" – which of course begged the question, what were trans women at the beginning of the day?

If you can wake for breakfast as a man and sit down for dinner as a woman, it only goes to show there's less to being a woman than one might have thought.

It turns out any old man can do it.

The cheerleaders for women's empowerment at UN Women said as much yesterday when they tweeted:

> *There's no wrong way to be a woman.*
> *There's no wrong way to be a woman.*
> *There's no wrong way to be a woman.*
> *There's no wrong way to be a woman.*
> *There's no wrong way to be a woman.*
> *There's no wrong way to be a woman.*
> *There's no wrong way to be a woman.*

The repetition is not a typo.

At first, I wasn't sure whether this was a real UN Women post or if perhaps a small child had been practice tweeting.

Tweet chanting, as if repeating a fallacy ad nauseam makes it true, is juvenile. Repeating nonsense doesn't magically make it science.

When Twitter doubled its character limit so that people could express themselves more fully, the wacky interns at UN Women decided to use the increased social media real estate to chant mantras.

Basically, they are saying, 'we will not even attempt adult discourse'.

But leaving aside the cult-like, repetitive doublespeak propaganda which has the distinct feel of compelled speech – a salient feature of totalitarian regimes – UN Women has become just another institution hijacked to remove biological fact from our minds.

It has never been more important for parents to be vigilant about actually parenting their children, a key part of which means keeping them well away from United Nations social media accounts.

If "there's no wrong way to be a woman" then UN Women have, true to form, effectively erased women.

One might suggest that having the Y chromosome would be a wrong way to be a woman. We should at least agree that being born a man is a pretty poor starting point.

We might also agree it is quite remarkable that we now live in a world where this has to be explained.

If, as UN Women insists, "there's no wrong way to be a woman", does this mean there's no wrong way to be a man? Are UN Women about to admit that the "toxic masculinity" they decried in 2019 was all a myth?

Apparently, there is a wrong way to be a man. We know this because once men want to wear make-up and dresses they seem to become women, instead of staying as men wearing make-up and dresses.

The United Nations is right that all women are different, provided – of course – that the one commonality is that all women are female.

I can put on a Sydney Swans jumper but that doesn't make me Buddy Franklin. "Woman" is not a costume, a feeling or an attitude. Being a "woman" is based on a fixed biology reality. To put it bluntly, women are born, not worn.

Which means there can't be a 'wrong way' to be something that you objectively are. Yet while there is not a wrong way to be a woman, there is a wrong way to identify a woman.

A biological man is not a woman – as any female athlete competing against a 6'4 bloke in a skirt will tell the activists at UN Women if they stop chanting long enough to listen to the people they claim to represent.

Oh, and there's no right way to be a failed, corrupt experiment in multilateralism. That only needs to be said once.

3

FREEDOM OF SPEECH IN WOKETOPIA

THE SAFE SPACE WHERE CULTURES GO TO DIE

When Catholic Archbishop of Hobart Julian Porteous wrote a booklet entitled "Don't Mess with Marriage", it never occurred to him that the Tasmanian Anti-Discrimination Commissioner was about to mess with him.

The Catholic bishop was merely doing what Catholic bishops do. He wrote a booklet outlining Catholic doctrine for Catholic parents interested in Catholic teaching.

That's when a transgendered activist and federal Greens candidate stepped in.

The activist complained to the Commission that the booklet was insulting. As well as an apology, she demanded that Catholic Education implement a 'lesbian, gay, bisexual, transgender and intersex awareness program' for all staff and students.

It's a mystery why 'she' did not go further and insist that Catholic boys and girls also be taught – in between learning to "love thy neighbour" and "do unto others as you would have them do unto you" – about asexuals, androsexuals, gynesexuals and pansexuals. But baby steps, right?

In Tasmania, it is illegal to engage in conduct that insults, offends or humiliates someone on the basis of their sexual orientation if it is reasonable to anticipate that someone might be insulted.

So you have to anticipate the feelings of complete strangers before you say anything. And failing to correctly anticipate how your words might make someone whom you've never met feel, can put you in breach of the law.

This was Bishop Porteous' mistake!

He should have anticipated that a transgendered activist might intercept his letter to Catholic parents and be suddenly offended by Catholic teaching that has been well known for 2000 years.

Tasmania's Anti-Discrimination Commissioner Robin Banks – a great name for a public servant if ever there was one – concluded that the complaint against Bishop Porteous had merit.

Ms Banks said the Bishop's booklet asserted "messing with marriage is messing with kids" and this was a problem because it "brings to people's minds child abuse."

Bishop Porteous was to be held responsible not only for the words he wrote but also for the thoughts that might come to mind when people, lacking in basic comprehension skills, read them.

So Tasmanian taxpayers were to fund an investigation into whether or not Catholic teaching on sex and marriage might be offensive to a transgendered activist with an eye on garnering much needed publicity for an upcoming tilt at a federal election.

The Anti-Discrimination Commissioner was not just robbin' banks!

Ms Banks attempted what the Anti-Discrimination Tribunal call "conciliation". Conciliation means the action of stopping someone from being angry.

If Catholic doctrine makes you angry, fear not! The Anti-Discrimination Commission will facilitate conciliation because the State is now responsible to help you manage your feelings.

Media reports at the time said that all the activist wanted was for the Catholic Church to make amendments to their booklet on marriage.

Bishop Porteous must have felt so stupid. How much time and trouble could he have saved himself if he had simply allowed activists to edit Catholic doctrine before he preached it?

And while he was at it, he could have had activists run an eye over the doctrine of the Virgin Birth, Crucifixion, Resurrection and Return of Christ, just to make sure they were all lesbian, gay, bisexual, transgender and intersex compliant.

When the Catholic Church refused to change their 2000-year-old doctrine on the say-so of an activist; and when the activist refused to accept the Bishop's statement of regret for causing offence, the Anti-Discrimination Commissioner decided the matter would go to a tribunal hearing.

A tribunal hearing would have discovered that Catholic Bishops and transgendered activists disagree on existential questions such as the definition and purpose of marriage. Who knew?

The Tribunal would have adjudicated on whether the complainant felt humiliated and whether the bishop intended to offend. That's right. Government bureaucrats would have investigated the emotions of the complainant and the inner thoughts of the churchman.

Presumably the outcome would be better for the bishop if he could prove he was not thinking malicious thoughts when he penned his booklet. The outrageous thing is that an unelected, unrepresentative public servant now has the power to probe the thoughts of a free man to determine whether a crime has been committed.

The activist eventually dropped the complaint, but only after Bishop Porteous had spent thousands of dollars on lawyers and wasted a year of his life agonising over whether he would be criminalised for expressing his sincerely held religious belief.

Commissioner Robin Banks didn't need to punish Bishop Porteous. The process was the punishment.

The activist could afford to drop the case against the Catholic Bishop because 'she' didn't need a favourable judgment in order to win. 'She' merely needed to make an example of one minister, and a thousand ministers across the country, not wanting the expense or the stress of being dragged before the courts, could be counted on to censor themselves.

Whilst the case against Bishop Porteous was dropped, the law in Tasmania remains. I was with pastors in Hobart earlier this year, and they were well aware that if they said the wrong thing, there was nothing stopping someone from claiming to have been offended and then hauling them before Robin Banks' successor.

Think about that for a moment. If you say the wrong thing in Tasmania – and by the "wrong thing", I mean the suddenly un-fashionable thing – there's a government bureaucrat who can punish you.

Israel Folau used to be known for his exploits on the rugby field. But one fateful day earlier this year, when asked a question on social media about God's plan for homosexuals, he foolishly gave his honest opinion – that gays would go to hell unless they sought forgiveness.

Well all hell *did* break lose, against Israel Folau.

Suddenly, a footballer's opinion about the afterlife created more outrage than the fact that Australia hadn't won a Rugby World Cup in almost 20 years.

Australian Rugby boss Raelene Castle said that Folau's religious belief about eternal judgment had been "the singularly most difficult thing" she had ever had to deal with!

Don't worry that Rugby, unlike AFL, is not on free-to-air television. Forget that NZ Rugby had asked the ARU to reduce the number of Australian Super Rugby teams because they were worried about the poor standard of our players ... the greatest challenge to Rugby Union in this country was a fullback's musings on eternal damnation.

The ARU boss told *The Australian* Newspaper: "I really wish I could sit here and say that by sanctioning him we'll fix it. But it really is not that simple because of the freedom-of-speech element."

Ah yes, that pesky freedom of speech element. You know, where people's speech can't be controlled by their betters. And trust me, our betters would love nothing better than to control our speech.

The former Human Rights Commission President, Gillian Triggs, told a crowd in Hobart last year that: "Sadly you can say what you like around the kitchen table at home."

Well what is this country coming to when, from Hobart to Cairns, families are still able to speak freely around the kitchen table!

If only a bureaucrat could sit at every dinner table around the nation, adjudicating what family members can and can't say to one another as they pass the casserole!

It sounds ridiculous. But the ridiculous people are not joking.

The same people who rightly insist that they should not be told what to do in their bedrooms, want the power to tell you what you can say in your kitchen.

The question is not whether you agreed with Israel Folau. The question is whether he should have the right to say what he thinks. And be careful how you decide. Because the same principle you use to deny Folau the right of expression is the very principle that may well be one day used to deny you of yours.

Australian rugby sponsors said their commitment to diversity and tolerance meant they could not tolerate Folau's divergent view. They would celebrate diversity by using their sponsorship to enforce conformity.

They insisted that Rugby must prove it was all about inclusion, and how better to celebrate inclusion than by excluding Folau .... because of his views on what happens after you die, for goodness sake!

It must have been a surprise to Folau to learn that corporations had such strong convictions about what does and does not happen after a person gives up the ghost.

The difference between Folau and the corporate sponsors was this – and it's significant. Whilst Folau said he believed homosexuals would be judged in the afterlife, those who disagreed with Folau wanted him judged now!

You tell me who is the greater danger; the religious footballer who, in answer to a question, says he believes some people will be punished after they die; or his detractors who say that someone must be punished in this life, merely for what they believe about the next?

A Qantas spokesperson said Folau's comments were disappointing. Well God forbid that any of us hold religious views that might disappoint an airline.

But here's the part of the Folau story which was truly frightening. And it didn't get anywhere near enough media focus. One of Australia's Human Rights Commissioners told the media he would make himself available to counsel Israel Folau about "how better to express his views".

How thoughtful.

We now have a government bureaucracy of highly paid public servants who make themselves available, via the media of course, to help you better express your religious views.

Here's a view. The Human Rights Commission should mind its own business. (Admittedly, I could have done with some help expressing that view).

Human Rights Commissioner Edward Santow told the media: "I will write to the Australian Rugby Union to offer to meet with Folau – to hear his side of the story, and to discuss how he can live out his faith while being conscious of the impact his words can have on others."

What qualifies Mr Santow to tell Israel Folau – or anyone else for that matter – how to "live out your faith"?

Here's the frightening thing; in a so-called 'inclusive' culture, it increasingly seems that the logical next step is for dissenting voices to need State permission to speak.

What seems to have been missed in this whole episode is that not a single Australian human rights commissioner sprang to the defence of a Polynesian Christian who was vilified and threatened with sanction for merely answering a question about his religion.

Just as not a single human rights commissioner sprang to the defence of a Tasmanian Bishop who was being vilified and threatened with sanction for merely saying what Penny Wong, Julia Gillard and Barak Obama had all been saying a few years earlier.

Raelene Castle from the Australian Rugby Union said that she was trying to find a balance between Folau's right to speak and other people's right to not be offended. She said that she was committed to helping Israel Folau "walk the line".

It all sounds very reasonable, doesn't it? Striking a balance. Finding the line.

But what's the point of free speech unless it's for speech that is over the line and unbalanced?

If everybody only says what everybody agrees with, then there's no need for freedom of speech. And if no-one is allowed to say anything that deviates from Government-policed parameters, then speech is not free at all.

To be candid, it doesn't seem like corporations or activists or government bureaucrats are that interested in striking much of a balance. They've drawn a line and they are increasingly outspoken about which side of that line they are on.

Whether it's climate science or gay marriage or gender fluidity – one side has gleefully swapped that Voltaire line about disagreeing with what you say but defending to the death your right to say it, for an easier two-word phrase: "Shut up".

This does not bode well for our future, particularly when it comes to the subject of religion.

Religion, properly understood, is our set of answers to the big questions. Where did we come from? What's the purpose of life? How do we determine what is right and wrong? What happens when we die?

If we are not free to honestly discuss those issues, without fear of being dragged before a government tribunal or pushed out of our place of employment, we are left with something far worse than a few people with hurty feelings. We are left with an eerie silence.

We are left with a world in which everything has been settled. Science is settled. History is settled. Truth is relative. Religion is neutered. There is nothing left to discuss, nothing left to learn and so nowhere left to go.

Free speech and a dynamic, growing, advancing culture are intimately linked. A culture that is too weak to bear a dissenting word on race or religion or gender fluidity or reef science is a society that will cease to grow, and then decay, and then decline, and fast. As author Mark Steyn once said, a safe space is where a culture goes to die.

WE HAVE BANNED HATE SPEECH. NOW WE MUST BAN HATE VOTES

Drongo alert: this piece may contain traces of satire and irony.

We have banned hate speech in order to protect minorities and it is now time to ban hate votes in order to protect democracy.

If America's experiment with Trumpism has demonstrated anything, it is that votes, like words, have consequences and so sensible restrictions should be applied.

Just as it is widely accepted that freedom of speech does not give a person the right to say whatever they wish; we must now agree that free elections should not give people the right to cast ballots however they choose.

There must be limits on voting in order to protect voters from themselves.

If it is illegal to speak in a way that offends or humiliates another person on the basis of race, gender, religion or sexual orientation, why should it be legal to vote in a way that offends or humiliates?

For instance, supporting any political party that refuses to remove gendered terms from official documents should be considered a hate vote against trans people.

If discriminating against women in the workplace is illegal, why should it be legal to vote for a party that does not insist on gender quotas? Voting for such a party should constitute a hate vote against women.

And casting a ballot for a politician who does not support Black Lives Matter must be deemed a hate vote against First Nations People.

Anyone found guilty of hate voting should face criminal sanctions.

If your voice can be cancelled on social media for the expressing the wrong opinions, why should your vote not be cancelled at the ballot box for voting the wrong opinions?

Just as free speech does not mean the right to be a bigot, the freedom to vote does not mean the right to vote for a far-right extremist, by which I mean anyone other than a progressive social justice warrior whose pronouns are listed in their social media bio.

It is only by banning hate votes that democracy can be protected from those who would destroy it by recklessly wielding their vote in such a way that values other than those espoused by progressives are able to be legislated.

I understand that some people will argue that there is no freedom to vote if people don't have the freedom to vote in a way that others disagree with. But that's too simplistic.

It's easy to say everyone should vote however they please when your socially progressive agenda's right to exist is not in the firing line.

Eliminating hate votes should not be thought of as limiting free elections. It should be thought of as a moral strategy to keep hate votes from escalating into something more dangerous – like the election of conservatives.

We have banned certain kinds of speech. We must now ban certain kinds of votes. It is the only way to remain free.

Big tech companies have demonstrated that hate speech can be quickly and easily eliminated from social media platforms by suspending or blocking users who violate speech codes.

Such a strategy could be applied at the polls. Hate votes could be quickly and easily eliminated from election counts.

After all, if we are willing to adjudicate what people can say, why would we not adjudicate how people can vote?

It's the logical next step. God help us all

A THREATENED PRIESTLY CLASS WANTS TO CRUCIFY FREE SPEECH

When you understand why the Jewish establishment wanted Jesus dead you'll understand why the mainstream media are now openly agitating for the crucifixion of free speech.

Jesus claimed to be God, communicating directly with people. This was Good News for the common man but for the privileged priestly class, it was hell.

Priests had, for thousands of years, mediated between God and man, placing them in a unique position to be able to control the conversation and mould society as they – er, God – intended.

But now that God was communicating directly with the masses, mediators were suddenly superfluous. Their opportunity to massage messages, manage narratives and manipulate outcomes was gone.

"Crucify Him!" they yelled. And so the priests ensured God was put to death so that they could continue to speak for Him.

Fast forward 2000 years and a new priestly class, suddenly under threat, is reacting with much the same venom.

The mainstream media have, for years, mediated between power and people, placing journalists in a unique position of power themselves.

But then along came a Tweeter-in-chief who used social media to speak directly to voters, sidelining journalists and, in so doing, threatening their ability to control the conversation.

(No, I am not suggesting that Donald Trump is a sinless, Christ-like messiah who can command the oceans and save the world from destruction. Every leftist knows that was Obama).

The High Priests of social media, Mark Zuckerberg and Jack Dorsey, are now actively censoring Trump posts – along with any other conservative messages they don't like – in a rearguard action designed to protect their role as arbitrators of speech.

But like Jesus, free speech is hard to kill.

And so it was that Network Ten's The Project warned ominously about the dangers of Parler, a new social media platform where speech is allowed to roam free of interference from big tech and mainstream media.

The segment was introduced like this: "Are you looking for a place for your misinformation, conspiracy theories and outright lies to be shared with millions, completely unchecked or challenged?" prompting many viewers to think it was going to be a promo for The Project itself.

Then the show's co-host Peter van Onselen identified the enemy of freedom: "It's getting a bit harder for fans of alternative facts, but not on Parler.

"Parler, launched in 2018, looks like Twitter and it functions like Twitter but there are some big differences starting with this catchy tagline: 'Speak freely and express yourself without fear of being de-platformed for your views'."

Now you might think a prominent journalist – not to mention journalism academic – like Peter van Onselen would like the idea of citizens being able to freely express themselves. He does, after all, count on this freedom for himself.

But you'd be mistaken. Ten's political editor loves free speech about as much as the Jewish priests loved Jesus of Nazareth.

Van Onselen sermonised: "In practice, this means things like unsubstantiated claims of voter fraud or QAnon material can be thrown around willy-nilly, without any fact-checking or mediation."

And there you have it — from the professor's own mouth. The problem with Parler is that it allows people to speak without any need for the priestly class to "mediate".

And without the Peter van Onselens of this world fact-checking our opinions, we're in danger of all sorts of "willy-nilly" thinking — which is a high priestly term for non-leftist thinking.

"The reason it's a good thing that platforms like Facebook and Twitter are starting to remove the completely unfiltered world is because it reinforces incorrect thinking and all sorts of problematic ways of having attitudes and that undermines democracy," he said.

Only a self-appointed priestly class who control the media would argue that the best way to protect democracy is to filter people's thinking and attitudes through the leftist bias of a self-appointed priestly class who control the media.

Van Onselen continued: "My natural tendency would be against censorship, but …"

Now when someone uses the word "but" immediately after insisting their natural tendency is to support free speech, you can bet their natural tendency is to think North Korea has a lot to recommend it. But I digress, " ... this isn't about censorship, it's about fact-checking and being able to keep discourse that's discourteous out of the platform."

In other words, it's about censorship.

Shouts of 'crucify free speech' were quickly echoed by The Project's co-host Lisa Wilkinson.

"When you consider how many people are still with Trump at this point and still believe that vote checking has to happen because they feel like the election was stolen from them, they're going to go on this (Parler) and there'll be no fact-checking whatsoever and I'm really worried about the future of the US," she said.

And so our priests in the media want to kill free speech so that they can continue to freely speak and think for us.

God save us from your priests!

VICTORIA MAKES FREE SPEECH UNAFFORDABLE

WHY should protestors have to pay the costs of police who prevented them from assaulting guests arriving to hear Canadian commentator Lauren Southern give a public speech in Melbourne?

Left wing activists should not be financially penalized for wanting to intimidate those with whom they disagree.

If police start charging activists for the disruption to life and property that their actions cause, they will no longer be able to stage violent protests at all, and this would not be fair.

Many of the protestors who harassed mums and dads wanting to hear Southern are likely unemployed and so lack the means to pay police costs. But if members of the Antifa-associated groups have to get jobs, they will not have the spare time to disrupt lawful gatherings in the first place.

Aware of the awful predicament protestors face, the Victorian Government has come up with a novel solution. They have decided to charge law abiding citizens for the crimes committed against them.

Instead of fining protestors who blocked a highway, destroyed private property and threatened people who attended Lauren Southern's July 20 event, police have invoiced the event organisers.

The $68,000 cost of posting 100 uniformed police officers between Southern's legal event and the pack of feral protestors trying to disrupt it is to be borne by Southern.

Victorian Police minister Lisa Neville calls it user pays policing. This innovative approach means that police and protestors can now work together to ensure Australia's most left-wing State remains that way, with their political opponents picking up the tab.

Whenever a conservative speaker comes to Melbourne, their ideological opponents can threaten violent protests outside the venue. If this fails to intimidate the speaker's audience, the Victorian police will threaten to invoice the speaker for any costs incurred policing protestors who have made threats.

The beauty of this arrangement will not be lost on the protestors. The more feral the protestors, the more police who will be required to control them. And the more police required, the higher the financial cost to those with whom the protestors disagree.

In this way, protestors get to intimidate people they don't like and hit them in the hip pocket, all at the same time.

Meanwhile, Victoria's left-leaning Government is able to turn the State into a no-go zone for conservative speakers. Rather than banning their ideological opponents from holding public meetings in Melbourne, the Andrew's Government can brag about its commitment to upholding free speech whilst actually charging for it.

Predictably, organisers of Lauren Southern's speaking tour, Axiomatic Events, have complained that, by charging them for the protestor's actions, police are "victim blaming".

But if conservative groups don't want to be charged for being victims of violent protests they should stop saying things that make them victims of violent protestors.

If right-leaning groups don't like this idea, they are welcome to hold a public meeting in Melbourne to argue for their right to free speech. Of course, their meeting will be protested and guests will be harassed and they will subsequently be invoiced for costs.

That's the way it now works in Victoria where free speech is no longer affordable and violent protests are increasingly profitable.

4

WOKETARDS EVERYWHERE

THE DICTIONARY IS NOW A POLITICAL WEAPON

The dictionary is now a political weapon, edited at will by sanctimonious progressives in order to dominate their ideological opponents.

Definitions are changed with breathtaking speed in order to make the perfectly acceptable thing a conservative has said at breakfast, evidence of bigotry by dinner.

The tactic – employed Tuesday with devastating effect against US Supreme Court nominee Amy Coney Barrett – is one with which Australians are familiar.

Macquarie Dictionary announced it would broaden the definition of misogyny a week after Julia Gillard's speech labelling the then Prime Minister Tony Abbott as a "misogynist".

Misogyny had been defined as "a hatred of women". The problem for Gillard was that Tony Abbott did not hate women – he was married to one. And he had three daughters. And a sister. And a female deputy.

So dictionary editor Sue Butler told the Sydney Morning Herald the definition would be "changed to reflect what Ms Gillard really meant".

Now that's power – the ability to imagine your own version of reality and then edit the dictionary to later wave around as proof that your reality does in fact exist!

What Macquarie Dictionary did in a week to damn Abbott, Webster's dictionary did in a day to trap Amy Coney Barrett.

Trump's Supreme Court nominee told her Senate confirmation hearing: "I have never discriminated on the basis of sexual preference and would never discriminate on the basis of sexual preference."

Later that same day the Democrats decided the term "sexual preference" – a term Joe Biden used without complaint as recently as May and that media and gay activists have used for more than a decade – was problematic.

Senator Mazie Hirono said it was "an offensive and out-dated term used by anti-LGBTQ activists to suggest sexual orientation is a choice".

MSNBC producer Kyle Griffin, who is himself gay, tweeted: "Sexual preference, a term used by Justice Barrett, is offensive and outdated. The term implies sexuality is a choice. It is not. News organizations should not repeat Justice Barrett's words without providing that important context."

Later that same night Webster's dictionary updated its definition of "preference" in order to be in lockstep with leftist ideology.

"The term preference as used to refer to sexual orientation is widely considered offensive in its implied suggestion that a person can choose who they are sexually or romantically attracted to," the dictionary now says.

Putting aside the fact that this meant Websters themselves were unaware the term was "widely offensive" prior to Tuesday, it was an awesome demonstration of cultural domination.

Progressives took the benign term "sexual preference" and turned it into an unspeakable slur in less than 24 hours.

Simply, the term was made offensive soon after someone the Left hates had used it, so that the hated one could be retrospectively accused of hate.

Perhaps the greatest commendation of Amy Coney Barrett is that Democrats had to go so far as adjusting the dictionary in order to make her look bad. But I digress.

It was unnerving to watch 1984 play out in real time, in real life, right in front of our eyes.

One side of the political divide has now been given free license to adjust language on the fly, however they see fit.

As everything becomes digital, reality becomes fluid and the past can be edited at a whim.

Orwell may have predicted the memory hole, but not even he could have predicted real-time public viewing of it in action. And yet it's still effective, even out in the open.

LET'S GO WOKE NOW, EVERYBODY'S LEARNING HOW

Is it just me, or does most social justice stuff seem to be a bunch of whining people looking to "problematize" everything, everywhere, all the time?

The most annoying social justice worriers are those who insist that everything must be diverse. You cannot escape the diversity police. There is no respite from their incessant harping ... not even in the ocean.

And so it was that on July 23rd The San Francisco Weekly published an article headlined: "California Surfing Has a Serious Diversity Problem".

Well of course it does. We're just amazed it has taken until now for the activists to notice.

Although to be fair, they've been busy toppling 200 year-old statues in a ritual of purification aimed at cleansing society while consolidating their own moral credentials.

Now with statues destroyed, police stations ablaze and Coon Cheese forced to change its name, they've decided to take their activist zeal off-shore.

With apologies to the Beach Boys ...

> "Let's go woke now
> Everybody's learning how
> Come and campaign with me
> Come and campaign with me
>
> "Early in the morning we'll be startin' out
> Some LGBT honeys will be coming along
> We're woke and we're diverse
> With bitter envy inside
> And headin' out righting all wrongs
>
> "Lets go woke now, come on and see
> I'm gonna make you woke like me
> Let's go woke now come on and see
> Let's drone on about diversity
> Let's get woke now, everybody's learning how
> Come on a campaign with me
> Come on a campaign and me"

And so Emily Zhang, an intern at the *SF Weekly*, goes on a woke safari insisting that the ocean is racist and that the waves off California's coast are homophobic because white guys outnumber black lesbians in the surf.

Emily has surveyed the ocean and discovered that pale skinned heteronormative cis-gender males are far more prominent than LGBTQ BIPOCs. And so the intern has found a brand new outrage that absolutely no-one was outraged about.

She writes: "Surfing, despite its roots in indigenous Pacific Islander history, has been seen as a sport for straight white men for far too long."

We look forward to Emily's next article that will no-doubt begin: "Basketball, despite its roots in white people culture having actually been invented by a white man, has been seen as a sport for straight black men for far too long."

We won't hold our breath.

Intern Emily interviews Mira Manickam-Shirley who complains that she is regularly one of the only women of colour trying to catch a wave.

Okay. So, white men are preventing non-white people from catching waves?

Or do the waves discriminate? Do the waves yell racial slurs at black people?

The article then focuses on Dionne Ybarra whom we are told "would have had a hard time seeing surfing as anything other than a white sport".

Why does Dionne feel this way? What terrors of discrimination must she have faced in the surf?

Intern Emily writes: "Her Mexican-American family would only venture out to the water once a year, on July 4th."

In other words, my mum didn't teach me to swim or take me to the beach ... so it's white people's fault that I don't surf.

I wasn't aware that only heterosexual white dudes were allowed to purchase surfboards and get in the ocean.

Emily's article should have included this handy three-step guide to ending white supremacy in the surf.

1. Buy a board
2. Get in the water
3. Get on the board while in the water

Thank goodness the *SF Weekly* – a publication you'd never heard of and now you know why – is finally getting around to the things that matter. Diversity in surfing is right up there with diversity in polo. We can't be truly equal until this wrong is righted.

Next it will be that the sharks are racist because black surfers are hardly ever attacked.

It is a strange person indeed who looks at an activity and says: "Not enough two-spirited gender queer vegan's do that activity and that's a problem. We need some sort of government agency to promote two-spirited gender queer vegans in the surf!"

How about just finding things you like to do and sharing them with people regardless of their race, or their sexuality?

Oh, and one more thing.

The *SF Weekly* article failed to mention when complaining that surfing has been "a sport for straight white men for far too long" that the reigning world champion is Brazilian Italo Ferreira.

Italo Ferreira is non-white. I can't tell you his sexual preference, but everyone at the *SF Weekly* hopes he is gay.

RUGBY LEAGUE'S HUMILIATION IS COMPLETE

Rugby Australia sacked their star player and trashed their brand to keep a sponsor happy. Now they have no star player, no brand and — as of today – no major sponsor.

Go woke, go broke.

Qantas announced today it would end its partnership with Rugby Australia, a year after it demanded the code ditch its best player for his views on homosexuality.

What fools the ARU who bent over to keep the airline's pink sponsorship dollar, alienating fans who wanted to watch rugby rather than receive a lecture on LGBTQI diversity.

Qantas had pressured the ARU to deal with Israel Folau after he posted on social media that homosexuals would go to hell unless they sought forgiveness from Jesus.

Suddenly, a footballer's opinion about the afterlife created more outrage than the fact that Australia hadn't won a Rugby World Cup in 20 years.

The then CEO of Rugby Australia, Raelene Castle, said that Folau's religious belief about eternal judgment had been "the singularly most difficult thing" she had ever had to deal with.

Never mind that Rugby, unlike the AFL, had no free-to-air television deal.

Forget that NZ Rugby had asked the ARU to reduce the number of Australian Super Rugby teams because they were worried about the poor standard of our players.

The greatest challenge to rugby union in this country was, apparently, a fullback's musings on eternal damnation.

Sponsors complained that their commitment to diversity and tolerance meant they could not tolerate Folau's divergent view. They would celebrate diversity by using their sponsorship to enforce conformity.

They insisted that Rugby must prove it was all about inclusion, and how better to celebrate inclusion than by excluding their best player ... because of his views on what happens when you die.

So Rugby Australia acted at the behest of sponsors to rid themselves of their best player in what became a publicity and legal nightmare, costing the code millions in lawyers' fees and many more millions in a settlement with Folau.

The loss of its star fullback did not help the Wallabies bid to attract a TV deal. Nor did it help them to progress beyond the quarter finals of the 2019 World Cup.

The fallout ultimately saw coach Michael Cheika resign.

Then Castle resigned.

And now, key sponsor Qantas has flown the coop.

The moral of the story?

Don't waste time pandering to fickle, woke organisations that care more about a footballer's views on the afterlife than a footballer's ability to run and kick and tackle and pass.

Not only will you lose your fanbase, you'll lose your woke sponsor the moment the wind changes.

Qantas chief customer officer Stephanie Tully said the COVID-19 pandemic meant the airline could no longer afford to support Australian Rugby.

"Like all Australians, we'll continue to cheer them on from the sidelines," she said.

News of Qantas' departure led some to wonder if Israel Folau might return to the Wallabies team.

But even if he wanted to, the code can no longer afford him.

Rugby Australia's humiliation is complete.

A BAD YEAR FOR GOODYEAR

THIS year has been a bad year for Goodyear.

Up until this year, Goodyear knew what their business was – making tyres. And that's what they've been doing since 1898.

But 122 years after Frank Sieberling started the iconic tyre brand, Goodyear tired of making tyres and decided to enter the exciting world of virtue signalling.

Goodyear has operated successfully for more than a century without needing a diversity training seminar.

For 122 years, blokes have come to the factory, made tyres and gone home.

Some of the blokes were white and some were black and some were Asian and some were straight and some were gay and some were probably men who wanted to be women. But none of that mattered, because they were just making tyres.

It's not rocket science. It's tyres. It's pretty simple. You fashion bits of rubber into circles that fit easily onto car and truck wheels. And Goodyear have been pretty good at it. Very good in fact.

But in 2020 the world went mad and everything became political, including the wheels on your car. And so the bosses at Goodyear decided they needed to hold a diversity training seminar so that their workers would be more focused on differences whilst trying to work toward a common goal.

I will never understand why organisations hold diversity training seminars. Diversity training does absolutely nothing to help a company achieve its aims. But it will serve to highlight differences between staff members and so divide them against each other.

A diversity training seminar excites the social justice warriors on your staff, giving them license to start agitating for their view of utopia in the workplace. And at the same time, it outs everyone else who just wants to make tyres – and doesn't care for all this 'woke' stuff – as dinosaurs and homophobes and racists and whatever.

Before diversity training, they were just blokes making tyres. But now they are part of the problem who need to be re-educated or retired, if you will.

And so it was that Goodyear's diversity training notes found their way to the media.

A worker who didn't like the wokie seminar leaked a power-point slide from the diversity training module that listed what was and what was not acceptable at the Goodyear factory.

Under the heading "Acceptable" was: "Black Lives Matter; Lesbian, Gay, Bisexual and Tansgender Pride."

Under the heading "Unacceptable" was: "Blue Lives Matter; All Lives Matter; MAGA attire and political affiliated slogans or material."

So at Goodyear, if you wear a "Black Lives Matter" shirt while making tyres you're creating an inclusive workplace, but if you wear an "All Lives Matter" shirt while making tyres, you're perpetrating hate.

And you can make tyres for police cars, as Goodyear does, but you can't make tyres for police cars while saying that police lives matter.

You can promote BLM, a group that advocates for destruction of property, taking other people's belongings as a form of reparations, killing or maiming of police officers, wide open borders, and the complete upheaval of the social construct.

And you can promote gay and lesbian and trans pride – which seek to redefine the family, re-write school curriculum and weaponize anti-discrimination law.

But you can't wear a MAGA hat, because that's political.

So Goodyear will balance your tyres but don't expect them to balance anything else!

As the employer who leaked the diversity training material said: "If we're talking about equality, then it needs to be equality. If not, it's discrimination."

Give that man a noble prize!

The result was Goodyear blimp meets the same fate as the Hindenburg Blimp. The whole thing exploded.

People announced a boycott of Goodyear tyres because Goodyear tyres kept pulling to the left.

Goodyear spokeswoman Melissa Monaco put out a statement staying: "Goodyear is committed to fostering an inclusive and respectful workplace cliché cliché where all of our associates can do their best in a spirit of teamwork.

"As part of this commitment, we do allow our associates to express their yawn support on yawn racial injustice and other equity issues but ask that they refrain from workplace expressions, verbal or otherwise, in support of political campaigning blah blah for any candidate or political party as well as other similar forms of advocacy that fall outside the scope of equity issues."

Everyone was a lot happier, not least Goodyear employees, when they were simply making tyres.

TEEN VOGUE OUTLINES NEW ECONOMIC THEORY: "GIMME, GIMME, GIMME"

Envy used to be one of the deadly sins. But it is no longer a sin, it's a virtue. And it's no longer called envy. It's now called "social justice".

Last month's edition of Teen Vogue featured an article entitled: "Abolish Landlords. Housing is a Human Right" by which the editorial team really mean, "Give Us Your Place to Live Rent Free".

Communist, er, columnist Kandist Mallet wrote: "While we're working to abolish the police, we must also work to dismantle what the police were put here to protect: property. What is more evident of the legacy of settler colonialism and its violence than the idea of the ownership of land?"

Ignoring the fact that it's disingenuous to argue against the abuse of indigenous people's property rights while simultaneously arguing for the abolition of property rights in general, reading this you couldn't be blamed for thinking: "Wow, there's free stuff up at the offices of Teen Vogue! Ignore security and the hipsters pedalling at their cycle desks, they want you to have that iMac Retina 5K."

I'm not sure how *Teen Vogue*'s advertisers feel about the magazine encouraging its readers to eschew possessions, but if Kandist Mallet feels so strongly about abolishing the idea of private property, why doesn't she lead by example and reassign her property to the collective?

Oh wait – Kandist doesn't own any property! Suddenly "abolish the police" makes sense.

Kandist wants to abolish police who, by her own admission, are the only ones standing between her greedy hands and your hard-earned property.

She writes: "We need a housing movement based on a rejection of the construct that any one person should own this earth's land."

Her use of the phrase "housing movement" is revealing. She is arguing for a world in which your house moves to her. "Give me your stuff" was always the goal of Marxism.

I'm not sure when *Teen Vogue* – which is supposed to be a fashion magazine for young people with a cervix – became the Romper Room edition of Pravda, but Kandist Mallet is a typical collectivist, by which I mean, lazy, envious and entitled.

Unwilling to work and save so as to own a property, she demands that others who have worked and saved have their properties taken from them and given to her.

Because "fairness".

Wait until Kandist finds out that State provided housing for all doesn't mean luxury condos with pools and gymnasiums; but three families per unit with bedsheets to divide among them and elevators that don't work.

Warming to her theme, the Teen Rogue writer continues: "We should cancel rent outright as this pandemic rages. And we should work toward a world where landlords no longer hold this sort of power over people's lives."

Good idea. We should also cancel rental car fees and work toward a world where Hertz no longer hold that sort of power over people's lives.

We should cancel grocery prices so we can work toward a world where Woolworths no longer hold that sort of power over people's lives.

And let's cancel room rates at the Hilton because five-star hotels shouldn't hold that sort of power over people's lives.

When Kandist argues that one group of people shouldn't have power over another group, what she really means is that no-one should be able to deny her anything she wants.

Kandist promoted her article on Twitter by asking: "If my rent money is paying for my landlord's mortgage, shouldn't I be part owner?"

No Comrade Kandist.

Your landlord owns the property because your landlord took the risk to build the house and your landlord lives with the responsibility to maintain the house. As a reward, your landlord gets to make a profit.

And for paying rent, you get to live in a nice place without any risk that property prices might fall and without any responsibility for rates or maintenance.

And if you don't like that, you could always try owning something.

But using Kandist's logic, if for some crazy reason I used my money to buy a copy of *Teen Vogue*, shouldn't I be her editor?

She ought to be careful what she wishes for.

An article in *Teen Vogue* calling for the abolition of private property just goes to show that communism is a fashion accessory for the young woke. Hopefully it goes out of style soon; like before we get to the millions of state executions part.

The good news for Teen Vogue and its journalists is that jellyfish have survived for millions of years without a brain.

OUR CULTURE IS A SELF-DRIVING TESLA

News of a fatal accident last week involving a Tesla electric car that smashed into a tree with no-one at the wheel raises the question: why do Teslas have a "full self-driving" feature if they don't fully drive themselves?

If I sold your mother-in-law a car and said it was self-driving, only for your mother-in-law to die after the car hit a tree and exploded into flames while operating in full self-driving mode, wouldn't you be furious?

Well, okay, imagine it was someone other than your mother-in-law.

Wouldn't you complain that a full self-driving car in which the driver had to sit in the driver's seat with hands fully on the wheel and eyes fully on the road isn't really a full self-driving car at all?

Wouldn't you say, "This car is not self-driving because it doesn't drive itself. It's just a normal car being sold at an exorbitant price. How can my friend get one for *his* mother-in-law?"

If a man puts on a dress and wears make-up, do you call him a woman and insist he should be allowed to play women's rugby? Or do you say, "That's not a woman. It's a man playing dress-ups. And there's no way I'm letting him tackle my wife."

And what if he was driving a Tesla? Would you say, "Look there goes a woman in a self-driving car" as it careered straight off the road into a tree?

Of course not.

Wouldn't he just be a strangely dressed man found in the passenger seat of the burnt-out wreckage of an exorbitantly priced Tesla, leaving the women's rugby team short a player, but not a female player?

Or what if there was a medical procedure that caused an unborn baby to be torn to pieces before being vacuumed out of the womb and thrown into a trash bin?

Would you say, "Isn't health care wonderful"? Or would you say,

"That's not health care. That's the barbaric killing of a human being. And it's wrong."

And if the abortion doctor arrived at his family planning clinic in a self-driving Tesla, would you say, "Look! It's the family planning doctor in his amazing self-driving car"?

Or would you say, "Look! It's the butcher in his very expensive Tesla purchased with money made from killing babies in the womb."

And if that doctor protested that no-one has the right to tell a woman what she can or can't do with her own body, would you agree? Or would you ask him whether he also believes no-one has the right to stop his self-driving Tesla slamming into a tree at speed with him as the passenger?

Or what about this? If there was a tax-payer funded broadcaster that employed no conservatives whilst pushing every left-wing agenda item you can imagine, would you call that media network fair and balanced? Would you say it was impartial? Would you call it unbiased?

Or would you say, "the ABC is an out-of-control Tesla that keeps pulling to the left" and demand to know "who the hell is driving this thing"?

And what if Australia had a political and media class that spent more time debating who was masturbating on whose Parliament House desk than they did addressing the erosion of civil liberties, the rising threat of China and the wisdom of record debt levels?

And what if sexual mores had become so confused that police seriously suggested an app be used for women to give consent before intercourse?

And what if a footballer who beats his wife can continue playing, but a footballer who quotes the Bible cannot?

Would you say, our country is headed in the right direction?

Or would you say, "Put me in the passenger seat of a full self-driving Tesla, because I like my chances better"?

YOU MUST STAY AWOKE

Students at Marymount Manhattan College are demanding a professor be sacked for falling asleep during a discussion on racism.

Theatre Arts Associate Professor Patricia Simon was one of 150 staff and students participating in a Zoom meeting on June 29 to discuss implementation of an "anti-racist framework" when she appeared to doze off.

Almost 2000 students have signed a petition to have the professor sacked.

Petition organiser Caitlin Gagnon wrote: "It has been brought to the attention of students that Patricia Simon was sleeping during the meeting ... these actions have proven to the students within the program that she does not have the best interests of all students in mind, and therefore, she should not be an educator any longer."

Well who could blame the poor professor for nodding off, listening to a bunch of young adults whinge and whine about how unconscious bias was all that stood between them and their dreams.

The professor was probably dreaming about what she would rather be doing – you know, like teaching theatre rather than listening to the theatrics of a bunch of moralising social justice warriors who still live at home with mummy and daddy.

The professor, who according to the New York Post has worked at the College since 1991, told students she had not been asleep.

"I was looking down or briefly resting my Zoom weary eyes with my head tilted back which I must do in order to see my computer screen through my trifocal progressive lenses. I listened with my ears and heart the entire meeting."

But neither the explanation nor the fact that Professor Simon was wearing "progressive" lenses were enough to placate the mob.

Social justice warriors have put the world on notice that you cannot be properly woke unless you are literally awake. And you must remain awoke at all times!

It is likely more of the Theatre Arts students - by Theatre Arts we really mean "Barista Science" since a degree in Theatre Arts most often leads to a job pouring lattes at Starbucks -would have signed the petition had they not been asleep in class when the document was passed around.

The saga brings to mind stories of Soviet dictator Joseph Stalin who would serve dinner around 1am and insist subordinates stay with him until dawn. Advisor Nikita Khrushchev wrote in his memoirs that he would nap in the afternoon to be prepared for the all night meetings. "Things went badly for those who dozed off at Stalin's table," he said.

He could have been writing about a university social justice meeting.

Of course, being punished for being sleepy during a wokey talk was predicted by George Orwell in his dystopian classic *1984*.

"The smallest thing could give you away ... to wear an improper expression on your face (to look incredulous when a victory was announced, for example) was itself a punishable offense. There was even a word for it in Newspeak: facecrime, it was called."

The Marymount Manhattan College meeting is reminiscent of a story from the Gulag Archipelago where, at the conclusion of a planning meeting, everyone rose to applaud. But no one wanted to be the first to sit down. So they clapped and clapped. Finally, on the verge of collapse, one man sat down and the rest quickly followed.

In the morning, the man who sat down first was arrested and shipped off to the gulag. The message: never be the first to stop clapping.

If he had fallen asleep they likely would have shot him. Much like the Marymount students have Professor Simon in their sights.

Wokeness is now much like an old-time religion, but harsher since there is no forgiveness to be found and no redemption offered.

Speaking of which, I confess that I once fell asleep during a church service. I wasn't bored or trying to be disrespectful. I was simply tired. I certainly wasn't making a stand for Satan!

As for the man across the aisle who was also asleep, I can't say who he was working for.

CRICKET AUSTRALIA'S WOKE ARROGANCE

The same cricketers who intend to snub Australia Day at home want priority receiving the Covid vaccine so they can represent Australia overseas.

Well played Cricket Australia. Well played.

They have a hostile quick, aiming bouncers at the national day from one end, and a spinner exercising guile to extract special treatment from the nation, operating at the other.

It's a two-pronged attack that is likely to win as many fans as they have won Test Matches this year.

None.

Cricket Australia announced last week that they would sandpaper away any mention of "Australia Day" from their promotion of Big Bash games on January 26.

The decision came after consultation with someone who said something about this being a powerful way of being seen to be doing something about racism or something.

Much like the now-familiar barefoot circle – where players begin each Test Match by standing around silently contemplating how standing around in silent contemplation will improve the lot Indigenous people – the decision to not say "Australia Day" on our national day is pointless.

It will not help struggling batsman Joe Burns get even one more run.

Nor will it save even one Indigenous woman from domestic violence.

It will, however, distract attention from the team's poor summer.

"Well yes, we lost at the Gabba for the first time in 20 years to an Indian team missing seven of their best players. But look over there, a social justice pantomime!"

When the Prime Minister, speaking for many cricket fans, suggested that Cricket Australia should have "a bit more focus on cricket" he was promptly told to "read the room".

In other words, how dare cricket fans demand their cricket team win games of cricket when what cricketers really need to do is to focus on their role as ambassadors for Cricket Australia's woke adventures.

It is surely only a matter of time until Cricket Australia change their name to just CA (in the same way that Kentucky Fried Chicken now calls itself just KFC) to avoid any obvious connection either to cricket or to Australia, both of which only seem to get in the way of really important things like inclusivity, diversity, equality, equity, sustainability and trans-whateverity.

Inner-city progressives will, of course, approve of the Australia Day snub. However, this too is pointless since inner-city progressives tend not to like cricket.

They are disgusted by the crowd's cultural appropriation of the Mexican Wave. They are horrified by the nationalistic chants of "Come on Aussie, Come on". And they are sickened by misogynistic cricketing terms such as "to bowl a maiden over".

In this regard, Cricket Australia has become almost indistinguishable from Rugby Australia – a sporting organisation that is world-class when it comes to alienating fans and losing games whilst impressing people who don't care with gestures that don't matter.

All of which makes Cricket Australia's request for players to receive the Covid vaccine before everybody else in the country a bit rich.

Cricket Australia's chief medical officer Dr John Orchard argued at the weekend that the team should jump the priority queue because its tour of South Africa in February was "vital to Australia's national and international interest".

So one minute they are snubbing Australia Day because 'national shame'; and the next minute they are elbowing their way to the front of the vaccination queue because 'national pride'.

If Cricket Australia want to receive funding from Australian taxpayers in order to represent Australia then they might like to honour Australia's national day.

And as for elite athletes aged under 35 demanding vaccinations before front line workers and the elderly ... what's that expression again?

Read the room.

PLAYING FOR DIVERSITY IS NOT PLAYING TO WIN

Netball Australia decided to hold an Indigenous Round last weekend to celebrate diversity and inclusion. What could possibly go wrong?

Games were opened with an Acknowledgement of Country. A didgeridoo was played before the start of each game. Match balls featured indigenous artwork; as did player uniforms.

So far, so woke.

There was even one indigenous player. The problem was that she sat on the bench – for the entire game.

And faster than you can say "cultural awareness", a weekend designed to show off the sport's woke credentials became prima facie evidence of the sport's systemic racism

Social media cried foul. Netball Australia were "racist trash". The much-publicised Indigenous Round was "a debacle" and a "kick in the guts" to the Indigenous community. Aboriginal and Torres Strait

Islanders had been "disrespected".

Besieged Queensland Firebirds coach Roselee Jencke issued a public apology, explaining that her decision to keep indigenous wing attack Jemma Mi Mi on the bench was one of strategy, not of bigotry.

She had naively approached her team's Super Netball game against minor premiers Melbourne like any other -- with a view to win. And they did win.

But this wasn't a game like any other. This was the Indigenous Round.

And during the Indigenous Round, you play the Indigenous woman whether she helps you win the game or not.

"The decision not to put Jemma on the court was the right one from a game-strategy perspective," Jencke said. "However we misread community expectations."

Jencke had been under pressure to get results after her team finished bottom of the table in 2019. She was coaching to win.

Netball Australia had been under pressure to get results after more than 20 years without an Indigenous player in the national team. They were playing to signal inclusion.

Caught between the coach's desire to win and the code's desire to send a culturally appropriate message was Jemma Mi Mi. She was playing to establish herself as an elite netballer.

Like I said, what could possibly go wrong? I mean, apart from the public humiliation of Jemma Mi Mi and vicious accusations of racism against her coach and teammates?

Sharon Finnan-White, the last Indigenous netballer to play for Australia, told the ABC:

> "There needed to be a bit more cultural sensitivity around the fact that Indigenous Round is really special for our people and Jemma should have been able to be a part of that win.

> "She should have had a chance to hit the court. They can't make finals. They weren't even in contention.
>
> What was supposed to be a wonderful celebration of our culture – her culture – turned into something completely sour."

Unintentionally, those comments highlighted the hypocrisy of both Netball Australia and of Indigenous sporting activists.

Netball Australia can hardly use their sole indigenous player to promote its Indigenous Round only to then have her sit on the sidelines watching all the non-Indigenous people play.

Netball Australia set Jemma Mi Mi up to look like a fool.

But by the same token (pun definitely intended), Indigenous activists can hardly demand "respect" while insisting that one of "theirs" gets court time at the elite level because skin colour and because 'the team wasn't going to make the finals anyway'.

Ignoring form and tactics in order to give an Indigenous netballer a few minutes of token game time is hardly a way to generate respect for Indigenous players.

Journalist Nancia Guivarra wrote: "An Indigenous Round without Indigenous players on the court isn't an 'Indigenous Round'. It's tokenism."

She's right.

But it's equally true that putting Indigenous players on the court because it's Indigenous Round is also tokenism.

Jemma Mi Mi told media prior to Sunday's game: "I've never played a netball game in an Indigenous dress before so it's going to be really exciting to step out on court at a home game to represent both the Firebirds and Indigenous community."

When game time came, the 24-year-old was all dressed up with nowhere to go.

It wasn't Mi Mi's fault. She was put in that position by virtue signalling sports administrators and by race obsessed activists who are as bad as each other.

And what of Jemma's teammates?

Shamefully, they were publicly accused of racism for not subbing themselves out of the game so that Mi Mi could get on the court.

Aboriginal scholar and Western Sydney University lecturer Robyn Oxley told SBS: "It really questions why white players do not remove themselves, even when they are cramping. These players would rather risk further injury than see an Indigenous person play in a round dedicated to promoting awareness of Aboriginal culture."

One has to wonder if Robyn Oxley watches any sport. Players want to play and are loath to sub themselves off – cramp or not.

And if a white player had taken herself off to get Mi Mi on the court, the goal attack would likely have been called a bigot for not swapping positions so that Mi Mi could score the goals.

Super Netball CEO Chris Symington responded to the controversy by saying that he understood calls for the Indigenous round to be scrapped.

But then, reverting to robotic woke-speak, insisted: "Indigenous Round provides an opportunity to celebrate Aboriginal and Torres Strait Islander culture and acknowledge the contribution that many Aboriginal and Torres Strait Islanders play across the entire netball system and we plan for this round to continue in future years."

The reaction to last weekend made one thing certain – the Indigenous Round is not a celebration of elite sport or of elite athletes.

If you want to see that, save your money for the following week, when social justice warriors are sidelined to create a safe space for professional coaches and athletes playing to win.

CNN – ALL THE NEWS NOT FIT TO PRINT

News is simple to write.

The introduction must be short and sharp and tell the reader what happened, preferably in less than 25 words.

But CNN prefer to camouflage the news rather than to report it.

Take this impressive piece of verbal contortion from a CNN report on August 31 ... "Two Chicago police officers pulled over a person suspected of having a gun, and all three ended up hospitalized with gunshot wounds, officials say."

According to CNN's headline, the act of pulling a suspect over resulted in everyone just "getting gunshot wounds".

Police pull over a car.

And yada, yada, yada.

And everyone ended up shot.

What happened between "officers pulled over a person" and "all three ended up hospitalized" doesn't seem particularly important to CNN's incurious reporter.

There they all were – suspect and police officers gathered together on the curb – when bullets started falling from the sky like rain.

"And all three ended up hospitalized with gunshot wounds".

Did the officers shoot themselves? Did they trip and fall on some bullets?

Maybe it was those damned magic gunshot-wound fairies playing their harmless pranks again.

Or – and this is just a wild guess – maybe the man stopped by police pulled a gun, shooting and wounding two officers before himself being shot by a third officer who came to his colleagues' rescue.

You would need to read eight paragraphs of CNN's report (most people don't read more than the first sentence of any news story) before discovering that the armed perpetrator opened fire first, taking out two police. He was then shot by a third officer arriving at the scene as back-up.

Imagine the mental contortions it took to write CNN's headline, doing everything linguistically possible to avoid saying that a person had a gun and shot two police with it.

Passive voice is discouraged when writing news headlines. Unless of course, it is to draw attention away from the fact that a suspect shot two police officers.

And why would CNN want to disguise the simple fact of what happened?

The fact that police can be ambushed at a run-of-the-mill traffic stop does not fit the CNN narrative.

The fact that a member of the public shot police, rather than police shot black members of the public, doesn't fit the CNN narrative.

The fact that policing is a difficult and dangerous job does not fit the CNN narrative.

So what do you do when actual facts from actual events do not conform to the pre-approved news narrative?

You twist and contort and you duck and you weave and you stand on your head and you call it news.

But we all know it's not. It's just CNN.

HOW TO WIN THE ASHES USING CANCEL CULTURE

The suspension of English cricketer Ollie Robinson for poor form – not on the field but on Twitter – should fill Australians with hope that we can win this year's Ashes series, regardless of how our players perform.

Thanks to cancel culture, our opponents can be easily dismissed without a single ball being bowled.

We don't need fast bowler Pat Cummins to take a wicket or spinner Nathan Lyon to even roll his arm over when the English team tours.

Cricket's ultimate prize can be won by a non-athletic social justice warrior hiding in the musty darkness of the MCG (Mother's car garage) from which he trawls through the Poms' social media archives.

A bit of offence archaeology is much easier than hitting boundaries or taking wickets, and far more effective.

Clean bowl an English player and he's out for an innings. Find a questionable tweet from ten years ago and you've dismissed him for the entire series.

This is exactly how English debutant Ollie Robinson has been sent packing from the current Test series against New Zealand.

While 27-year-old Robinson was busy collecting seven wickets on debut at Lords against the Kiwis this week, a woke warrior was busy collecting tweets from when Robinson was a teenager.

Back in 2012, he made a joke about Muslims and a joke about Asians. There was a tweet using the 'n' word. And there was an observation that "females who play video games actually tend to have more sex".

Thank you woke folk for pointing out that before Robinson was an international cricketer, he was an immature teenager. Cue outrage!

The woke police – who can neither bat nor bowl, but who are pretty handy with a Google search and a stern look – screamed "howzat?", and Robinson was immediately suspended by the England and Wales Cricket Board.

He's a great cricketer but, you know, views.

That the everythingphobic tweets surfaced during a test match that began with the ECB lining up its players dressed in t-shirts bearing slogans rejecting various forms of discrimination did not help.

And so, Robinson's cricketing deeds – he took 7/101 with the ball and made 42 with the bat – were declared irrelevant.

The scorecard will forever read: "Robinson caught Twitter bowled Wokestapo for almost nought".

As a result, England will now play the second and deciding test against New Zealand without their talented all-rounder who is now being "educated", as they like to say.

Well, the whole cricketing world has been educated. We've learned that beating the Poms at cricket requires neither runs, nor wickets. Why bowl when you can troll?

If we simply find something their players said as teenagers that offends current sensibilities, they will enthusiastically dismiss themselves.

The Ashes are as good as ours.

A BISEXUAL BACHELORETTE FIXES EVERYTHING

Channel Ten have announced that the next Bachelorette will be an indigenous bisexual woman, proving that crap television and inclusive television are not mutually exclusive.

Bisexual aboriginal Brooke Blurton will "make television history" when the show is aired later this year, according to Ten Network publicists.

No, not "television history" in a man lands on the moon kind-of-way. More in a brown queer girl who, having already featured as a contestant on the Bachelor, now stars in the Bachelorette kind-of-way.

(If you didn't just get a shiver down your spine, you clearly don't appreciate history)

Reacting to the historic announcement of the historic casting for the historic season of the Bachelorette, Macquarie University academic Amy Thunig said: "This is history-making stuff and the kind of representation that saves lives."

Indeed.

"I was at the end of my rope and about to do myself in when I saw a First Nations bisexual trying to find love on reality TV and, suddenly, I knew life was worth living," said no one, ever.

Imagine your life being so bland and artificial that a brown person – of whom the most interesting thing that can be said is that she can't decide whether to bed a man or a woman – being cast as a token diversity hire in a dating reality show is considered to be some kind of victory.

It does raise the question, though: have Channel Ten gone far enough?

After all, a bisexual is a pretty safe choice. Of all the letters in the LBGTQIA acronym, B is the most common. All the cool kids swing both ways these days. Yawn.

Are we really to believe that no indigenous trans or gender non-conforming people were available?

How will their lives be saved if they cannot see themselves represented in the few dregs that remain of commercial TV?

Do black pansexual lives not matter?

And if the Bachelorette is to be a model of inclusivity, why isn't she a size 18 or, even better, a size 20? And why isn't she in a wheelchair? And why doesn't she have Tourette syndrome? Where is their representation? We can play this game all day.

If Channel Ten wants to parade their diversity credentials, they should get back to us when the Bachelorette's final rose ceremony features an Asian transgender Muslim wearing a Hijab, choosing a left-handed, cross-dressing homosexual Jew.

Until that happens, I don't care how many indigenous bisexuals they beam into our living rooms, Australian television is nothing but an instrument of CIS gendered white supremacy.

Buzzfeed journalist Julia Willing reported: "Blurton identifies as bisexual, which means producers will be casting a mix of both men and women for her to woo – and we can only pray this step forward for diversity extends to the contestants too."

Well, yes. Let us pray.

"Dear Lord Jesus, we ask that you would direct the producers of this season's Bachelorette to give their bisexual lead the choice of both men and women, with diverse sexual tastes ..."

Wait. What?!

Scott Morrison may have closed the borders but the woke plague from America has made its way over here anyway and now infects everything – even the Bachelorette.

As if we needed a reason not to watch.

WOKESPEAK: A POCKETGUIDE

With the ascendency of Joe Biden and the rise of Leftism around the Western world, it is vital that every person hoping to survive the next four years becomes fluent in the mysterious language of Wokespeak.

Failure to become proficient in Wokespeak can result in job loss, social ostracisation or worse.

To help you navigate the Leftist's brave new world, I offer the following helpful guide.

Anti-racism

This is a completely meaningless term since almost no-one is pro-racism.

But just because a term is meaningless does not mean it is useless. In fact, the repetition of meaningless terms – as if they were utterances of profound thought – is a key feature of Wokespeak.

The more meaningless a term, the more useful it is likely to be since its meaninglessness makes it difficult to rebut. How do you argue against a mist?

Letting people know that you are anti-racism automatically positions anyone who disagrees with anything else you say as being "for racism", and therefore wrong.

Overrepresented

This term implies that the number of people of a particular gender, ethnicity or sexuality performing any task – or found in any situation – should be proportional to their numbers in the general community.

If 90 per cent of SAS troops are men, then men are overrepresented. This is deemed to be a problem because it suggests there is a difference between the sexes.

Since almost no women are physically capable of qualifying for the SAS, the entry standard must be lowered to allow more women to qualify and so prove that they are exactly the same as men.

If the number of indigenous people in jail is proportionally higher than their numbers in the general community, they are said to be overrepresented in the justice system. This is a problem since it could suggest some cultures are different to others.

The courts are pressured to show leniency to indigenous offenders so as to keep them out of jail and thus prove that no culture is worse than any other.

Another example of overrepresentation is the number of African Americans playing in the NBA. But this is not something Leftists talk about.

Diversity

Diversity is how the Woke justify the number of blacks, women or gays in desirable positions to be out of all proportion to their numbers in the general community, without being accused of overrepresentation.

The more people of colour, women and LGBTQ members on a corporate board, for example, the better – though no-one really knows why.

It is vital to realise that diversity does not apply to thought. In fact, diversity of thought has the power to completely nullify actual diversity.

For example, if the black man on your corporate board does not believe cultural appropriation is a real thing, then he is not really black and so he does not contribute to diversity. In this case, he must be replaced with a black man who thinks like all the other Leftists in the room so that diversity can be maintained.

Cultural Appropriation

This is when people from one culture borrow something from another culture, without giving due credit.

For instance, a white man who wears dreadlocks or who performs rap music, would be guilty of cultural appropriation. And a white woman creating dot paintings would be guilty of cultural theft.

But you would be wrong to think that an indigenous woman playing piano, or a black man playing golf, were examples of cultural appropriation.

Cultural appropriation only happens when an oppressor group borrows from a victim group; and never the other way around. Those are the rules.

Equity

The beauty of this word is that it sounds like equality, so people will readily agree to it without ever realising what they are agreeing to. It's a bit like how the Greens sell themselves as environmentalists. But I digress.

Equality is the out-dated, now discredited idea of treating everyone the same. The problem with treating everyone the same is that not everyone ends up at the same place. And this is unfair.

Equity means treating everyone very differently – penalising some and rewarding others – in order to make certain they all end up in the same place no matter what they do. Because this is fair.

That the elites decide who is penalised and who is rewarded is not fair. But they don't care about fair and there's nothing you can do about it, so stop whining about what's fair and what's not.

Hate Speech

This is any speech that members of the Left hate.

Violent Speech

This is any speech that causes members of the Left to become violent toward the speaker.

Unconscious bias

Some people (by whom we mean all white people) are so biased that they are not even aware of their bias. Or to put it another way, they are rotten to the core.

When a white person protests that they do not have unconscious bias, they prove that they have it.

Any suggestion that Leftists made up the idea of unconscious bias because they themselves are deliberately biased against white people is an example of violent speech.

Structual Racism

This term is used to describe racism that is so deeply entrenched that actual examples are impossible to find.

When asked to define structural racism, Leftists will give what sounds – to non-Leftists – like vague generalisations but which are actually convincing proofs to those who are already convinced and so don't need any proof.

The presence of structural racism makes it necessary for Leftists to dismantle everything and to build a new society in which every institution is biased toward non-Whites, thus replacing so-called structural racism with actual structural racism.

LGBTQ Community

This phrase is important since it convinces people that lesbians, gays, bisexual, transgendered and queer people all exist in one happy, united, playful rainbow family – unlike heterosexuals who everyone knows are always miserable. But in reality, the LBGTQ Community does not exist.

L's think G's are irresponsible and immature. G's regard L's as stuffy and arrogant. Both L's and G's think B's are in denial. Neither L's, G's or B's really understand T's. And none of the L's, G's, B's or T's are exactly sure what a Q even is.

Micro-aggression

This magical phrase enables us to turn a race or gender-based prejudice so small as to be imperceptible into something so egregious as to be a hanging offence.

Something as seemingly innocuous as a facial expression or even a momentary silence can, with the right training, be identified as code that gives one away as an ugly racist or as a terrible misogynist.

Those trained in the art of detecting micro-aggressions are able to find offence everywhere, and usually do. As a result, the number of friends they have can be written on a micro list.

THE ABC WANTS TO REFINE PAEDOPHILIA FOR THE SAKE OF 'SENSITIVITY'

The problem with so-called Progressives is that the very term they use to describe themselves begs a question that they can never answer – progress towards what?

The answer "towards more progress" is hardly adequate since there can be no progress without direction and there can be no direction without a fixed point.

But progressives are so inclusive that they have done away with fixed points.

Objective truth does not exist in their brave new world where fuzzy notions of "my truth" and "lived experience" mean that the only thing which can be ruled out is the idea that anything can be ruled out.

A love of novelty, a penchant for sentimentality and an unnatural fear of hard thinking have combined to produce a culture of juvenile free-thinkers.

Having insisted there was no difference between God and ourselves we have enlarged our broadmindedness into a sweeping synthesis that says reality is whatever we declare it to be.

We have become like sailors who, having agreed to ignore the stars, have hung our lamp on the ship's mast and agreed to navigate by it. The port we arrive at will be whatever rock we hit right after the last one we crashed into.

And so progressivism has no endpoint. Every time we think that we have finally arrived at the woke nonsense terminal, another passage opens up.

We have redefined marriage because diversity.

We are currently in the process of redefining women because inclusivity.

And our national broadcaster now wishes to redefine paedophilia because sensitivity.

Well, why not?

Journalists at the ABC were told this week to "avoid" referring to child sex abusers as paedophiles so as to not marginalise people who had been clinically diagnosed with paedophilia but who had not acted on their impulses.

"Instead use serial sexual offender/predator, or a sexual abuser of children and young people," reporters were told, according to a report published in *The Australian*.

Don't think the idea is too silly for our national broadcaster.

In January the ABC referred to violent street crimes and home invasions committed by teenage gangs marauding through Melbourne suburbs as "youth network offending".

It is only a matter of time before we are urged to stop calling criminals "criminals" for fear of creating a stigma around those who wish to commit crime.

Perhaps it is time we stopped calling ABC journalists "journalists" and instead referred to them as activists. But I digress.

The edict to not call paedophiles "paedophiles" lest we marginalise paedophiles ignores the fact that some people need to be marginalised.

And it begs another question for progressives.

Just how long does it take to go from "Don't marginalize paedophiles" to "Respect Diversity"?

DON'T CANCEL ME. I'M SORRY.

With the way things are going, I wonder if we might start issuing apologies before we get cancelled. You know, get in early. It could go something like this.

I have not yet been cancelled, but I am sure it is only a matter of time before something I said 20 years ago triggers someone today.

I have therefore decided to provide this heart-felt and sincere apology in advance of even knowing what it is I will be cancelled for, in the hope that you will give me the chance to learn and to grow and to do better at whatever deficiencies my Twitter history may find in me.

And so I want to extend an apology to every single person who was hurt by the meme I posted, the meme I failed to post, the unacceptable phrase I used, the tasteless joke I told, my failure to speak out, my silence or whatever else it is that I will be found to have done, omitted to do, said or thought.

I am sorry.

No matter what it turns out to be, I take responsibility. And I extend that apology to every single person

But most importantly I extend that apology to my black brothers and sisters, to my disabled friends, to full-bodied extra-large people, to beloved members of the LGBTQI+ community, to vegans and, of course, to women whom I now agree include trans women, especially if it was not including them that led to me being cancelled in the future, as I anticipate I will be.

I didn't realise how truly harmful my words were, whatever they turn out to be, and I feel deep contrition.

Let me be clear. Black lives matter. Trans women are women. Coal is bad. Obesity is beautiful and we need more of it, especially on magazine covers. Gay is good and normal and everyone should try it. Men can have periods. Down with the patriarchy. You're born that way. Believe all women. Capitalism is evil.

And if, at this point, I have not uttered the key phrase that proves I am onboard with whatever narrative we are doing at the time I am cancelled, please know that I agree with it and I believe it.

Whatever it is.

Like so many people, I am heart-broken about whatever is happening in our world right now. And one of the things I am most heartbroken about is my own bigoted or racist or misogynist, or Islamophobic or homophobic or transphobic or white supremacist or fascist or vegaphobic attitudes.

It is quite likely that, at some point in the future, I will be found to have been a contemptable combination of three or more of those things. And for this, whatever this turns out to be, I am truly sorry.

I am committed to doing the hard work of undertaking a journey of continued learning and growing in these areas.

I will seek to listen and learn and understand and grow and any other verb that emphasises my humility.

I hope that I can use what I have learned through whatever this painful process turns out to be so as to seem part of the solution rather than the problem.

I promise to use whatever influence I have left after being pilloried on social media, hounded out of my job and ejected from polite society to help other people such as whites, heterosexuals, Christians and especially men to learn these important lessons too.

I now understand the reality of things like white privilege, unconscious bias, inequity, systemic racism or whatever other hot button progressive issue I have failed to treat with the seriousness they deserve. And I still have a long way to go.

I acknowledge that I sit where I am today largely because of centuries of gross injustices done to everyone who is upset at me for any reason.

And I take responsibility for any injustices anyone else has suffered anywhere at any time for any reason, even before I was born which was no excuse.

I am responsible. I am truly sorry for the hurt and suffering that I caused, even if I didn't.

Finally, thank you for letting me apologise.

My only focus from this day forward will be to learn, to understand, to stay engaged, to be educated and, yes, to say whatever the hell I need to say in order to not lose my livelihood because of you crazy, easily triggered, deeply miserable, cancel-happy, utter nut-jobs.

EDDIE MCGUIRE TRIED TO SMOKE AN EXPLODING CIGAR

The Collingwood Football Club is like the man who ordered an exploding cigar and then smoked the exploding cigar only to be caught by surprise when it exploded in his face.

What did they think would happen when they commissioned Indigenous activists to investigate whether or not their AFL club was racist?

A 35-page report on racism, written by academics with a history of race activism, found evidence of "systemic" and "egregious" racism.

Who would have thought?

I'm not sure how a list of six racist incidents over the past 50 years, detailed in the report, amounts to systemic anything.

Unacceptable? Definitely.

Regrettable? Of course.

Evidence that Collingwood is the AFL equivalent of the Ku Klux Klan? Hardly.

But let's be honest, it's difficult to imagine any organisation that would not be called racist in the current environment where Critical Race Theory insists that no white man can do any good, no matter how hard he tries.

The report, entitled Do Better, began by asserting that "if racism is endemic through the broader community, it is not surprising to find it within institutions such as sporting clubs".

So there you have it.

Investigators seeing racism everywhere were invited to run their eye over Collingwood and saw racism everywhere.

That the authors felt the need to begin their report by acknowledging the "elders and their ancestors" upon whose land the report was typed was an early clue that the Club's attempt to get some honest feedback was always going to be hijacked by a politically driven agenda.

I'm not sure about systemic racism, but there was certainly naivety at the board level.

And Collingwood president Eddie McGuire, calling the release of the report "a proud day" for Collingwood, deserves a special award of his own.

He is now the subject of a massive social media campaign calling for his resignation. Even a one-eyed – one toothed – supporter saw that coming.

And Australia's most famous sporting club is now stuck with recommendations that may well hinder their core business, but that they cannot reject.

Those recommendations include ensuring that players and coaches are recruited, not simply for their footballing ability, but for their ethnicity – "particularly First Nations and people of colour".

From now on it will concern Collingwood recruiters that they need a key position player to kick goals just as much as that they need an Indigenous player to tick boxes.

And when drafting white players, the club will have to ensure these young men can run and jump and kick as well as express "genuine support of anti-racism".

Further, the club will now be expected to "undertake an audit to ensure its membership, though their behaviour and beliefs, reflect its goals of diversity".

How the "beliefs" of Collingwood supporters will be audited the report does not say, but an Expert Group on Anti-Racism will be formed to ensure the thought-audit happens.

Collingwood smoked the cigar and, predictably, it blew up in their face. Now they must live with the mess.

ONLY A FOOL FEEDS THE WOKE BEAST AND THINKS IT WILL NOT DEVOUR HIM

Collingwood Football Club President Eddie McGuire played the woke game for years but he could not outrun it.

Yesterday he was forced to quit by the very people he spent much of his 22-year tenure trying so hard to impress – not the footy fans, but the woke social justice worriers.

It was telling that in his final, teary speech as club president, McGuire listed numerous achievements, not one of which related to the actual game of football.

Rather than celebrate Collingwood's glorious 2010 premiership – played in front of nearly 100,000 frenzied fans at the MCG – he boasted about the women's game played last Saturday to promote "gay pride".

He used his last press conference as President to reminisce about "rainbow flags in the Collingwood cheer squad, alongside the black and white! Women of all types of size, religion, sexual orientation and cultural background".

"It reminded me of the journey from when we established our LBGTQIA+ support group, the Pink Magpies back in the 1990s," he said.

McGuire went on to list an impressive number of progressive causes that the Club had championed during his time in charge – from Indigenous rights issues to programs for the disabled and the homeless.

Oh, and don't forget all the work he had done to promote the LBGTQIA+ agenda.

McGuire said that since becoming club president in 1998 "my sole motivation was to heal unite, inspire and drive a new social conscience – not just into this club but sport and the community in general".

"I try my best and I don't always get it right," he cried. "But I don't stop trying."

The unspoken question was: 'Do you not see how hard I have tried? After all that I have done, how is it that I find myself here?'

'Here' was standing before a woke firing squad with which he had previously spent a good deal of time flirting.

McGuire's fate was not decided by Collingwood's 85,000 paying football club members, but by a grab bag of less than 100 political activists and virtue signallers from the Greens, ALP and indigenous industries who love to cry 'racist' at every opportunity.

Like jackals coming in to finish a lion, they had been baying for McGuire's blood from the moment he held a clumsy press conference to talk about an internal investigation into racism at the Club.

The investigation's 35-page report, written by academics with a history of race activism, found six racist incidents over the past 50 years and concluded this was evidence of "systemic racism".

McGuire called the release of the report "a proud day" for the Club.

Reasonable people knew what he meant – he was proud of the report, as opposed to proud of the culture that had occasioned the report. But since when does the mob have time for nuances?

There was blood in the water and not even McGuire could avoid the feeding frenzy, as the Left devoured one of their own.

Of course, the self-righteous mob could have paid for Collingwood memberships and voted him out. But who has time for natural justice when you're busy doing social justice? And besides, it's cheaper to tweet.

#eddiesgottago started trending on social media.

The Twitterati labelled McGuire a "white-splaining white male dripping in his own privilege and unrecognized bias, who with breathtaking cognitive dissonance insists with the issue of one report he's proud to have fixed racism".

Journalist Barrie Cassidy condemned "the club's descent into racism".

A group of "prominent" Australians – by which they must have meant 'prominent in their own minds' since hardly anyone had ever heard of them – published a letter demanding that McGuire be sacked. They even insisted that Collingwood sponsors, such as Coles and Nike, needed to demonstrate their anti-racism credentials.

Like most sensible people, I hate the Collingwood Football Club, but this was a massive over-reaction. It was Coon Cheese all over again.

When McGuire fell on his progressive rainbow coloured sword, Greens Senator Lydia Thorpe tweeted: "Well, it's a proud day for all those who have been racially vilified in this country. The fight doesn't stop here."

The Senator, crowing like a rooster taking credit for the sun rising, could cross 'claim the scalp of a high profile alleged racist' off her to-do list.

This doesn't exactly appear to be what John Howard once called "practical reconciliation", but Thorpe was unimpressed by McGuire's teary resignation.

"We refer to them as white tears" she told an ABC radio host who was not at all curious at the racist rhetoric from the anti-racism campaigner who had just forced McGuire to resign for racist rhetoric.

The Senator, along with her "prominent" activist friends, can now glory in the delusion that they have improved the lot of indigenous Australians by destroying a man who has done far more for minority groups than they will ever do.

And Eddie McGuire will be left to ponder how different things might have been if his sole motivation as President of Australia's biggest football club had been winning games of football.

Club members would have been more than happy to have gone to the football and enjoyed the game and a meat pie, without the woke lectures.

And they would have loved McGuire far more than the woke mob he spent far too much time romancing.

Meanwhile, every other sports administrator in the land with eyes to see and ears to hear will have made a mental note... Only a fool feeds the woke beast and thinks it will not devour him.

WHERE'S THE DIVERSITY AT THE ABC WHEN IT'S ONLY WHITE PEOPLE TALKING LEFT-WING DROSS?

Former Race Discrimination Commissioner Tim Soutphommasane yesterday slammed the ABC for using too many white-skinned Leftists to present its news and current affairs programs.

Above a photo of white ABC personalities he tweeted: "A very long way to go before we see our diversity on screens. Let's remember the ABC has it in its charter that it should reflect the cultural diversity of the Australian community. So where is it?"

The anti-racism campaigner is right to be outraged. There will be no diversity at the ABC until journalists of every shade are presenting news from a far left-leaning perspective.

How can the taxpayer funded ABC represent the broader community while every Leftist host has a pale face?

And it is difficult to defend the ABC against charges of political bias when everyone pushing the collectivist point of view is fair-skinned.

If the ABC is to provide balanced reporting, as its charter demands, then everyone promoting the same socialist agenda cannot be of white European descent.

Where are the brown-skinned Marxists? And why isn't the ABC showing exotic-looking, really dark-skinned progressives?

It's not enough for ABC chair Ita Buttrose to talk about diversity, we need to see it!

Mr Soutphommasane is absolutely right to insist that the ABC provide the public with a wide variety of views.

People need to be able to view Asians and view Islanders and view Africans all saying the same woke things.

Flagship programs like Q&A and The Drum should have panellists who are diverse like a packet of M&Ms – lots of different colours and all with the same flavour.

Mr Soutphommasane should be applauded for pointing out the need for the ABC to represent Australia's pluralistic society with a plurality of faces.

There is a real danger that when everyone in the ABC newsroom is white that reporters will start to suffer from group face. And when everyone's looking the same, no-one's looking different. Mr Soutphommasane is bravely ensuring that the national broadcaster does not get away with it.

But Mr Soutphommasane's skin-deep critique of the ABC does not go far enough. Someone with a real talent for reducing everything to race would have noted that the ABC's diversity problem is not confined to its flagship television programs.

It is to our national shame that ABC radio presenters use the same broad Australian accent to push progressive ideas.

Every ABC personality sounds exactly the same on air. And that's not good for democracy. We need to hear lots of different voices.

Why aren't we hearing about the climate emergency from someone with an Asian accent? Or that Trump is Hitler from someone who sounds Mexican? Or that Christians are a bunch of homophobes from someone with a really cool South American twang?

That foreign accents might make it difficult for listeners to understand ABC news and political commentary would not matter since everyone knows in advance exactly what they are going to say.

OUR VERY WOKE WALLABIES

Having gotten rid of their star black player, the Australian rugby team is set to take a knee at the start of their next game in support of Black Lives Matter.

The Australian Rugby Union chased Israel Folau out of the sport and eventually out of the country for his supposedly outdated minority views.

Now, with Folau out of the way, the woke Wallabies plan to signal their support for minorities.

Confused?

That's because you're thinking. To enjoy performative virtue you must be woke enough to feel, but never conscious enough to think.

Senior Wallaby Dane Haylett-Petty revealed this week that the team will consider taking a knee during the national anthem before the third Bledisloe Cup Test against the All Blacks on October 31.

"We've got a very diverse group and we see that as a big strength of ours," he said.

Not strength enough to tolerate diverse views though, or Folau would still be playing for Australia rather than running around for the Catalans Dragons in France.

But again, you're overthinking things. And that's no way to enjoy politically correct sport.

Rugby Australia chairman Hamish McLennan said the Wallabies would be wearing their new Indigenous-designed jersey for the October 31 game.

"We're very proud of our Aboriginal and Indigenous heritage, and we're going to promote it proudly," the proud chairman said with pride.

Except that no player of Indigenous heritage has been picked in the squad.

"I think it shows that we've got to open more player pathways for indigenous rugby players, but what it also says is that we're very committed to an inclusive culture," he said.

So there are no indigenous players included in the squad but the non-indigenous players will wear jumpers featuring indigenous squiggles to prove rugby has an inclusive culture.

It makes complete sense, provided you don't think about it.

The Wallabies also made a big deal about the fact that new coach Dave Rennie has been encouraging players to embrace different cultures, even teaching them to sing Fijian and Tongan songs.

If this news makes you wonder how much better the Wallabies would be at singing Tongan ditties had they not punted their star Tongan player for expressing views commonly held in Tonga, stop it.

You can't square a circle any more than the Wallabies can beat New Zealand.

And there is no point wondering why, if our footballers are going to sing, they don't instead learn the words to the Australian national anthem so that they can actually sing it before games rather than pretend.

Of course, the winless but very woke Wallabies could ditch all the virtue signalling and focus on winning rugby games.

But that thought doesn't seem to have occurred to them for a long time now.

5

EVERYTHING IS RACIST IN WOKETOPIA

DO THE MOB TOPPLING STATUES EXPECT THEIR OWN MONUMENTS?

It is only a matter of time before someone pulls down a statue of Mother Teresa because she was silent on transgender rights.

Admittedly, the Catholic Saint did some good work amongst the poor of Calcutta, but did she ever use her international profile to campaign for gender-neutral bathrooms? No. And so her statue must go.

And statues of Florence Nightingale will likely be demolished because she failed to speak out about the climate emergency.

Little matter that the founder of modern nursing lived and died before the effects of the industrial revolution were known. Her silence was violence.

How dare she, to borrow a line from Saint Greta, waste time fussing over hospital sanitation when the planet itself was soon to be on fire.

And while we are Talibaning, monuments to William Shakespeare must be toppled.

It is of no interest to us that the famed English playwright lived long before Captain Cook ever set foot on Botany Bay. If white people living after James Cook are to be held liable for every ill of colonisation, why not white people living before James Cook?

Just as we must look back and divorce ourselves form the sins of our ancestors, Shakespeare should have looked forward and disavowed the behaviour of his descendants. But he did not. So he must go.

It is a glorious thing to be able to sit atop history and judge all who have gone before.

Of course, it requires a certain amount faith to believe that we are the pinnacle of humanity and therefore fit to be judge and jury and executioner. But it isn't that hard to do if you insist that the history of humanity is inevitably one of progress toward a kind of heaven on earth.

And here we stand.

It is in the very nature of Progressives to engage in a sort of chronological snobbery, judging against the past for no reason than because it is the past.

We are the Woke. We see clearly where others were blind. We have no time for humility and no need for self-examination. The only truth is "my truth". And the only banner we will march under is "Pride".

We have arrived. And so we stand outside of history; the perfect platform from which to view everything objectively.

It never occurs to us, as we search out and find the needle of imperfection in the haystack of other people's accomplishments, that one day we too may be judged by unforgiving narcissists.

We wouldn't dare post an image of ourselves without first applying the right filter. But the past is afforded no such filter. The past will be judged in the harsh light of present sensibilities.

In doing so, we have found a way to feel good without having to be good. Much easier to denounce Churchill than to be Churchill. Much cheaper to pull things down than to do things worth memorialising.

We are the art critic who never produced a painting and the movie critic who never directed a film.

Our opinion is our achievement. Our posturing is our legacy.

The next generation will not pull down our statues for there will have been no reason to erect any.

IT'S NOT OUR RACISM BUT OUR VIRTUE THAT RACE ACTIVISTS FEAR

In Reconciliation Week and on Sorry Day we acknowledge that Australia is a racist country, and to say that it is not is to prove that it is.

Since we know that only racists would say they are not racists, it is necessary to prove you are not a racist by acting like you are guilty of racism, even when you feel no actual guilt.

Doing this enables you to experience an incredible sense of self-righteousness since, by apologising for racism, you prove that you are not a racist like those people who refuse to apologize for the racism they are not guilty of; which is itself a form of racism.

Racists argue that we don't have to apologize for racism since Australia is no longer a racist country.

Whilst they agree that bigotry occurred in the past, they insist that we have made moral progress and have eliminated racism from our institutions.

They will point to Indigenous sports starts like Cathy Freeman, politicians like Neville Bonner, actors like Deborah Mailman, singers like Jessica Mauboy and journalists like Stan Grant as proof that indigenous Australians are free to achieve anything they set their mind to. Of course, they only say such things because they are racist.

They want indigenous people to see themselves as autonomous agents who, through hard work and personal responsibility, can make anything of their lives, just like the rest of us. But this is racist.

It is only by encouraging indigenous people to make an identity out of grievance and inferiority that we can help them to realise how much they need our help to succeed. This is vital since, in helping indigenous people succeed, we give ourselves an opportunity to prove we are not racist.

We must also convince indigenous people that protest is the best way to cash in on the entitlement they are due as a result of their collective grievance. This way indigenous people are able to call for help and we are able to answer.

We will undo the bigotry of the past, which insisted indigenous people were inferior and so we could push them down, by insisting indigenous people are helpless so we can lift them up.

But if indigenous people begin to believe that institutional racism does not exist, there will be no paternalistic role for the rest of us to play. This would be particularly unfair for those of us not old enough to have voted in 1967 to remove discrimination from the Australian Constitution.

We long for an opportunity to demonstrate our virtue by changing history. This means we must deny our country's moral progress and manufacture modern-day grievances that we can then heroically campaign against.

The trick is to insist that a litany of racial disparities prove racism still exists in this country. For instance, Indigenous people die, on average, 10 years younger than non-indigenous people. Only 60% of Indigenous youth finish high school. And an indigenous man is 15 times more likely to be jailed than a non-indigenous man.

Racists say that It is wrong to conflate past oppression with present oppression. They argue that today's racial disparities are likely due to dysfunctions within the indigenous community. We must not even entertain such ideas. Instead, we must insist it is the height of racism to suggest even the possibility that indigenous people might be responsible for their own condition.

Racists also point out that – with everyone eager to prove they are not racists by offering deferential treatment to minority groups — indigenous people are more likely to receive racial preferencing than racial discrimination. Drawing attention to this is racist since it implies that indigenous people don't need white people's help.

To suggest that indigenous people don't need our help is to subvert black victimization and with it, our identity as "woke" social justice warriors.

If, as racists insist, there are no social evils from which we must heroically liberate indigenous people, where then is our claim to real political and cultural power? Power we need to create social programs by which we can re-engineer society on a national scale?

This is why it is vital to continue to say that Australia is a racist country and to paint those who say it is not, as proof that it is.

The truth is that, for we social justice advocates, the real agitation is not racial injustice. To the contrary, we relish evidence of racism since it justifies our own political identity. Racism gives us something to protest and, with it, our own historic purpose.

The real agitation is not racism, but the suggestion Australia might have evolved beyond its racist past.

It is not our nation's evils but our moral growth that frightens us, since it will turn us into an irrelevancy.

RACE CAMPAIGNERS, PLEASE LEAVE MY BLACK KIDS ALONE

I spend more time lately protecting my black sons from well-meaning people concerned they might be victims of racism than I do protecting them from actual racism.

I am not afraid that my sons might experience occasions of racism. I am afraid that they might see racism everywhere.

As hurtful as moments of racism might be, a lifetime of imagined victimhood would be ruinous.

But the activists claim that if my sons' black lives matter, I should purge my fridge of Coon cheese.

When the boys ask for their morning Coco Pops, I should explain that I rose early and burned the box, since the monkey on the front had been mocking them each morning these past few years. And I will apologise for having allowed this to happen to them in their own home.

When my sons arrive home from school and ask why I am emptying my cans of Colonial Beer down the drain, I should explain to them that I had been inadvertently glorifying their oppression every time I drank it.

And later tonight, when the boys ask to watch Summer Heights High, I should explain that we don't watch it anymore.

When they protest, "But it was funny", I will sit them down and gently break it to them that the entire time, the joke had been on them.

Because when a white Chris Lilley pretended to be a black Jonah Takalua ... well, honestly, I'm not exactly sure what the problem was, but I will do my best to help them understand that an Australian actor pretending to be a Tongan character is a slur on them as Ethiopians because of skin colour.

No!

I contend that because my sons' black lives matter, I will refuse to see racism everywhere.

It is because I hate the evil of racism that I refuse to minimise it by teaching my sons that Derek Chauvin and a box of breakfast cereal are the same thing.

And it is because I love my sons that I refuse to minimise them by teaching them to think they can't breathe for the weight of the Coco Pops monkey on their neck.

My sons live in the freest country on earth where they have the opportunity, if they are diligent to develop their unique gifts and talents, to create an incredible life for themselves.

There is not a white supremacist lurking in every pantry. There is not a racist hiding behind every police uniform. There is not a historical grievance creating every challenge they face. And there is not a racial slight that can explain every setback they will experience in life.

I want my children to live free. So I will do all I can to protect them from those virtue-signalling do-gooders who would shackle them in the chains of victimhood.

It is because my sons matter so much that I would respectfully ask the Black Lives Matter crusaders to please, leave them the hell alone.

WHY DON'T WE LEAVE THE CHEESE ALONE – AND TACKLE VIOLENCE AND SEXUAL ABUSE IN INDIGENIOUS COMMUNITIES INSTREAD?

I'VE managed to go through my whole not so short life without ever associating the name of Coon Cheese with anything but cheese. Until now.

Thanks to Darwin race activist Stephen Hagan, I now understand that Coon Cheese is racist because the word "coon" has sometimes been used as derogatory name for Aborigines.

"First Nations people and people of colour shouldn't have to tolerate the visual ugliness of Coon cheese products positioned prominently in the dairy aisles in supermarkets," he told today's *Australian* newspaper.

Mr Hagan appears to have been successful with his demands that the famous cheese name be "consigned to the past of outdated racist brands".

Some people look at Coon and see cheese while others, like Mr Hagan, read Coon and see a racist statement. Whose thinking needs adjusting?

If Mr Hagan is adamant that Coon Cheese is a racist brand because name, then I imagine the next item on his list of things to improve the lives of Indigenous Australians will be lobbying local governments to change town names Coonawarra, Coonabarabran and Coonalypn.

No doubt issues like high levels of domestic violence and sexual abuse of children in Indigenous communities will also be tackled, but after the important issue of cheese is dealt with.

The difficulty is that Coonawarra is an Aboriginal word meaning "honeysuckle". Coonabarabran is an Aboriginal word meaning "inquisitive person" and Coonalypn is an Aboriginal word meaning "barren woman".

Will Mr Hagan damn these Aboriginal words as offensive because name?

Coon Cheese was named, not as a personal affront to Mr Hagan, but in honour of Edward William Coon, of Philadelphia, who patented a method for fast maturation of cheese.

But Mr Hagan is not so sure. He wants an investigation as to whether Edward Coon was actually a cheesemaker in the 1920s or a factory hand used "as a cover" for a racist brand.

This is a bit lazy. It would take Mr Hagan less than a minute to download a copy of the patent application made by Edward William Coon.

And it beggars belief (that's a turn of phrase, not a slight against people short of cash) that a manufacturer looking for profit would allow a patent to be made and secured by a factory hand. It's a silly argument. But the whole thing is silly isn't it.

Is every Australian with the surname Coon (there are dozens) now to change their name or be cancelled?

Should the AFL be taken to task for awarding the 2008 Brownlow Medal to Adam Cooney?

Should Julia Gillard be apologising for employing a speechwriter with the same name?

Should caterpillars be evicted from their cocoons?

Must coloured pencils now be called "pencils of colour"?

Of course, I'm mocking the whole thing now. And that's the point. When you label as racist something you know full well not to be racist, you trivialize racism and turn the whole thing into farce.

I would love Mr Hagan to explain to me, the parent of black children, how turning racism into a joke helps to protect them from racism.

Too many race activists are making too much noise for the wrong reasons and soon, like the boy who cried wolf, they will find no-one is listening anymore. Some of us have already stopped.

And when proposals for Constitutional Recognition and for an Indigenous voice to Parliament are rejected by the Australian people, it will not be because of racism but because of weariness with rubbish like this.

Oh, and one more thing. My teenagers didn't even know "coon" was a racist term until activists like Dr Hagan started going on about it. So well done Mr Hagan on giving racist terms to a new generation. Talk about an own goal.

STILL NOT CHEERED BY THE CHANGE FROM COON

Every parent knows that if you give in to your toddler's temper tantrums, you will receive as your reward even more temper tantrums.

So I was not surprised to learn that the Indigenous activist who protested Coon Cheese was racist is now stomping his feet because he wasn't consulted on the new name.

Stephen Hagan has spent the better part of 20 years complaining that he couldn't go to the supermarket without being racially abused by the dairy fridge.

And so it came to be that Coon's owners, Saputo Dairy Australia, eventually acquiesced and this week announced they would change the name from Coon to Cheer.

"Our decision to change the name of Australia's much-loved cheese reinforces this commitment to build a culture of acceptance, inclusion and respect where everyone feels a sense of belonging," the company's chief executive officer said.

But if Saputo was expecting Cheer would elicit cheers from a placated Mr Hagan, they were quickly disappointed.

The perpetually offended academic was only encouraged to engage in another dummy spit, telling journalists: "I would have liked it to be something a bit more inclusive of First Nations people. We weren't even consulted on names. We would like to have contributed."

Mr Hagan further complained that the Cheer Cheese packaging was too similar to the now discarded Coon Cheese. "I wish they'd changed the packaging too. If you look at the packaging quickly, you'd think it was still Coon cheese," he grumbled.

Had they called it Bush Tucker Cheese and wrapped it in a gum leaf, Mr Hagan would still have found cause for grievance.

Yet he is wasting no time moving on to his next brain haemorrhage – this time over an iconic board game.

Dr Hagan said words derogatory words like "abo", "coon" and "boong" could be used to score points in Scrabble because game manufacturer Mattel endorsed the Collins dictionary which defines a number of racial slurs.

"If you normalise those words, you're really normalising bigotry," he said, as if it should be obvious to everyone that the next issue facing Indigenous Australians were senior citizens plotting to score five points with the word "abo" in retirement village Scrabble games across the country.

Why wouldn't Mr Hagan kick up a stink about this non-problem? He will be duly rewarded with the attention he craves.

But when the nation is finally cleansed of white supremacist Scrabble players, will it be enough to cheer him? I doubt it.

CRICKET AUSTRALIA TALKS BALLS

Australian cricketers proudly announced yesterday that they will begin every game this summer with a barefoot circle ceremony that will not improve even one Aboriginal person's life.

A Cricket Australia wokesperson said the empty gesture would serve to signal the team's commitment to demonstrating their intention to doing something that would do nothing to change anything for anybody in Australia.

"We can probably put our hands up and say we haven't done enough virtue signalling in the past, but we believe standing barefoot in a circle will go a long way toward rectifying this," he said.

"In Australia, we think the most marginalised group is the First Nations people and we think the barefoot circle is a great way to celebrate them because a lot of them got around barefoot before white colonisers oppressed them with shoes. Or something."

The wokesperson denied the ceremony was a chance for umpires to check whether Australian cricketers were hiding sandpaper between their toes.

"We are very sincere about our desire to tackle a serious issue like racism by reducing it to a pantomime," he said.

"And besides, I think everyone knows we hide sandpaper down our pants. But the bare butt circle ceremony is not something the players were keen on doing."

It is believed members of the Australian cricket team agreed to participate in the gesture against racism after a team meeting to brainstorm new sledges to be used against the touring Indian squad finished early due to an overwhelming number of suggestions.

"This was a player-led initiative," the Cricket Australia wokesperson said, "And after we explained that dissenters would be outed as racists and made to field at silly mid-on for the entire series against India, the players unanimously agreed to participate."

He said the players' commitment to popular social justice causes would extend further than wandering around the MCG barefoot to end racism.

The barefoot warriors would also remove their shirts in acknowledgment of climate change and moo like cows to protest the live cattle export trade.

They would remain in the circle formation before each game for exactly 153 seconds to draw attention to the 153 countries in which tampons attract a Goods and Services Tax that unfairly penalises people who menstruate.

All of this would be followed by a rousing rendition of John Lennon's Imagine which players had agreed should be substituted for the racist national anthem because "feels".

The players would continue to wear their traditional cricketing "whites" but they would be called "off whites" to signal there was something "a bit off" about white people.

"They may not win a Test match but this will be the most tokenistic team to ever represent Australia and we're very proud of that," the wokesperson said.

IT'S AN EVIL COP OUT CLAIMING DOMESTIC VIOLENCE IN ABORIGINAL COMMUNITIES COMES FROM COLONISATION

When a black man hits a black woman it's a white man's fault, according to Diversity Council Australia.

The Council, quoting Indigenous activist Kelly Treloar, yesterday tweeted that a high rate of domestic violence in Aboriginal communities was the result of colonisation.

Well, of course.

And high rates of alcoholism in those same communities is the result of Advance Australia Fair. Not really. But you wouldn't put such a suggestion beyond Diversity Council Australia after yesterday's effort.

The Council tweeted: "Statistics show that First Nations women experience higher rates of #familyviolence than other women but this is a complex issue stemmed from issues of colonisation, trauma from displacement and legacy of intergenerational trauma."

The first part of the tweet is indisputable. Statistics show that Indigenous women experience extraordinarily high rates of domestic violence.

The Australian Institute of Health and Welfare reports that Indigenous women are 32 times more likely to be hospitalised as a result of family violence than are non-Indigenous women.

But statistics also show that critical race theory and social justice scholarship will do less than nothing to fix the problem.

The second part of the tweet – the bit where it says the causes of domestic violence are "complex" and then immediately blames Arthur Phillip – is disgraceful.

It is the racism of low expectations that suggests certain people have no autonomy and that their actions have been pre-determined by historical events because, you know, melanin.

Personally, I would love to blame my own failures on the intergenerational trauma of convict transportation.

But I'm white, so unlike my Indigenous brothers, I am considered able to take responsibility for my actions.

It is just this kind of rubbish that permits suffering to continue unabated – suffering which is essential for groups like Diversity Council Australia to exist.

Blaming domestic violence in Indigenous communities on colonisation ensures that domestic violence in Indigenous communities can never be stopped. It's a classic case of ensuring that you never fix the patient so that you always have a patient to fix.

The Council may as well have tweeted, "Statistics show that First

Nations women experience higher rates of #familyviolence than other women but we don't care unless it fits our divisive identity politics".

"A boat arrived at Sydney Cove 222 years ago" is no excuse for beating a woman.

And, "if it wasn't for January 26 this would never have happened to you," is no consolation to a battered woman.

Domestic violence in Indigenous communities always was, always will be the responsibility of Indigenous men to own and to fix.

But as long as activists suggest that Indigenous men in 2020 are victims of white men from 1788, indigenous women – whose deaths by family violence far outnumber the Indigenous men who have died in custody and yet they receive none of the attention – will continue to suffer.

Diversity Council Australia imagines that Indigenous people had never known violence until whites showed up in boats. This, of course, is nonsense. And everyone knows it.

Bone fracture pattern analysis of pre-settlement indigenous women, as well as testimony from the first settlers, has shown that brutal levels of violence existed in Indigenous communities long before 1770.

Diversity Council Australia though, to their credit, do ensure a diversity of views. There's the truth, based on facts, and there's the politically correct, self-serving fiction that the Council tweets.

FINALLY, SYSTEMIC RACISM IN THE MATERNITY WARD HAS BEEN BROUGHT TO PUBLIC ATTENTION

Last Ship, *Nightflyers* and *Queen & Slim* star Jodie Turner-Smith gave birth at home rather than in a hospital because of "systemic racism", according to a report in the *New York Post* this week.

The black British-born actress and model told the Post: "We had already decided on a home birth because of concerns about negative birth outcomes for black women in America."

"According to the Centre for Disease Control, the risk of pregnancy-related deaths is more than three times greater for black women than for white women, pointing, it seems to me, to systemic racism."

Turner-Smith could have given birth by a river to be more culturally attuned. But I digress.

Frankly, I'm surprised it's taken two months since the death of George Floyd for someone to finally bring systemic racism in the maternity ward to public attention.

I say that because I well remember the day after I was born and placed in the recovery room with the other newborn babies. The "N" word was just flying around the room.

Of course, I only heard it because I was in the front row. All the minority babies were made to lay in cribs up the back.

I'll never forget lying on the white sheet they had provided for me and thinking, "Wow. They're not even trying to disguise it."

But before we defund hospitals we might want to consider that the pregnancy-related death rate for black women may be due to factors other than white supremacist nurses lurking menacingly in post-natal suites.

Asthma related deaths are three times greater for African Americans than for whites. Does this mean asthma is racist? Perhaps the inhalers discriminate.

Diabetes related deaths are also more common in blacks than in whites. Defund insulin.

Blacks have a much higher rate of teen pregnancy which is a factor in higher rates of death during childbirth. But rather than call attention to this social problem, it's much easier just to make stuff up.

I once had a bad case of indigestion bought on by systemic racism and eating too fast. But mostly I blame systemic racism.

What exactly is Jodie Turner-Smith, who is married to former Dawson's Creek star Joshua Jackson, suggesting when she says systemic racism in hospitals is responsible for black women dying in childbirth?

Are hospitals turning away black women? Are midwives targeting black mums for death?

If we want to talk about blacks dying in pregnancy, we might have a conversation about the fact that blacks represent 13% of the American population and yet account for five times as many abortions as whites.

Abortionists, who typically set up in poor black neighbourhoods, kill 1000 black babies every day.

This is the one form of actual systemic racism in America and the only form of systemic racism no-one wants to talk about.

It's not Planned Parenthood killing black babies every day but hospitals assisting black children to be born in a safe, professional environment that is the real race problem in America.

Just don't tell Beyonce, who reportedly took over an entire hospital floor when she last gave birth.

As for home births, a report published in the American Journal of Obstetrics and Gynecology in February found that nearly 14 newborns per 10,000 live births died following planned home births – more than four times the rate for babies born in hospitals.

When you endanger the life of your newborn in order to engage in post-natal virtue signalling, you've done nothing to end imagined systemic racism, but you've certainly proven that endemic stupidity is a thing.

DAMN THOSE WHITE PEOPLE AND THEIR ... VEGANISM?

Vice magazine published an article on August 14 headlined: "Dear White Vegans, Stop Appropriating Food."

"Veganism is going through its own racial reckoning that's a long time coming, considering white vegan influencers have appropriated traditional foods forever," the article said.

It goes on to quote Afia Amoako who complains that she doesn't see herself reflected in the vegan community, which she says, is dominated by wealthy white women. "They often touted recipes – "African peanut stew" or "Asian stir fry" – that rely on racial stereotypes," Amoako said.

"One, they don't look like you, and, two, they are appropriating your food. Those are ways to turn racialized people away."

Well there's Amoako's problem. She's racialized. Maybe if she was less racialized and a bit more, you know, human, she'd be able to look at food without being oppressed!

When you can't think of a single thing more racist than some cracker eating a tofu dumpling, you're the problem!

When you feel like vegetables and salad have that micro-aggression of racism built into them, you're no longer eating the plants, you're smoking them.

If Amoako has her way, we won't be able to eat anything without first making certain that what we are eating was first eaten by someone who shared our skin colour...or else!

Come to think about it, there's a Japanese noodle restaurant in my city that serves Kimchi. I don't know whether to wokesplain to them why this is wrong, or just set fire to the place.

Vice Magazine said that Amoako, a vegan Instagrammer and blogger based in Toronto, wasn't the only racialized vegan who felt sidelined by the community.

"Black vegan influencer Tabitha Brown told Vice that before she cut out meat and dairy, she thought vegans were "white ladies who do yoga." White people and their blogs dominate the results when key terms like "vegans," "vegetarians," or "vegan recipes" are plugged into Google."

Well, let's ensure some black women eating spicy Chinese eggplant are bumped up the Google search results – or George Floyd will have died in vain!

Wait a second, I thought veganism was about eliminating as far as practically possible the use and abuse of animals. The fact these people are choosing to look at veganism through the lens of race means they have zero care for the actual cause of vegans.

It's almost like they sat down and thought: "Damn white people and their ... shuffles deck ... veganism!

Cooking and enjoying food from another culture is not cultural appropriation so much as cultural appreciation.

But the geniuses at Vice Magazine seem to think learning something from another culture and using it yourself is a heinous act of racial oppression.

I was actually very close to going vegan. But after reading the article in Vice, I decided to honor my whiteness with another helping of ribs and bacon.

Maybe it's a good thing I don't cook any of that foreign rubbish. I'm accidentally Woke!

I do look forward to Vice Magazine doing a story on cultural appropriation of things like pants, and air travel. And the telephone, internet, the PC and the stuff like that. They could start with the cultural appropriation of "Desk Top Publishing".

REPARATIONS: WHERE PEOPLE WHO NEVER OWNED

SLAVES PAY MONEY TO PEOPLE WHO NEVER WERE SLAVES

America's mayors this week backed a national call for reparations to black people, a program that could cost taxpayers $6.2 quadrillion.

The U.S. Conference of Mayors released a letter Monday backing a Democratic plan to form a reparations commission to come up with a payment for slavery.

The Washington Examiner reported that the issue of repatriations had been raised afresh in response to the Black Lives Matter movement.

The report said: "Long at the centre of the debate has been the potential price tag of paying slavery descendants, for which studies broadly include most or all of the 41 million black people in the country."

The paper quoted a new study by three college professors that said the ultimate cost could be $6.2 quadrillion."

For those who don't know what a quadrillion looks like, here you go: $6,200,000,000,000,000

The study - which calculated unpaid hours that slaves worked as well as a price for massacres and discrimination and then added interest - suggests a payment of $151 million to every African American. The cost to whites would be $18.96m per person.

(All of the above is true)

But another study – based on looting during the Black Lives Matter protests – suggested that cigarettes, a 60" flat screen, Jordan's, and some Apple products would be sufficient reparations for some.

The Jewish community backed the proposal and issued their own reparation bill for 100 quadrillion gazillion dollars. But this was immediately dismissed by anti-racists as "just more victimhood by money-hungry Jews".

It is believed Irish Americans, many of whom claim their ancestors worked as slaves, are expected to launch their own reparation claim. A spokesman said they would be happy to be paid in pints of Guinness.

"And since we are just making stuff up," the spokesman said, "I think a quadrillion trillion billion pints, per person, should suffice."

Democrat spokesperson Lately Woke, whose pronouns are they/their, privately admitted no-one in the Party seriously believed the money would be paid.

"Oh we know it will never happen," they laughed. "It's political theatre of the first degree. But proposing a dollar figure roughly 72 times the entire world economy positions us to be able to act appalled when it's ultimately shot down.

"This proposal costs us absolutely nothing but dangles the empty promise of a fortune in front of every vote we want to buy."

Responding to the charge that Democrats were "completely unserious people who should be wholly dismissed", Lately said: "We should not be wholly dismissed".

A spokesman for Normal People, an oppressed group being systematically hunted down and cancelled throughout America, said the idea of paying reparations was unfair.

"You cannot demand people who never owned slaves, pay money to people who never were slaves, to punish them for people in the past," he said. "It's unethical and it's racist."

When his comments were reported by local media his employer fired him from his job and a group of mostly peaceful protestors burned down his house.

MASTERCHEF IS DEEPLY RACIST. APPARENTLY ...

Next time an Asian makes the final of MasterChef, I'm turning the TV off. If my team – by which I mean whites – are not winning, then I'm not watching. That's sarcastic humour, by the way.

Yet imagine if I meant that. I'd be crucified on social media as a bigot and likely hounded out of my job.

Actually, I probably wouldn't suffer for those terribly racist views because no publication of repute would ever agree to print them, and so you'd never know what a jerk I am.

All of which makes me wonder why the Sydney Morning Herald, a former newspaper, ran a column by Jessica Zhan Mei Yu expressing those exact views, but against Caucasians.

The Australian born Chinese-Malaysian wrote that she refused to watch the MasterChef finale because the finalists were white.

"It hurt so much when Reynold Poernomo, the only Asian-Australian to make the top five was eliminated from the competition, making the finale a showdown between two (talented) white chefs," she wrote.

"It suddenly didn't matter who won because my team had already lost."

It's apparently very racist to ask a person of Asian appearance where they come from since it assumes they were not born here. But Jessica Zhan Mei Yu can root for her "team" when it suits. A classic case of tribalism for me, but not for thee.

Moreover, I had never realised MasterChef was a competition between Team Asia and Team White.

Apparently you have to be a self-proclaimed anti-racist to think in those terms.

I'm just what they call a Quiet Australian who thought he was watching a cooking show in order to keep his wife happy.

But for Jessica, MasterChef is more than cooks cooking. Rather, "MasterChef is all you've really got if you're looking for Asian-Australian faces on TV."

Here's a conversation that has never been had in our house:

"What do you want to watch on TV tonight, babe? White faces? Or should we look for Asian? We watched a Will Smith movie last night so I'm not really in the mood for black again. Are you?"

I never go "looking" for particular faces on TV. I've always thought the content of the program was more important than the colour of the faces. But hey, that's just me. And Dr Martin Luther King.

That Jessica's preferred face didn't win this year's cook-off – despite the fact that Asian-Australians have won the past three seasons – was proof of a "bamboo ceiling", she said.

If the writer wants to experience an actual bamboo ceiling – one built by the Party over a concrete floor and steel walls – she might try complaining in China that her Wuhan bat came with a side of virus.

NOW WALKING IS RACIST

Just when you thought claims of racism could not get any more puerile, the World Economic Forum has published an article alleging black people are excluded from the outdoors.

That's right. Hiking is racist.

The evidence? UK author Rhiane Fatinikun went for a walk in a park and didn't see many black people.

White privilege now extends to going outside!

"The lack of representation in hiking is clear for all to see", Fatinikun said.

"I wasn't keen on the prospect of venturing out alone or joining a typical hikers' group where there'd be nobody I could identify with."

This point says far more about the author than it does about the white supremacists guarding hiking trails and the "whites only" signs posted along footpaths in order to keep blacks isolated indoors.

Why would the author not "identify" with other humans, regardless of melanin, based on a mutual love of hiking?

The only way she could possibly feel excluded from hiking is if she herself is so racist that she cannot form meaningful relationships with people of different skin colours.

Imagine needing to see a reflection of yourself wherever you go. That Fatinikun identifies only with people who look like her is evidence of a problem with her, not with the outdoors.

But no, black people have been systematically excluded from the outdoors and so Fatinikun founded Black Girls Hike "to encourage black women to explore the UK countryside in the safety of sisterhood".

So the Manchester resident has decided to tackle exclusion by creating a group that determines membership based on skin colour. And the World Economic Forum want to champion this!

The article doesn't say what precisely it was about the outdoors that Fatinikun believed excluded her. By her own admission, she just didn't want to go walking with people who weren't black.

"I'm proud we are challenging stereotypes and showing people that the outdoors is for everyone," she said.

Walking is for whites has never been a stereotype. And forming a 'blacks only' walking group doesn't show that the outdoors is for everyone.

The only words in that quote that could possibly be true are the first two.

Fatinikun complains that walking in parks is "not even marketed at black people".

What would such a marketing campaign look like?

"Don't let the racist grass intimidate you. Ignore the white supremacist trees. Open the front door, start walking and keep going!"

If the marketing campaign doesn't work, perhaps governments should force black people to hike. Or bribe them with tax incentives. Or maybe whites should be excluded from bush trails until the quota of back people increases.

Maybe local mayors could stand at the end of hiking trails and pat black people on the head as they conclude their walks.

Too far?

This infantile obsession with skin colour has gone way too far. It's not enlightened, it's stupid. It's not progressive, it's divisive and regressive.

A black British hiker looks for a problem that doesn't exist so she can cry "racism". And the World Economic Forum, right on cue, shouts "Wokey wokey, rise and shine!"

Speaking of which, the only thing British walkers are regularly excluded from is the sun. And that applies to people out for a stroll regardless of their skin colour.

THERE'S NO RACISM IN BASKETBALL? WELL NEVER MIND, ALL IS NOT LOST

A Human Rights Commission report into racism within Basketball Australia, released at the weekend, is a solution in search of a problem.

A five-month investigation by the HRC found pretty much zero evidence of racism.

In fact, the report itself lamented that only 21 people had even bothered to make submissions to the inquiry.

It said the poor response indicated "a lack of interest in the topic by the basketball community or no concerns about racial equality in basketball".

Well, there you go. That's good news, right?

And the few who did respond to the HRC's call for evidence of racism said that the sport could "sometimes be exclusionary". And – wait for it – that "progress can sometimes depend on who you know".

In other words, basketball is a lot like life generally.

The report also said: "The small sample size means that the feedback drawn upon and reflected in this report cannot be considered representative of the experiences of any relevant cohort — national players, coaches, or staff."

Right. So an inquiry that few people could be bothered participating in produced vague generalisations that were, for all intents and purposes, meaningless.

Hardly a slam dunk.

But, of course, none of this stopped the HRC producing a 49-page report containing 12 sweeping recommendations requiring "a whole of ecosystem commitment" to change.

With no obvious racism to tut-tut, the HRC noted that "for the purposes of this Review, racial equality within such a sporting context means actively valuing diversity".

There's no racism at Basketball Australia? Well never mind, all is not lost. We will redefine terms and insist that it is not enough to not be racist. You have to be "actively valuing diversity".

And with that sleight of hand, the HRC justify the cost of the report and the glossy paper it is printed on.

The HRC urged Basketball Australia to set targets for diversity among board members. Basketball Australia needed to "embed racial equality in all policies" (whatever that means) and implement "regular anti-racism training".

Indeed. What better way to help a sporting organisation that has no obvious racial problems than by insisting those running it start to focus on race.

There were nine other incredibly important action points without which the future of basketball in this country was doomed, but you get the idea.

Yada, yada, diversity, yada, inclusion, pathways, organisational culture, systemic approach, yada, yada, whatever.

Less than a quarter of the way through reading the jargon-ladened report my main worry about the organisational culture at Basketball Australia concerned the fact that someone had paid the HRC good money for this.

But that won't be the end of the spend.

The Racial Equality Review of Basketball Australia 2021 concluded that: "Racial equality alone will not result in making basketball an inclusive sport and the recommendations should be considered and implemented in conjunction with broader diversity and inclusion efforts.

"This is critical, as the effects of exclusion can be compounded when race intersects with other characteristics such as gender, sexual orientation, disability, or socio-economic status."

And so we look forward to the LGBTQ Equality Review of Basketball Australia, the Gender Equality Review of Basketball Australia, the Disability Equality Review of Basketball Australia and, of course, the much anticipated Socio-Economic Status Equality Review of Basketball Australia.

Because it's not enough to not be racist or to not be homophobic when playing basketball. You have to shoot hoops in such a way that you are actively valuing approved identity groups.

And it just so happens that the Human Rights Commission, unable as it is to find many actual cases of abuse in the freest country on earth, have free time on their hands to help out with that.

WHO ARE YOU CALLING RACIST?

So it turns out that six men ejected from the third cricket test in Sydney for racist conduct weren't racist after all

They were just in the wrong place at the wrong time – by which I mean Australia in 2021, where an allegation of racism is as good as proof; and where self-righteous preeners will gladly denounce their fellow man if it means a chance to parade their own anti-racism credentials.

Three weeks after spectators were escorted from their seats and thrown out of the Sydney Cricket Ground by police for hurling racist insults at an Indian player, investigations by both Cricket Australia and NSW Police have found that the men did no such thing.

Well, Indian fans in the crowd could have told them that. In fact, they did.

But eyewitnesses were ignored as television cameras zoomed in on the latest examples of what we are continually told is rampant racism in Australia.

Seven Network cricket commentator Lisa Sthalekar said: "So disappointed with a very small part of the SCG fans, totally embarrassed."

Well no.

Embarrassing was the way in which everyone raced to tar and feather a group of sports fans whose only crime was to not have thought to wear body cameras to the cricket in order to protect themselves from baseless charges.

Nine Network news showed what the reporter called "disgraced spectators" being led from their seats after play was stopped for ten minutes when Indian fast bowler Mohammed Siraj complained that he was being racially taunted by the crowd.

Nine news might have waited for charges to be laid before deciding the men were "disgraced", but who has time for such technicalities when the witch hunt is already well underway?

Cricket Australia's Head of Integrity and Security, Sean Carroll, immediately released a statement, saying "Cricket Australia condemns in the strongest possible terms all discriminatory behaviour. If you engage in racist behaviour you are not welcome in Australian cricket."

One might have imagined that "integrity" meant not condemning in the strongest possible terms something that never happened in the first place.

Former prime minister Kevin Rudd immediately took to twitter, describing the men as "boneheaded racists".

"Cricket Australia should throw the book at these fools," he thundered.

(How did you refer to Chinese, Kevin?)

NSW Labor leader Jodi Mackay rushed to join what was rapidly becoming a social media pile-on.

"India is watching how we respond to the racial slurs being directed at their cricketers. Ban those responsible for life. I stand with the Indian team."

It's a pity Ms Mackay didn't stand with her beleaguered constituents. Or at least wait until the accusation was confirmed before advocating life bans for men who would later be found to have done nothing wrong.

But the principle of innocent until proven guilty does not apply to charges of racism since any hesitation to condemn those accused is itself taken as just another form of racism.

Indeed, when NSW One Nation leader Mark Latham tweeted that perhaps the cricket fans had not done what they were accused of doing, he was – right on cue – accused of defending racism.

But what is surely as bad as racism is wrongly accusing people of racism.

How is it that a group of mates can go to the cricket, be forcibly removed from seats they paid for while being shamed on national television and on social media, only for authorities to belatedly announce three weeks later that the men didn't in fact do anything wrong?

Will they get an apology?

If people were calling for a life ban for something that didn't happen, perhaps the men deserve life membership for what did happen.

Perhaps the next time our woke cricketers perform their bare foot circle ceremony to contemplate victims of racism, they could spare a thought for their own fans who were victims of the so-called anti racists.

Amazingly, Cricket Australia were still insisting that racist comments were made by the crowd, even as they admitted the men removed from the game were not the culprits and that they had no idea who the culprits were.

Well they would say that, wouldn't they. Because the alternative – that Aussies aren't obviously racist – just doesn't fit the narrative.

ABORIGINAL IMPRISONMENT: DON'T CONFUSE A SOCIAL ISSUE WITH A JUSTICE ISSUE

Those who insist that too many indigenous people are in jail confuse a social issue with a justice issue, and so make both issues worse.

West Australian Police Commissioner Chris Dawson is the latest public official to demand indigenous incarceration rates be reduced.

He told *The Australian* newspaper yesterday: "Too many (indigenous people) are being arrested and charged."

It's hard to imagine what law-abiding West Australians must think when hearing their top cop complain that police are arresting too many criminals.

Although, to be fair, that's not exactly what he suggested. It was more along the lines that police were arresting too many of the wrong *kinds* of criminals.

There was an "over-representation" of indigenous people in the state's prisons, he said.

Well, he is absolutely right if the point of the justice system is to ensure that the number of different kinds of people behind bars is more or less proportionate to their numbers in the wider community.

As a side note, if indigenous people are over-represented in prison it begs the question as to which group is under-represented. Which ethnicity should law enforcement police harder in order to balance things out? But I digress.

Unless West Australian police are going around arresting people for being indigenous – which plainly they are not – then the only explanation for the disproportionate number of indigenous people in prison is that indigenous people are committing a disproportionately high number of crimes.

And if that is the case, then indigenous people are not over-represented, but accurately represented in jail.

But no one wants to say that.

So, instead, we say that police have arrested, and the courts have jailed, too many indigenous criminals. That's far easier to say because it saves us from insisting that people ought take personal responsibility for their decisions whilst giving us the chance to yell "racism" and so prove we are not racists.

Now you might imagine that an easy way to avoid being arrested and charged is to obey the law. But such ideas are too simple for those in public office to entertain.

Commissioner Dawson blamed his own police force for the high number of Aboriginals in jail saying "we are not doing enough" to divert offenders from arrest and court and prison.

I wish police would blame themselves when I am caught speeding. But again, I digress. (See how insisting that a social issue among indigenous people is a justice issue only serves to undermine faith in the justice system whilst doing zero to fix the social issue?)

It does not seem to occur to Commissioner Dawson that, just as it would be racist to put people in jail because they are Aboriginal it would also be racist to divert criminals from jail because they are Aboriginal. Again, holding any kind of public office seems to prevent obvious thoughts from occurring.

Commissioner Dawson did say that "a crime is a crime," which would have momentarily heartened victims of crime because let's face it, the skin colour of the thief who steals your car doesn't change the fact that your car is missing from the driveway and you're rightly mad as hell.

But having insisted that "crime is a crime" the Commissioner then went on to insist that the justice system should play social worker by treating some crimes as something other than crimes depending on the ancestry of the criminal.

He said young Aboriginal offenders should be dealt with by leaders within the Aboriginal community.

"It would allow a child here to be dealt with by Aboriginal leaders, exposing them to the shame and sanction of their own communities," he said.

Now I'm just asking for a friend, but are these the same communities where sexual assault and domestic violence is thirty to fifty times higher than in the broader community? And just how are the Aboriginal leaders dealing with *that* problem right now?

At every public event we pause to "acknowledge elders past, present and emerging". I always wonder where they are and what they're doing.

But a better question is why the police chief is talking about the role of community leaders rather than the responsibility of parents.

That's not a police siren you hear. That's the sound of crickets.

If the Police Commissioner wants to involve indigenous leaders, he might like to involve Alice Springs Deputy Mayor Jacinta Price, a rare public official who does not choke on the obvious.

Writing in *The Australian* last week she said: "No amount of adjusting targets to reduce incarceration by developing race-based legislation will prevent crime. As long as there are no targets to reduce family violence and the abuse and neglect of our children, incarceration rates will continue to climb."

Jacinta Price is, as usual, spot on. When you confuse social issues with justice issues you only end up undermining confidence in the justice system while allowing social dysfunction to grow ever worse.

OUTING YOURSELF AS A RACIST IS GOOD FOR BUSINESS

Drongo alert: this piece may contain traces of satire and irony.

Nestle yesterday took the unprecedented step of complaining that its own product was racist, after seeing the publicity other companies got when accused of racism.

Company spokeswoman, Candy Crush, told reporters she was "deeply sorry" no-one had been offended by their raspberry-flavoured Redskin confectionery.

"Because Redskins are only sold in Australia and New Zealand there has been no outrage from American Indians at all," she said. "And for that we are deeply sorry."

It is believed anger about the iconic lolly's name began last week – not among American Indians, who had never heard of the chewy sweet, but among staff in the company's marketing department.

"Our team saw the national coverage Colonial Brewing got when they were accused of racism," Ms Crush said. "It certainly triggered us. We were suddenly woke to the idea that our brand would be just as offensive, if anyone was actually offended.

Ms Crush said Nestle executives hoped the Black Lives Matter movement would inspire a Red Lives Matter protest against their product, sparking a media frenzy.

But when Australians proved too sensible for that, the company decided it's confectionary needed confected outrage.

"We take outrage over racism very seriously," a stern Ms Crush told assembled media. "And so we thought, in the absence of any outrage, the only option left was for us was to be outraged at ourselves."

Ms Crush said not everyone at Nestle was comfortable with the idea.

"Our chiefs had reservations," she said.

"But our marketing team convinced them the product name was out of step with our values which are rooted in respect and boosting sales."

Ms Crush said she didn't know the background of why the Australian-made product had been given its name.

"I have no idea whether there were actual racial undertones or not," she said. "But for the sake of the news, let's just say there probably were because the one thing we can agree on is that everyone from the past was racist.

"I really want to emphasise that this is our moment of growth and respect and that we acknowledge our need to learn and to listen and to be on a journey and, you know, all that wokie stuff."

Television and radio news bulletins all ran the story that Nestle was cancelling the Redskin name amid concerns it mocked Indian Americans.

The brand immediately started trending on twitter as people pledged to buy the company's product in a show of support for the name.

"This decision to cancel the iconic Redskin brand acknowledges the need to ensure that nothing we do marginalises our friends, neighbours and colleagues – whilst taking full advantage of the incredible marketing opportunities presented by cancel culture," Ms Crush said.

Packaging for the 'Red Skins' lollies previously featured a photo and cartoon of Native Americans, which were removed in the 1990s.

Ms Crush said a new product name would come later. "We want to soak up this moment first," she said with a broad smile.

FAIR SUCK OF THE SAUCE BOTTLE, KEV. THAT'S NOT RACIST

Is Kevin Rudd really stupid, as he expects us to believe? Or is he just a rank opportunist who manipulates the serious issues of race and sex in order to score cheap political points?

The former PM was all huff and puff today when triggered by a cartoon in *The Australian* that depicted Joe Biden introducing his presidential running mate Kamala Harris as "a little brown girl".

The Democrat presidential nominee was shown saying: "It's time to heal a nation divided by racism."

In the next frame, Johannes Leak's cartoon shows Biden, standing in front of Kamala Harris, saying:

"So I'll hand you over to this little brown girl while I go take a lie down."

This was enough to enrage Kevin Rudd who, engaging twitter before first engaging brain, ranted: "So how on earth does Murdoch editor Chris Dore justify publishing a racist and sexist cartoon about a US Senator who is likely to be the next Vice-President of the US? Murdoch is a Trump mouthpiece. But this is gross even by Murdoch's gutter standards."

Fair shake of the sauce bottle, Mr Rudd. It's a miracle you were able to run the country for even an hour when you evidently cannot comprehend a simple cartoon.

The cartoon was not mocking Kamala Harris. Harris was not even its object. Leak's clever cartoon used Joe Biden's own words to point out how racist and sexist Joe Biden was.

Yes. It was Biden who said, after selecting Harris as his running mate, that: "This morning, little girls woke up across this nation — especially Black and Brown girls who so often may feel overlooked and undervalued in our society — potentially seeing themselves in a new way: As the stuff of Presidents and Vice Presidents."

Joe "if you don't vote for me you ain't black" Biden has a long history of racial and sexual gaffes. This was merely the most recent and Leak rightly called it out.

But of course, Mr Rudd knows all of this. The real outrage is Mr Rudd's caricature of the Australian public – whom he believes to be so stupid they will mistake his faux outrage for moral virtue.

Even worse, Mr Rudd manipulates the public's genuine concerns about racism in a bid to mobilise them for his own ends – his personal vendetta against News Limited whom he blames for his failed prime ministership. Er, prime ministerships.

Not to be out-virtued, other Labor and ABC figures (but I repeat myself) joined in.

Shadow Attorney-General Mark Dreyfus tweeted from on high: "If *The Australian* has any respect for decency and standards it must apologise immediately, and never again publish cartoons like this."

Sure, sure Mr Dreyfus.

When Joe Biden told a black radio host that if blacks didn't vote for him they weren't black, you were silent. When Joe Biden said that "poor kids are just as talented as white kids", you were silent.

When Joe Biden described Barrack Obama as "the first mainstream African-American who is articulate and bright and clean" you were silent.

But when a cartoon in *The Australian* points out Biden's racism you suddenly find your anti-racist voice by screaming "racist" at *The Australian*, and thinking we are fool enough to take you seriously.

What is indecent is your cynical manipulation of the public conscience; trying to leverage our genuine concerns about racism for your political point-scoring. Everyone who has ever been the victim of actual racism ought to be appalled at civic leaders engaged in such cynical antics.

Fellow Labor MP Andrew Leigh tweeted: "Racism has no place in

Australian public life. *The Australian* should pull today's offensive cartoon off their website, and issue an immediate apology."

Issue an immediate apology for what? For quoting the 2020 Democratic nominee?

ABC News Breakfast host Michael Rowland, referring to the cartoon, tweeted: "I feel really sorry for those good journalists when their stories appear in the same paper as this. Shameful."

The rest of us just feel sorry that our taxes go towards a national broadcaster that doesn't even pretend to be fair-minded; employing journalists who prefer to massage the news than report it.

LOWERING INCARCERATION RATES

Drongo alert: this piece may contain traces of satire and irony.

Australia must address factors that make criminals more likely to go to jail than other members of the community, activists say.

While the Australian Institute of Criminology has found the rate at which criminals die in custody has been decreasing, data from the Australian Bureau of Statistics shows the proportion of prisoners in Australia who are criminals has remained steady at 100 percent.

This is despite the fact that 100% of prisoners claim to be innocent.

"Criminals are over represented in our prisons," activist Ima Lawless told thousands of peaceful protestors who had gathered to loot department stores in the city centre.

"We must work together to address the factors that contribute to high incarceration rates among criminals. These include leaving behind too many clues, a failure to avoid CCTV and boasting about their crimes on Facebook."

Ms Lawless said Australia needed to look closely at the factors contributing to incarceration rates and the way in which our systems were handling criminal incidents.

"This requires a co-operative approach," she told reporters. "Specifically, we want to see the police co-operating more closely with those who commit crimes by giving a nod and a wink, or simply looking the other way when they see a crime committed."

Ms Lawless said reducing the number of criminals in contact with the justice system was key in addressing the number of criminals in custody.

"That's why we want to defund a range of activities such as policing; to improve justice outcomes for criminals in Australia," she said.

"For years we've thrown money at this problem and it has made no difference to criminal incarceration rates. We are now urging the Government to take funding away from the police, and you just watch outcomes improve for criminals."

Police Commissioner Rob Banks said he was not concerned about a decrease in funding since the recently introduced "cops on bicycles" program had reduced spending on vehicles "and, more importantly, made us feel a lot better about the environment".

But he said that despite awareness of the disproportionate level of criminals inside detention centres, programs implemented to address the issue had failed.

"Not that long ago we thought tying officers up in copious amounts of paper work would help to reduce the number of offenders being arrested and jailed," he said.

"More recently we have redirected police away from fighting crime and had them focus on the important work of becoming allies of minority groups."

Commissioner Banks lamented that such programs had made little difference to anything at all but "the Police Department float at last year's Mardi Gras is something all Australians can be very proud of".

"Oh, and it got us plenty of favourable coverage on the ABC," he added as peaceful protestors chanting "a good cop is a dead cop" burned his bicycle.

"It's only property," he said, "And there's no harm in it. They're just letting off a bit of steam. In fact, I want to congratulate protestors on observing social distancing rules while rummaging through high end stores. They've adhered to our strict one looter per 4 square metre rule."

Meanwhile, Wokeopia University Vice Chancellor Professor Cognitive Dissonance said it was difficult to disentangle crimes committed – such as theft, assault and murder – from legal issues that contribute to the incarceration of criminals.

"Laws that see criminals put behind bars are out of touch with common decency. Australia is lagging behind the rest of the world," she said. "It's not right that we are criminalising people for committing crimes."

"The Government must set targets for lower incarceration rates and, if the targets are not achieved, cabinet ministers should be locked up."

WHEN YOU VIEW ALL OF LIFE THROUGH THE PRISM OF OFFENCE, YOU'LL FIND OFFENCE IN EVERY SUPERMARKET FRIDGE

The Indigenous activist who forced Coon Cheese out of Australian fridges now wants Paul's to stop producing "Smarter White Milk" because it is offensive to Aborigines.

Dr Stephen Hagan has told The Daily Mail Australia that the brand name insinuated it was for "for smart, white people, not for smart, black people".

"There's a lot of Aboriginal people who take offence," he said, leaving the world confused as to whether he was trying to end racism or satire.

Of course, smart people of any colour would realise the adjective "smart" was a reference to the product's low fat content.

And the adjective "white" was simply describing the milk; which is, you know, white.

Apparently not everyone is smart enough to understand Smart White Milk, but it has nothing to do with one's skin colour.

A chip on the shoulder, however, does seem to affect cognitive ability.

When you view all of life through the prism of offence, is it any wonder you see offence peering out from every fridge in the supermarket?

And can we really blame Dr Hagan for seeing racial taunts everywhere? We all knew the campaign against Coon Cheese was ridiculous – but we acquiesced anyway, out of a misplaced desire to be kind.

"It's only the name of a cheese," we thought. "What does it really matter if we change the name? If it makes Dr Hagan happy, why not? And besides, inclusive."

And so we did. We binned the iconic cheese and wished Dr Hagan well.

But like the parent who gives the foot-stomping toddler everything he wants, we just encouraged increasingly ridiculous tantrums.

Emboldened by his ability to scream "racism" on a whim and see the world pander to his sensibilities, Dr Hagan is not even slightly embarrassed to pout and stomp his feet all over again.

If we really cared about Dr Hagan, we would tell him to stop being ridiculous and to grow up. If we really cared about Indigenous people, we would do the same.

Tantrums in the supermarket are normally thrown by children.

But children like the five-year-old boy allegedly gang-raped on a Cape York beach last month by other Indigenous children don't have the luxury of throwing tantrums as children do.

That has instead been left to the activists who are supposed to be helping them but who prefer, instead, the thrill of raging against groceries.

Enough is enough.

COLOUR ME BLUE

The Washington Post announced this week that its reporters would uppercase the B in Black to identify African Americans in news stories.

The use of "Black" rather than "black" was an acknowledgment of shared cultural and historical bonds, the paper said.

In other words, Black is to be a noun rather than an adjective.

Black will denote not merely the colour of a person's skin, but importantly for journalists at the Washington Post it seems, the group to which that person belongs.

Of course, *The Washington Post* could just call everybody "American", but then how would the media pit people against each other?

The paper went on to announce:

> "This style change also prompts the question of how America's largest racial community should be identified. Stories involving race show that White also represents a distinct cultural identity in the United States. As such white should be represented with a capital W."

Which "stories" involving the White race, *The Washington Post* did not say. But we can take a Wild with a capital W guess.

Hmmm ... I'm guessing stories involving the White race feature things like colonizing, mass murder and slavery. Stuff like that.

But I digress.

The Washington Post essentially admits that having decided to lump everyone with black skin (now known as uppercase Blacks) into one bucket, they reckoned they might as well throw all the whites into their own special container.

The Post's uber-consciousness about race is starting to sound like it will contribute to, yes, racism.

At a time when America needs to come together, the Washington Post manages to find new ways to emphasise difference.

Wait. Maybe that's unfair. Perhaps citing skin colours is a great way to demonstrate a rich understanding of race and ethnicity.

Actually, no.

Imagining that Kenyans and Somalis are basically the same because Black, or that Italians and Australians are identical because White is not enlightened, it's backward.

The Washington Post did "recognise there are individuals who prefer not to confine themselves to identity based solely on the colour of their skin".

You think? Who are these people who don't want their humanity reduced by the media to melanin?

The Washington Post says that if any such people exist, they "will have the opportunity to identify as African American and biracial, or something more ethnically specific".

The option of simply identifying as "human" was not mentioned.

If you're wondering what the Washington Post will do if you are neither Black nor White, fear not; they haven't forgotten you.

The Post informed readers: "We will limit the uppercase version of the racial categorization Brown to direct quotations and use it sparingly in other instances. Although the term has gained general acceptance, the designation is seen by many as a catchall to describe people of colour of vastly diverse ethnic and cultural backgrounds who are not Black."

Right.

Because we wouldn't want to use colour as a catchall to describe people would we!

The Post goes on to say: "Other colours as racial identifiers have not been commonly adopted by members of the ethnic groups they are often used to portray, as many consider the terms insults or slurs. Those identifiers will remain lowercase."

So if your appearance is other than Black, White or Brown, you don't get your skin colour capitalised and underlined and written in bold in large font in front of your name in order to tell us everything we need to know about you.

Oh to be blue!

RACISTS AS ANTI RACISTS ARE IN VOGUE

British *Vogue Magazine* published an article on August 2 promoting the idea of a blacks only university under the heading "anti-racism".

Which just goes to show, socially acceptable racism is very one-sided. If Vogue journalists suggested a whites only university, they would be chased through the streets!

The article began: "In the wake of anti-racism protests the world over The Black Lives Matter movement has reignited fresh calls to decolonise higher education. Statues of colonialists on university campuses are set to be removed ... but efforts haven't gone far enough ... Plans are underway to establish the UK's first ever Black university."

Segregation! There's an idea that hasn't been tried before!

"Maybe Apartheid was a good system" is not something I expected from British *Vogue* in 2020.

Why is it that everything Progressives do ends up taking us backwards? They love to run full speed ahead, in reverse.

The article quotes students who complain that there are "not enough black faces" on university campuses in the UK.

Someone might like to suggest to these rocket scientists that, with a UK black population of around 4%, there will always be less black faces on campus. That's not racism. That's demographics.

The article doesn't say exactly how a black university would work. Perhaps they will use a colour wheel to determine whether young people are black enough to attend. Or maybe they play some music and if you dance, you're in.

Ultimately I imagine everything will depend on whether you identified yourself as black or white at the beginning of the academic year.

But if they can't create a black university, maybe these so-called anti-racists could convince universities to start having separate areas for blacks and whites. You know, like separate toilets, separate water fountains, separate seats on busses. It's the future!

This is what happens when you teach gender studies rather than history and consequences. You end up with gold standard Woketards!

ARE FRAUD ALLEGATIONS LESS SERIOUS IF THE VICTIM IS WHITE?

See if you can finish the following sentence. Guy Sebastian is one of Australia's most talented and highest-profile ....

Did you say "singers"?

Did you say "entertainers"?

You might even have said that Guy Sebastian is one of our most talented and highest-profile "Australian Idols".

All of those answers would seem reasonable, even obvious. Competing on Australian Idol is how Sebastian came to national attention. Singing is what he does.

But apparently these are not the first things that come to mind if you are a journalist with the national broadcaster.

When the ABC's Jason Om tweeted Thursday that Sebastian's manager had been arrested for allegedly defrauding him, the 7.30 journalist wrote: "One of Australia's most talented and highest profile POC should not have been treated this way."

There is exactly zero evidence that the alleged fraud had anything to do with the colour of Guy Sebastian's skin. But Jason Om looks at a story about alleged financial deception and immediately sees race.

He makes the connection faster than you can say "why the hell are my taxpayer dollars being used to divide me against my neighbour?"

And what if Guy Sebastian was not a person of colour? Is fraud more acceptable if the victim is white?

The ABC's obsession with race is not just unhealthy, it's pathological. And it is why we must regard most journalists at the ABC as activists rather than professionals.

Guy Sebastian is a highly talented musician – nothing to do with skin colour. His former manager allegedly defrauded him – nothing to do with skin colour.

That's the news – nothing to do with the ABC.

BLM PROTESTORS AREN'T MAKING HISTORY, JUST SHALLOW GESTURES

Many are saying the events of the past fortnight – with marches against racism being held around the world – constitute a historic moment. I disagree. I don't think much has actually happened.

Scratch beneath the sound and fury of the protests and what have you got? A proposal to defund the police? An idea so irresponsible it could only be imagined by people whom police had kept safe long enough to become so incredibly stupid.

So what are we left with?

My social media feed is filled with posts from friends, who have always believed racism is wrong, affirming that racism is wrong.

This might be important if there was an argument. But everyone agrees racism is wrong. One might as well announce on Facebook that you believe the sky to be above us.

The desire to be part of a truly history-making moment is strong. But this isn't it.

It isn't a history-making moment because no history is being made. Everyone agrees that black lives matter. And even the police agree that the misuse of police power by rogue police is wrong.

This may be a historic moment only in the sense that it is the first protest in history in which protestors protested against people who agree with them.

The past fortnight was not this generation's civil rights moment, as much as we might desire one since there are no civil rights, long denied, that are now being demanded.

The fact is, in Western countries, black people have never been less oppressed than they are today.

This is proved by the fact that no legislation is being proposed and no examples of discrimination in law have been offered, other than an all-encompassing anger at "systemic racism".

You couldn't do better than to invite Dennis Denuto, the bumbling small-time lawyer from *The Castle*, to summarise the protests. "It's justice, it's law, it's the vibe and, no that's it, it's the vibe. I rest my case".

Many were emotionally moved to see white people repenting before black people for the sins of colonialism. But this is not new and it is certainly not history-making.

One might argue that such displays of collective guilt are indulgent and do nothing but condemn blacks to repeat history by continuing on as victims, though they actually live at a time when there has never been less oppression.

When a group of people apologise for things for which they bear no personal responsibility, the very concept of a virtuous person is changed – from one who exercises virtue to one who expresses correct sentiment. The most virtuous person in the past few weeks has been the one who expressed the right emotion the loudest, and to the most people.

It used to be the case that a man felt most responsible for his own behaviour and was judged by how he behaved toward those in his own house. From there rippled ever-decreasing areas of moral concern, of which he was also increasingly ignorant. Now, though, it is the other way around.

Influenced by social media and cheered on by the mob, a man is more likely to judge himself – and be judged – by the opinions he holds on events far from his immediate concern.

So a man might be a terrible person at home, but that is more than compensated for by his outrage at George Floyd's death.

There is another pernicious aspect to this penchant of those with no personal responsibility for wrong apologizing to those who have suffered no personal wrong – the diluting effect it has on the morals of those receiving the apology.

It allows a man to be a terrible person at home, and blame history.

"What can I do wrong to compare with the wrongs that my forebears suffered at the hands of your forebears?" is the response when someone dares to complain that looting and setting fire to property and beating old ladies with lumps of timber is unacceptable behaviour.

I'm struggling to think of anything specific or concrete that we can come away with, in this entire episode, that is meaningful or particularly helpful.

But a lot of feelings have been expressed in a kind of collective case of emotional incontinence.

So we feel like we have made history. And for a generation that thinks with its feelings and reasons by way of its emotions, that is probably good enough.

BLACK MILLIONAIRE LIFESTYLES MATTER

Black millionaire lives matter - so the NBA will not display social justice messages on the court or on player singlets next season.

Television ratings for NBA games are at record lows this year with people complaining the world's premier basketball league has become too political.

The NBA embraced the Black Lives Matter movement only to find that fans aren't keen to watch men earning millions of dollars for throwing a ball in a metal hoop complain about how oppressed they feel.

Moreover, fans find it hard to stomach being hectored about the importance of diversity from a sport in which 75 per cent of players are African American.

And then there is the hypocrisy of a sporting league that damns America for civil rights abuses while cosying up to Communist China in return for billions of dollars.

The league has seen its viewership drop enormously during the NBA playoffs with ratings down 20% on the previous year.

A poll in September found that 38% of fans said they were not watching because the league had become "too political."

Things got worse from there when Game 1 of the NBA Finals between the Los Angeles Lakers and the Miami Heat recorded the lowest ever viewership for a Finals game.

That record was broken a couple of days later when the ratings for

Game 2 were lower still, and was broken again just days later when Game 3 attracted even fewer fans.

NBA bosses have belatedly realised that the league's edgy, woke stance on social issues is simply unsustainable as a business model. People don't want to watch politically correct basketball.

And so on Tuesday, NBA Commissioner Adam Silver announced that BLM messages would likely not be displayed in 2021.

He said: "I understand those people who are saying 'I'm on your side, but I want to watch a basketball game.'"

In other words, basketball players need to focus on being basketball players rather than social justice warriors who happen to dribble a ball.

As the sport's ratings plummet, advertising revenue dries up, owner profits go down and finally black millionaire contracts fall.

NBA players will know all about oppression if their multi-million dollar player contracts are cut in half and so wokeball will be abandoned in 2021 because black millionaire lifestyles matter.

YOU'RE NOT RACIST. CNN JUST HATES YOU

Pretty much everything is racist now; especially you.

Over the weekend I read published articles stating that ...

- Chess is racist because white always goes first
- Church statues are racist because they depict Jesus as white
- Cartoons are racist because black characters are voiced by white actors
- Coronavirus is racist because it has a disproportionate effect on blacks
- Skin care is racist because whitening products encourage people not to be black

- Finding black people attractive is racist because it is evidence of "racial fettish"
- Not finding black people attractive is racist because white supremacism prevents you from imagining that they might be attractive
- Climate change is racist because it affects people in majority black population countries most
- Eskimo pies are racist because Eskimos
- Biological sex is racist because it reflects white people's desire to categorize everything
- Air pollution is racist because minorities breathe in air pollution caused mostly by whites
- Trying not to be racist is racist because if you weren't racist you wouldn't have to try not to be
- Dogs can be racist because they pick up biases from white owners
- Fighting obesity is racist because it ignores unique health challenges faced by African American women
- Toy Story 4 is racist because the main toys are Caucasian.

And on July 7 CNN helpfully published a list of "Everyday Words and Phrases that Have Racist Connotations".

The article warned "many racist words and phrases are so entrenched that we don't think twice about using them".

Well there I was, playing Chess whilst eating an Eskimo pie as my kids patted a racist dog and watched Toy Story 4. And as if that wasn't peak racism, I was likely using racist words and phrases without even realising, so entrenched is racism in my darkened heart. (I mean no offence by the term darkened")

So you can imagine my eagerness to know what racist words and phrases I had been inadvertently using.

First on the list was the phrase "Master Bedroom"

The CNN article, which took two correspondents to write, said: "While it's unclear whether the term is rooted in American slavery on plantations, it evokes that history."

Right. So it's not actually a racist term. But it evokes history.

The next item on CNN's list of racist words and phrases was "Master/Slave" – terms used in computer programming.

CNN's reporters wrote: "Though the origins of those terms don't appear to be directly connected to race, some argue that they reinforce notions that black=bad and white=good.

So it's actually nothing to do with race, but "some argue". Who argues? CNN don't say.

Next on the list was famed golf tournament, "The Masters".

CNN reported: "The name appears to have been a reference to golfers with great skills, but its connotations have brought the name under scrutiny."

Are you sensing a pattern here? The name is not racist at all ... but (drum roll) "connotations".

The CNN article goes on to say: "Sportswriter Rob Parker recently called on the tournament to change its name. Parker argues the name evokes slave masters in the US South."

So these "connotations" were concocted by Rob Parker.

This is the same African American Rob Parker who was suspended from his role at ESPN in 2012 when he argued that a black Washington Redskins player was not a real black man because he was engaged to a white woman.

CNN's next example of racist speech that you and I engage in without a second thought – important because there is no-one so racist as the one who is completely oblivious to his racism – is the phrase "Black Mark"; as in "there was a black mark against his name".

And you guessed it, CNN admit that "black mark" is not actually a racist phrase.

"The phrase didn't originate in times of slavery, but the use of "black" to describe things that are wrong is subconsciously racialized," the article said.

"Black has connoted evil and disgrace, while white has connoted decency and purity. Those colours and their connotations may well reinforce social norms pertaining to those groups of people."

You know who has a problem with racism?

Not me.

Not you.

The people who have a racism problem are the people at CNN who can't engage in a normal conversation without "connotations" because, unlike you and I, they see race everywhere.

You have to wonder about a media organisation that pays two journalists to come up with a list of everyday words that are not racist – but that could possibly, subconsciously have connotations of racism – in order to prove how racist you are.

You're not racist. You're just hated by CNN.

DID A LACK OF DIVERSITY IN THE COMMENTARY BOX SPOIL YOUR GRAND FINAL TOO?

It was difficult to sit through the AFL grand final knowing all the television commentators were white.

I had been so looking forward to the historic first night grand final and, were it not for the lack of diversity in the commentary box, I would have enjoyed the game.

The atmosphere was electric and the game thrilling. But not a single Channel Seven commentator was black. Not even one. Can you believe it?

To my great shame, the issue of skin colour in the commentary box had not even crossed my mind until just before the opening bounce when ABC presenter Patricia Karvelas tweeted:

> "As the #AFLGF approaches it's worth reflecting on the lack of diversity in the ranks of those commentating on the sport that boasts so many successful Indigenous players."

As the AFL grand final approached, I had been reflecting on whether Geelong champion Gary Ablett would win a premiership in his last game or whether Richmond star Dustin Martin would win a third Norm Smith Medal.

But suddenly, the important issue of racial diversity amongst the commentary team was all I could think about.

The white but woke Karvelas continued: "Proud that the @ABCaustralia has hired @Tonaayy but the rest of the media needs to do better #Indigenous".

Indeed. The sheltered workshop which is the ABC has token people. Why not commercial media?

This is meant as no offence to Tony Armstrong who was mentioned in Karvelas' tweet. Armstrong is a former Collingwood footballer whom the ABC poached from Triple M radio in Melbourne where he was calling football for "the rest of the media that needs to do better".

But wouldn't it be better to be proud of Armstrong for being a great commentator than for being a diversity hire?

Replying to Karvelas' tweet, former Australian netball coach Lisa Alexander added: "Also perhaps more women as well."

And why not! I think we can all agree that the Grand Final would have been much better if it had been called by a black man. Or a woman. Or a black woman. Or a black trans woman. You get the idea.

Instead, we were stuck with a supremacy of white men whose only qualifications to call the biggest game of the year were decades in sports broadcasting and/or stellar football careers that gave them expert insights into the game.

Way to ruin the AFL grand final Channel Seven.

That Abbey Holmes was part of the commentary team is no credit to the commercial broadcaster.

The former AFLW player was used to give expert commentary from the boundary ... in the rain.

Presumably because the patriarchy didn't want her indoors with them.

Hopefully, next year's grand final commentary team will better reflect the diversity in the general community. And if the approved melanin and genitals happen to correspond with commentary ability and football knowledge, then even better.

But the next AFL grand final is a year away. So in the meantime, perhaps we could reflect on the lack of diversity in the ranks of those commentating politics on the ABC.

I wonder what percentage of ABC broadcasters and regular panel guests would be conservative?

6

LIFE IS CHEAP IN WOKETOPIA

ABORTION IS BAD FOR GIRLS

The brave new world in which we live makes it difficult to know how to react to research that suggests certain ethnic groups might be aborting girls because they prefer boys.

A Latrobe University study of more than a million births in Victoria found that, in key migrant communities, there were as many as 125 boys born for every 100 girls. This was a male birth rate 20% higher than if nature was left to take its course.

Lead researcher Dr Kristina Edvardsson said the results were evidence that "systematic discrimination against females starts in the womb".

"We believe that some women may be terminating pregnancies after discovering they are expecting a girl," she wrote.

Feminists should be outraged. There can be no worse form of misogyny than using ultra sound technology to track down females and kill them before they have a chance to be born.

But don't expect females in the womb to be defended by feminists in the Parliament. The same women's rights activists who were screaming "misogynist" at Tony Abbott when he dared to glance at his wristwatch while the then Prime Minister Julia Gillard was speaking will, themselves, not say a word to save the lives of their unborn sisters.

How can they?

If abortion is a matter of personal choice, as feminists insist, then the choice some ethnic women make to kill an unborn female for simply being female must be beyond criticism.

Feminists cannot very well yell at Catholic Nuns to "Keep your theology off my biology" whilst imposing their own ideology – non-discrimination against females – on those same pregnant women.

And whilst "Not Your Uterus, Not Your Business" fits nicely on a bumper sticker, "Not Your Uterus, Not Your Business ... Unless I'm Killing a Female for Being a Female in Which Case I'm a Misogynist Whose Uterus Should Be the State's Business" does not.

So feminists will continue to sacrifice their unborn sisters on the altar of "choice" in order to preserve women's access to abortion so that more females can be targeted for termination by mothers wanting sons.

But then, who is to say that the females showing up on ultrasounds are in fact female?

In our brave new world of gender fluidity, the females being aborted may in fact be males whose gender was wrongly assigned by a doctor, gung-ho on science and not nearly attentive enough to gender theory.

How could a doctor with an ultrasound, observing nothing more than genitals, possibly know if the baby in the womb - about to be aborted - is actually female?

If gender is a social construct, then no-one can be sure that the unborn baby, with a vagina and XX chromosomes, about to be aborted by an ethnic woman desperate for sons is actually female.

But even if we were to believe that objective, scientific evidence available to doctors is still valid in determining gender, who are we to impose our Western cultural values on the ethnic communities we have welcomed here?

Dr Edvardsson said that the Indian Government estimated two million girls "go missing" from its population every year because of gender-selective abortion. The custom of paying a dowry when a daughter marries means that giving birth to a girl is simply uneconomical. So the ancient dowry tradition has entrenched a modern day preference for male children, a preference that migrants might bring with them.

Dr Edvardsson concluded that there was "evidence that prenatal sex selection may be taking place following migration to Australia".

But who are we to criticize? Have we not agreed that the West – supposedly founded on genocide and the theft of land – is the last culture that should be lecturing others about what ought and ought not be done?

We will not talk about the targeted termination of unborn females within certain ethnic groups for the same reason that we will not talk about genital mutilation of born females in other ethnic groups. We haven't the cultural confidence to say what is or is not acceptable.

So the Latrobe University research will be quietly filed away – even as unborn girls are quietly aborted for simply being girls – because abortion is sacrosanct, gender is fluid and Western values have been undermined to such an extent that we are no longer confident enough to articulate them, even in defense of defenseless females.

ABORTION LAWS REVEAL PROGRESSIVIST SCHIZOPHRENIA

New Zealand law now views an unborn child depending on whether or not it is wanted.

How else to interpret the latest example of progressivist schizophrenia from our cousins across the ditch?

Just one year after legalising abortion laws to permit the killing of babies up until 20 weeks for any reason at all, New Zealand politicians have passed a law to provide bereavement leave for women who experience a miscarriage.

No decent person would begrudge a woman who miscarries time to grieve the loss of her baby.

But surely Kiwi lawmakers understand that a woman who miscarries at 19 weeks and a woman who aborts at 19 weeks have exactly the same thing inside them!

The two laws, when considered together, effectively mean that the status of an unborn baby is determined entirely by the whims of the mother.

If a baby in the womb is wanted, it is a human being. But if that same baby in the womb is unwanted, then it is just a clump of cells.

Imagine having your status as human decided by the health or mental state of someone else.

Actually, you don't have to imagine. Just think back to Germany in the 1930s. But I digress.

Let's apply that same principle to the same human being 80 years after birth and see what we think ...

If a senior citizen in the retirement village is wanted, he is a human being, with all the rights that entails. But if that same senior citizen in the retirement village is unwanted, he is a piece of meat that may be quietly disposed of.

Is it any wonder that when the same politicians who liberalise abortion start salivating at the idea of euthanasia, sensible seniors grow nervous?

If an unborn baby is just a clump of cells, as New Zealand's abortion laws assume, then offering taxpayer-funded bereavement leave for a miscarriage is ridiculous.

But if an unborn baby is a human being, as New Zealand's newly legislated bereavement provisions assume, then decriminalising abortion is obscene.

DANIEL ANDREWS' ABORTION DOUBLETHINK

Cognitive dissonance, thy name is Victoria.

How else to explain a state in which the miscarriage of a wanted baby is commemorated with a certificate, while the killing of an unwanted baby is protected by law?

Premier Daniel Andrews last night announced the creation of a certificate for parents who lose a child through miscarriage.

"Parents who have experienced early pregnancy loss can now apply for a commemorative certificate from Births, Deaths and Marriages Victoria," he announced via Twitter.

"Hopefully it'll help bereaved parents mourn the child they never got to meet."

A message on the government's website says: "To be able to provide these certificates to parents is such an important way to acknowledge their baby, and to acknowledge their loss."

The initiative is to be applauded. But it does make one marvel at the mental gymnastics required to accept that an unborn child is a "baby" when miscarried, and something else when aborted.

It's a classic case of doublethink.

Or is it? Perhaps the clump of cells growing in a womb magically becomes a baby when it is wanted.

Daniel Andrews last night lamented that "around one in five pregnancies ends in miscarriage before 20 weeks" leaving "bereaved parents."

But on the other hand, Mr Andrews is responsible for laws permitting abortion on demand up until week 24 of a pregnancy and, where two medical practitioners agree, right up until birth.

The definition of human, like gender, is now seemingly fluid – blowing this way or that according to an individual's sensibilities or, in this case, the audience Daniel Andrews is addressing.

What becomes of a society that decides the value of one human being on the basis of whether another human being wants them to exist?

If an unborn baby is a mere lump of cells, then we are lying to the bereaved parents by presenting a commemorative certificate lamenting the child they never got to meet.

But if an unborn baby is human, then we are lying when we assure the woman seeking an abortion that it's all about her 'choice' concerning her body and her 'reproductive health'.

Both positions cannot be true.

So is the commemorative certificate from Births, Deaths and Marriages Victoria confirmation that the unborn are indeed human, just as two and two are four?

"Sometimes, Winston. Sometimes they are five. Sometimes they are three. Sometimes they are all of them at once. You must try harder. It is not easy to become sane."

TASMANIA'S EUTHANASIA DIEHARDS

Euthanasia is being considered by the Tasmanian Parliament for the fourth time in 11 years, proving that some things just won't die.

So-called Voluntary Assisted Dying, first killed off by the State Parliament in 2009, was resurrected in 2013 only to bite the dust when it was put to the vote.

The legislation rose again in 2017 but was quickly snuffed out by two-thirds of Tasmania's MPs who declined to support it.

Anyone who thought then that the issue was well and truly buried was dead wrong.

Now, with almost as many reincarnations as Shirley MacLaine, euthanasia has come back to life in Tasmania – this time as a private members bill passed in the state's eclectic upper house this morning and expected to be voted on in the lower house before the end of the year.

Tasmanian progressives, who like to accuse their opponents of being "on the wrong side of history", have themselves been on the wrong side of history more often than a tabloid astrologer. And yet they persist.

In 2009 the Tasmanian Greens called euthanasia "Dying with Dignity" though they themselves refused to do so when their bill was defeated 15 votes to 7.

"I will put this bill up, or a similar bill, again and again and again," Greens MP Nick McKim told the ABC at the time.

In a classic case of 'if at first you don't succeed – die, die again', the Dying with Dignity Bill was twice reincarnated as the Voluntary Assisted Dying Bill and, in its latest incarnation, has been wheeled out as the End of Life Choices Bill.

The bill's sponsor, independent MP Mike Gaffney told *The Australian* last Friday: "In Tasmania, we've had bills in 2009, 2013, 2017 and now 2020. The bill should progress as quickly as it can and I'm sure the Premier will do that."

In other words, we've been told 'no' so many times, we're due for a 'yes'.

While general fatigue is not a valid reason for being euthanised under Gaffney's proposed laws, it does seem to be reason enough for Gaffney to insist the laws are passed. While the Bill differs from earlier versions, the main argument for it seems to be, 'Come on already!'.

Gaffney rejected calls for a public inquiry into the Bill saying: "There's nothing left to analyse – it's all there."

The Australian Medical Association has analysed the bill and described what's all there as poorly drafted, poorly conceived, riddled with ambiguity and rushed.

The Australian Nursing and Midwifery Federation has also expressed concerns about the bill as it was first presented, which among other things:

> Did not require a person to be terminally ill – there was no time limit as to when the person's condition may cause death.
>
> Did not require a person to be currently suffering – the mere anticipation of suffering at some time in the future was enough to qualify a person to be killed.
>
> Anticipated children would be able to access euthanasia in the near future – the legislation as it was originally presented mandated a review of the law in two years must consider extending the law to include minors.
>
> Obliged Christian hospitals and aged-care providers to allow people to be put to death at their facilities.

On this last point, Gaffney told *The Australian* last week that he was "unashamed", saying: "They shouldn't be able to (stop voluntary assisted dying occurring at their institutions) in a secular society."

Translated, this means Christian values will be subjugated to progressive values because no one has the right to impose their values. Did you get that?

Gaffney seems bewildered that Christians would object to people being killed at facilities they created to care for the living.

Gaffney said: "If this becomes law, it is ... a legal choice, so why would any institution deny a person access to adequate or correct medical assistance? VAD is not suicide; it's a legal, medical option."

So death, which is has never been an acceptable treatment outcome and which offers no net gain in health, is to be redefined as "correct medical assistance".

George Orwell would be proud.

Does it never occur to anyone that euthanasia enthusiasts, who repeatedly prester parliaments until they finally get the answer they want, are they exact same people who promise that when euthanasia is legalised, vulnerable people will never be pressured to push off?

ANASTACIA PALASZCZUK'S EUTHANASIA PLEDGE AND THE CULTURE OF KILLING FOR CONVENIENCE

In the same week that Stevie Nicks boasted there would have been no Fleetwood Mac had she not aborted her baby, Queensland Premier Anastacia Palaszczuk has vowed to legalise assisted dying.

Stevie Nicks confirmed what honest people have always known – that, despite the fog pro-abortionists like to create, abortion destroys human life for the convenience of others.

She told *The Guardian* she had conceived a child with The Eagles singer Don Henley in 1979 but that "there's just no way that I could have had a child then, working as hard as we worked constantly."

"I knew that the music we were going to bring to the world was going to heal so many people's hearts and make people so happy. And I thought: you know what? That's really important."

So Stevie Nicks had an abortion.

As Fleetwood Mac famously sang, "Loving you isn't the right thing to do. How can I ever change things that I feel. You can go your own way."

Freed from the inconvenience of a child, she went on to sell more than 120 million records and to be twice inducted into the Rock and Roll Hall of Fame.

"If I had not had that abortion, I'm pretty sure there would have been no Fleetwood Mac," she said.

And we all thought the cost of a Fleetwood Mac album was around $20.

When you feel no shame admitting that you judged the life of your unborn child to be of less value than the possibility of a pop music career, you are acknowledging that our culture has crossed a moral line.

But our obsession with individual autonomy – celebrated by Stevie Nicks – is something that should give Queenslanders reason for pause as Labor promises to legalise euthanasia.

If people applaud Stevie Nicks for judging another human's life worth sacrificing for a Grammy Award, what is to stop those same people judging our lives worth sacrificing for their own peculiar reasons?

This is not a question the Queensland Premier wants anyone to seriously consider which is why she waited until the middle of a pandemic and just two weeks before the state election to announce her euthanasia policy.

Better for voters to feel rather than think when it comes to euthanasia. And what better time to feel the argument for death than after suffering for months at the hands of a stubborn virus and soul-destroying lockdowns.

The argument for euthanasia derives its emotional power from the picture painted of a terminally ill patient with nothing but intense suffering standing between him and death.

The picture is largely false since there are ways to manage pain for the terminally ill.

Moreover, there are many people in discomfort – physical or emotional – but who are not terminal.

Are they to be denied the permanent relief euthanasia provides for want of a terminal illness? But I digress.

The euthanasia candidate will be in a diminished physical condition and probably frightened or despairing, or both. All of which means that his will and his capacity for independent thought will also be weakened.

He will be flat on his back with his relatives and the authority figure of the doctor looking down at him. There can be few better subjects and settings for subtle or not-so-subtle psychological coercion.

The patient will know and will probably be informed that prolonging his life – which the physician says will be brief – places an enormous emotional and financial burden on his family. Many people in this position are likely to accept premature death under coercion.

This is what progressives call "death with dignity".

There is also the very real prospect that some people who request euthanasia are really looking for reassurance that they are loved and valued despite their physical decline. If the family and the doctor fail to pick up on this, the patient may become trapped by the request and feel that he or she has no choice but to die.

Is this the autonomy of the patient that euthanasia supporters insist is their object?

The systematic killing of unborn children in huge numbers is part of a general disregard for human life that has been growing for some time. Abortion on its own did not cause the disregard, but it certainly deepens and legitimates the nihilism that is spreading in our culture and that finds killing for convenience acceptable.

We crossed lines, at first slowly and now rapidly. We killed unborn children for convenience and harvested their foetal tissue – for science of course – all the while calling it "reproductive health".

As Stevie Nicks would sing: "Tell me lies, tell me sweet little lies."

Abortion has coarsened us.

If it is permissible to kill the unborn human for convenience, it is surely permissible to kill those thought to be soon to die for the same reason.

And it is inevitable that many who are not in danger of imminent death will be killed to ease their families of burden.

Convenience has, for some time, been the central theme of our culture. Humans tend to be inconvenient at both ends of their lives.

7

CELEBRITY WOKETARDS

MADONNA: OVER THE BORDERLINE

Madonna, terrified of dying from the plague, has taken the vaccine. And no, we are not talking about Covid-19.

The Queen of Pop complained at the weekend that she was a victim of "the Patriarchy" – signalling that she should be protected from the woke plague currently sweeping the West cancelling all in its path.

"The Patriarchy continues to try to crush my neck with their heavy boots, cut off my life force and take away my voice," she tweeted, in what sounded more like a struggle with old age than with men.

But before anyone could tell her, 'Madge, the only Patriarchy you're fighting is Father Time', she continued: "DEATH TO THE PATRIARCHY! Now and Forever."

It is a tactic as old as civilisation itself. "Don't attack me. I'm one of the good guys!"

How else to explain one of the most successful entertainers of all time – worth a reported $850 million dollars and with mansions in multiple nations – whinging about being oppressed?

Death to the patriarchy? Madonna has nearly enough money to buy the patriarchy!

In an industry in which six of the 10 wealthiest singers are women, it's hard to know exactly which patriarchy Madonna is imagining.

When the pop icon complains about being hard done by, you could well be forgiven for thinking 'Who's that Girl'?

But when the whole world is being divided into victims and oppressors, those at the very bottom of the supposed victim ladder kick and scream, hoping others will perceive them as having been hopelessly oppressed and so grant them immunity from being cancelled.

Harry and Meghan will tell you it's the new vogue. Strike a pose, there's nothing to it.

Madonna is an empowered woman who has manipulated men by exploiting her own sexuality in order to make squillions.

> *They can beg and they can plead*
> *But they can't see the light (that's right)*
> *'Cause the boy with the cold hard cash*
> *Is always Mister Right*
>
> *'Cause we are living in a material world*
> *And I am a material girl.*

Whatever patriarchy exists, the material girl has played them at their own game and won big.

But now she is just another oppressed sister, suffocating in her Lisbon mansion – or is it the Hollywood mansion, or the London Mansion, or the New York apartment? – under the heavy boot of patriarchy.

The suffering that she has endured at the hand of the patriarchy is unconscionable. Imagine how many more homes Madonna would own if it wasn't for men. Imagine how wealthy she would be if men would just let her be free to succeed.

Madonna's complaint is ridiculous. We know it. She knows it.

Was it the patriarchy who suggested she offer oral sex to anyone voting for Hillary Clinton in 2016? (An oft-overlooked explanation for Clinton's shock defeat.)

And why did the patriarchy wait until after 2017, when Madonna fantasised out loud about blowing up the Whitehouse, before trying to take away her voice?

Her 'life force', whatever that is, seemed just fine when only last year she released a video of herself in a milky bath sprinkled with rose petals opining about Covid-19 as someone played piano in the background.

Incidentally, the video now has 497,000 views, and counting. Not bad for a woman who has been silenced.

If the crushing jackboot of misogyny helps one to amass a billion-dollar fortune, give me a little of that encrushment I say!

Madonna is the best-selling female musician of all time. She publishes books, she has her own record label and she attracts a massive social media following.

She is not oppressed – and she knows it.

But just as no-one is going anywhere in the 'new normal' without a Covid vaccine, she understands that no-one is going anywhere in Woketopia without having first established their victim credentials.

And so Madonna is singing a new song …

> *Like a victim, hey*
> *Oppressed for the very first time*
> *Like a victim*
> *With your heartache*
> *Matched only by mine*

TAYLOR SWIFT ENDORSES JOE BIDEN

Taylor Swift – who has made a career of writing songs about her terrible choices in men – has officially endorsed Joe Biden for President.

In news shocking to no-one, the pop singer has told V Magazine she will be voting Democrat in the US election.

Taylor Swift's announcement means Americans now only need to hear from 15 more celebrities before they will have enough information to be able to vote.

In an interview just published, Swift said: "The change we need most is to elect a president who recognizes that people of colour deserve to feel safe and represented.

"Women deserve the right to choose what happens to their bodies, and the LGBTQIA+ community deserves to be acknowledged and included. I'll be voting for Joe Biden for president."

If only all those 12 to 15 year-old girls who listen to her music were old enough to vote.

CNN described Taylor Swift's endorsement of Biden as "fearless", which had more to do with the fact that she once recorded an album entitled "Fearless" than with the courage it must surely have taken to do what most of Hollywood has already done.

Swift cannot lose by declaring she will vote for Biden. If Biden wins she can say she backed the winner. And if things don't work out with Joe Biden, at least she was on the right side of woke. And she can write a song about breaking up with him too.

Taylor Swift is a gifted musician. She has 10 Grammy Awards to prove it. But having a great set of pipes doesn't give her any special political insight. Infact, her celebrity likely makes her less informed than she might otherwise be.

Celebrities typically live in an alternate reality with little understanding of what everyday people have to endure. Taylor should walk the streets of New York, Chicago or Portland without her security team and then explain how she will vote.

The media breathlessly report the pronouncements of celebrities as if expertise in one area of life (in Taylor Swift's case, recording songs) makes them an authority on all areas of life.

But Swift's political views are no more relevant or newsworthy than the political views of her local school's janitor.

If my child swallows a coin, I'm not calling my accountant. Don't get me wrong, my accountant is brilliant with coins. He can stack them in neat piles, tell me how many there are and which accounts they belong in.

But just because he is good at counting coins doesn't mean he is qualified to remove them from my toddler's throat.

And just because Taylor Swift can hold a tune doesn't mean she has anything to say about the Presidential election.

If we insist that the person fixing our pipes knows something about plumbing and that the person repairing our car knows something about engines why do we not insist that the people the media give a platform to instruct us about voting know something about politics?

THEIR ABC PRESENTS JIMMY BARNES, THE CHINA EXPERT OF THE LARGS PIERS HOTEL

Jimmy Barnes is better known for his screaming than for his expertise on foreign affairs which, of course, makes him the perfect person to pontificate about international diplomacy on the ABC.

The ageing rocker told Q&A on Monday that Australia's feud with China could have been avoided if Prime Minister Scott Morrison had been more culturally sensitive.

Well sure. And England's feud with Germany could have been avoided if Neville Chamberlain had spoken in softer tones to the Fuhrer.

Jimmy Barnes didn't mention the 'cultural sensitivity' displayed by China when, having realised coronavirus had escaped (or was it released) from a wet market (or was it a lab) they shut down domestic travel but continued to export the virus overseas.

He ignored the 'culturally sensitivity' on show when China's Ministry of Foreign Affairs spokesman, Lijian Zhao, accused the US army of seeding the virus in China.

And he failed to mention the 'cultural sensitivity' demonstrated by China spreading fake photographs depicting an Australian solider beheading an Afghan child.

None of that was relevant. It was Scott Morrison who needed a lesson in manners.

Jimmy 'The Last Plane Out Of Wuhan' Barnes said the PM's call for an inquiry into the origins of the Chinese Flu, which spread from China to the world, had needlessly upset the Chinese.

"We can't just expect... if we're Australians and we say, 'This is wrong, we've got to bloody stand up to it' that may not culturally be the same way to speak to the Chinese," he said, in a monologue that almost made Joe Biden look articulate.

Warming to his new-found role as a geo-political expert, Barnes, likened China's expansionist plans to those of the British after the Industrial Revolution and to the US after World War II.

"China is doing what the Americans did, what the British Empire did – empires get strong," he said. "Whoever's financially doing that well, they grow and they try to take over the world. This is the nature of things."

As Barnes himself once sang, "He's a simple man with a heart of gold in a complicated land", but not even a working-class man drunk on cheap wine and sporting a three-day growth would be so simple as to suggest a moral equivalence between China and the West.

You could more credibly suggest a vocal equivalence between Jimmy

Barnes and Frank Sinatra.

I'm not sure that any of the Uyghur people currently wallowing in Chinese re-education camps, given the chance to come under American or British rule, would shrug their shoulders and reply "Meh. What's the difference?"

But in fairness to Jimmy Barnes, he has never claimed to be an expert on politics. It was, after all, the ABC who invited him on television to talk about foreign affairs.

Next time Q&A decide to discuss the intricacies of international diplomacy and foreign relations, they might want to try someone else. There's a new JJJ favourite who calls herself Alex the Astronaut. She might be able to bring a big picture perspective.

ODD. CELEBRITIES HAVEN'T SOLVED THE MIDDLE EAST CRISIS

Celebrities and woke corporations have not done enough to end the violent conflict between Israelis and Palestinians.

As the death toll from days of violence in the Gaza Strip and Israel mounts, celebrities have largely ignored the conflict, instead using their powers to change the weather and to end racism.

But it doesn't have to be this way.

Imagine if Prince Harry and Meghan Markle, for example, had used their earnest chat with Oprah Winfrey to focus on peace in the Middle East.

It is not unreasonable to think that a heart-to-heart with the Duchess of Sussex and her ginger handbag would have convinced Hamas militants to turn their swords into ploughshares by now.

Or what if Greta Thunberg had jetted into Jerusalem and given both sides the same stern talking to that she gave world leaders at the United Nations?

"Islamic militants – how dare you!"

You can't tell me Hamas operatives would continue launching rockets at Tel Aviv if they knew that in doing so they were stealing Greta's childhood and robbing her of her dreams.

Suitably chastised by the Swedish teenager who knows a thing or two about lowering temperatures, both sides would surely have cooled down enough to sign up for the two-state solution that has eluded politicians for decades.

At the very least, Michelle Obama could have started a social media hashtag to usher in a new era of harmony for the world's most troubled region.

Back in 2014, she famously freed more than 200 kidnaped Nigerian school girls using nothing more than a selfie in which she held up the hashtag #BringBackOurGirls.

One can only dream of the powerful effect a similarly disapproving selfie might have in this current crisis.

If a look of dismay from the former First Lady worked so well on Boko Haram (it didn't, but don't tell her fangirls that) then it would surely melt the hardened hearts of Islamists in Gaza.

And while we are at it, why hasn't our very own Magda Szubanski employed her considerable tweeting skills to bring an end to the Middle East mess?

Instead of working to free our Prime Minister's wife from her husband's creepy Christianity, Szubanski could have used her considerable powers to free the people of Gaza from their terror-loving overlords.

A well-placed tweet or three comparing the women of Gaza to those depicted in the Handmaid's Tale – women brutally subjugated by power-hungry leaders in a militarized, hierarchical regime of religious fanatics – would make all the difference.

It would at least be more accurate than the highly partisan, anti-

Christian bile that normally fills her Twitter feed.

But alas, celebrities can only solve one world problem at a time. And besides, having exposed the horror's of Pentecostalism, Magda's got a television game show to focus on.

What then of our woke corporations that continually lecture us on learning and listening and doing better? Where are they in the Middle East's hour of need?

Gillette single-handedly ended toxic masculinity in Australia with a powerful advertising campaign that taught us not to play fight in the backyard and not to excuse blokey jesting as just 'boys being boys'.

As a direct result, Aussie men are now the best a man can be – clean-shaven and very in touch with their kinder, gentler, more feminine selves.

You won't see us flinging explosives across the ditch at our New Zealand cousins because we now know that's not the best a man can be.

Which begs the question, if a razor company can do that for us, why won't they do it for the guys in Gaza?

The advertisement they created to neuter toxic Aussie men requires only the smallest tweak in order to powerfully change the attitude of rocket-ladened Hamas males.

With a soaring musical score playing in the background, a fatherly voice could tell Palestinians: "Hiding amongst civilians to lob missiles at Jews has been going on for far too long. We can't laugh it off, making the same old excuses. We believe in the best in men. Gillette — the best a Palestinian man can get."

You can't tell me a pep talk like that from a major corporation would not immediately convince Islamists to down their weapons and take up shaving instead. The path to peace, not to mention faces across the region, would suddenly be smooth.

Peace in the Middle East is only a Tweet, a rendition of John Lennon's *Imagine* or even a condescending selfie away.

It's probably unrealistic to think that our cultural betters can solve every human ill. And they have already done so much to improve us. But if they could just use their heady influence, hectoring tone and superior perspective one more time – we mortals, not least of all in Israel and Gaza, could sure use their help.

BETTE MIDLER: THE MALICIOUS MODEL OF A MODERN 'PROGRESSIVE'

Hollywood legend Bette Midler has become the embodiment of everything she professes to hate.

The actress who has spent the past four years accusing Donald Trump of xenophobia took to Twitter yesterday to label his foreign-born wife as a mail order bride who can't speak English.

"I'm surprised Trump wants to destroy the Post Office. He got all his wives from it," Midler tweeted while watching Melania Trump speak at the Republican Convention.

As the first lady spoke about the need for civility, Bette Midler was working the Democratic mantra "when they go high, we go low and then we go lower".

"Oh, God. She still can't speak English," Midler tweeted.

Funnily enough, Melania was literally speaking English. And with more fluency than Joe Biden.

English is one of several languages she speaks.

Perhaps Bette Midler just didn't realise that Melania speaks with an accent. You know, like Democrat Ilhan Omar.

We certainly understand that Bette Midler thinks with an accent.

The self-proclaimed anti-racist loves diversity so long as blacks and immigrants behave exactly the way they are all supposed to.

Last year Midler tweeted a photo of a Trump rally with the caption: "Look, there are African American men in this shot. How much did he pay them to be background?"

The Hollywood star and Democrat supporter – but I repeat myself – knew blacks could not possibly be at a Trump rally by choice because she knew blacks would never do that because they are blacks.

It's not that Democrats believe you can tell what a person thinks based on the colour of their skin.

Rather, Democrats believe you can tell a person what to think based on the colour of their skin.

Didn't Democratic presidential nominee Joe Biden recently say that if African Americans don't vote for him "you ain't black"?

As a sidenote, Bette Midler was an enthusiastic supporter of Harvey Weinstein so, in fairness to the Hocus Pocus star, judging a man by the content of his character is not exactly her strong suit. If Washington is the swamp, Hollywood is the cesspit. But I digress.

What Midler really hates about the Slovenian immigrant who became the first lady of the United States is that she is a Republican. And every Democrat knows that immigrants are not meant to become Republicans or else you might as well have a wall at the border.

"Get that illegal alien off the stage," Midler tweeted in disgust that Melania Trump did not conform to the loving, tolerant, diverse and inclusive Democrat narrative.

Imagine if a conservative tweeted about an immigrant: "Oh, God. She still can't speak English".

But Bette Midler can happily mock people from non-English speaking backgrounds without fear of being cancelled because progressives are the Cancel Culture judges, juries and executioners.

Midler accusing Trump of xenophobia whilst sneering at his

immigrant wife's accent is a classic case of "mirror, mirror on the wall …"

The only thing that can be said in the 74-year-old actress' defence is that when you're that near the end, capitalising the G in "God" was the smart play.

HOW TO HATE THE OSCARS MORE

I will continue to not watch the Academy Awards after it was announced this week that inclusion, rather than artistic merit, would determine whether a movie could be considered for Best Picture.

A movie that does not use the requisite number of women, LGBT or non-white people – no matter how brilliant – will be ruled ineligible for Best Picture under new rules to apply from 2024.

So the Oscar for Best Picture will not go to the best film but to the best woke.

Expect a headline in 2024 along the lines of: "Tarantino film hailed as 'instant classic' by critics is ruled ineligible for Oscars due to Inexplicable lack of transgender double amputee Pacific Islanders in cast."

Under new rules for Best Picture eligibility, films must meet at least two of four benchmarks. They include featuring actors from minority groups in significant roles or accounting for at least 30% of the cast. Similar criteria exist for those working behind the scenes.

It's not yet clear whether the rules will be applied to Hollywood's sexual predators, requiring them to make sexual advances to people of all races and with all kinds of disabilities.

Nor is it clear whether the criteria will be expanded to include other categories such as Best Actor which could be replaced with Best Nonbinary in a Diversity Hire Film.

The new rules signal a move away from entertaining audiences toward collecting people based on their skin colour and/or genitalia.

We can only imagine the 2024 awards ceremony: "The Academy Award for Best Picture – a film starring three lesbians, a bi-sexual and a couple of gays and featuring a production team comprising three Asians, a black South African in a wheelchair and a half Italian/half Indonesian who identifies as a unicorn – goes to ..."

The name of the film will not be heard for the sound of Hollywood millionaires cheering at the outstanding level of inclusion.

But that won't matter because few people ever remember which film won Best Picture as it is, and even fewer people actually bother to see it.

Critics will enthuse: "It cost $100m to make, tanked at the box office and scored just 18% on Rotten Tomatoes – but it had the highest number of victim group members of any film this year! Eight Oscars!"

The Academy announced Tuesday that, prior to the 2024 Oscars, movie makers will have to submit a confidential "inclusion standard" form detailing which minority groups were employed in the making of their film.

So a remake of the 1994 Best Picture, Schindler's List, would need to be accompanied by a Schindler's Intersectional List to even be considered in 2024.

This is not the first time people have dictated what must be included in art. A particularly uptight German tried it in the 1940s, as did a murderous Russian. Movies were not improved.

Who knows – maybe Hollywood could use a yellow star to mark a certain ethnicity, or a pink triangle to indicate sexual orientation.

Hollywood studios will be patrolled by inclusion and equity inspectors checking who is on set to ensure representation compliance.

"Show us your papers. Schnell!"

You can bet that filmmakers who fail to meet the inclusion standards will be made to attend the Academy Awards ceremony and confess their bigotry.

Inclusion is nice but mandatory genetic check-ins before rewarding art is creepy as hell. And rewarding chromosomes over merit is just wrong.

Excluding someone on the basis of skin colour is, of course, racist. But considering someone on the basis of skin colour is also racist. So Best Supporting Racist Award goes to ... the Academy.

Fighting racism and gender inequality by choosing employees based on their skin colour and gender makes as much sense as cancelling cinematic excellence in favour of feelings.

People do not want to be preached at by adult pretenders, they want to be entertained.

The Oscars was already a night when a mostly useless group of people gather together in a room to tell each other how absolutely fabulous they are and how absolutely awful the people they think are watching them are.

The live television audience for the Academy Awards was at an all-time low last year. Rebranding the event the Affirmative Action Awards – where a diversity check is prioritised over character development and story – will surely continue that downward trend.

Imagine losing a ton of money because of Covid-19 and then saying: "How can we devour ourselves even more? I know, let's enforce strict identity-based quotas for film making because telling great stories and delivering astounding performances just isn't enough."

It's almost as if they focus-grouped how to make the public hate the Oscars more.

The Academy are happy to be rid of us, and we are increasingly happy to be rid of them.

We now await news that, as of 2024, songs will only be Grammy-eligible if at least 73.5% of the instruments used to record them were made by left-handed gender-fluid Pacific Islanders with club feet and chronic fatigue syndrome.

Art is no longer about art. It's about feelings.

BREAK A LEG. REALLY.

Actress Octavia Spencer has said only disabled actors should play disabled people.

The Academy Award-winning actress told a disability advocacy organisation last month that: "Casting able-bodied actors in roles for characters with disabilities is offensive and unjust."

Right. Because if an able-bodied actor plays a character with a disability he will have to ... act.

Octavia Spencer – demonstrating that actors should never open their mouths without a script – is saying that acting is unjust. She is so woke she has just cancelled herself!

The Oxford Dictionary defines acting as "playing a part, pretending to be a particular kind of person".

But Octavia, who played the role of God in The Shack, said: "Nothing can replace lived experience and authentic representation."

That she felt qualified to play God tells you something! But I digress.

According to Spencer's logic, the role of Helen Keller in the 1962 film The Miracle Worker should have been played by a deaf mute.

Jodie Foster should have never played Nel. Sean Penn should have never played Sam. Dustin Hoffman should have never played Raymond.

And it was offensive to watch Tom Hanks pretend to be a dim-witted Forrest Gump. An actual dim-witted person should have been cast in the role.

And the part of Lt Dan in that same movie should have been played by two actors ... an able-bodied actor before he lost his legs and a disabled actor in the scenes after he lost his legs.

Pretty soon criminals will have to be played by criminals, rocket scientists will have to be played by actual rocket scientists, characters that are dying will have to be played by actual dying people and sex fiends can be played by pretty well anyone in Hollywood.

I'd hate to be casting the next Justice League movie. Finding a cyborg to play Cyborg is going to be all sorts of difficult!

For Hollywood's sake, let's hope they never insist that only straight actors can play straight characters or most of tinsel town will be out of work.

You may laugh, but Hollywood studios aren't laughing.

According to The Hollywood Reporter, CBS recently promised to audition actors with disabilities for every forthcoming production. And the BBC promised to increase the percentage of its workforce who are disabled.

That old show biz expression: "Break a leg" developed out of a superstition that wishing a person well would create bad luck. So as someone was about to go on stage, they'd be told "break a leg"; a kind of reverse psychology on fate.

But not anymore.

When we tell an aspiring actor to "Break a Leg", we really do mean, break a leg ... or your neck. Trust us. It'll help your career. And I promise you, it'll hurt less than watching Octavia Spencer's last movie, Ma.

CELEBRITY SERMONS

Beyonce urged Americans to "continue to take action to change and dismantle a racist and unequal system" when she was honoured at the BET awards Sunday.

Was I the only person who saw the irony in a black millionaire who is married to a black millionaire, in an industry overflowing with black millionaires, speaking about racism and inequality at an awards show given specifically for black entertainers?

The media breathlessly reported Beyonce's words as if she was an authority on inequality, rather than a best-selling recording artist who – with husband Jay Z – has a net worth of more than $1billion.

It is symptomatic of an infantized culture that we treat people who are successful in one area of life as if they must therefore be an authority on all areas of life.

On September 23, just before Trump's 2016 election victory, Rolling Stone Magazine ran an article headlined: "Bruce Springsteen Calls Donald Trump a Moron".

Now as singer/songwriter's go, there are few people alive who can match The Boss. Springsteen has more musical talent in his little finger than most of us have in our entire family tree.

But just because you play guitar well doesn't give you special insight into the mind of the US President.

Maybe Trump is a moron; maybe he's not. The point is that Bruce Springsteen's opinion on the President of the United States is no more valid than that of the janitor at my local high school.

Springsteen told Rolling Stone: "The republic is under siege by a moron. Without overstating it, it's a tragedy for our democracy."

No. The tragedy for democracy, without overstating it, is when the media equate strumming a guitar well with expertise in political commentary.

On September 9 of the same year, Fox News tweeted: "In a recent interview Brad Pitt said that he seeks to understand Donald Trump's appeal."

Brad Pitt is trying to understand Trump's appeal? I'm still trying to understand The Curious Case of Benjamin Button!

"Most Americans don't have time to watch CNN and Fox and Al Jazeera," Pitt explained. "And so suddenly when this voice comes in - and it doesn't have to be a voice of substance - saying he's fed up with all of this, that's the part that hooks into the DNA."

Brad Pitt was certainly right that the media doesn't always promote "a voice of substance".

Take Pitt, for instance. He is an actor; and a really good one. He is paid millions of dollars to pretend to be someone he is not, reading words written by others as if they were his own. When it comes to pretending, few people do it as well as Pitt, and he has an Academy Award to prove it.

But a career in pretending doesn't make you a political analyst, let alone a sociologist. So why do the media fawn like he is one?

Not to be outdone, news outlet The Hill ran a lead story on May 23, 2017 headlined: "Pink Floyd Singer: Trump's Wall a Ridiculous Idea"

I remember wondering why the media would ask a washed-up 73-year-old English rocker his opinion on Trump's proposed wall. And then I remembered that 1979 Pink Floyd released an album called ... "The Wall"!

Evidently, releasing an album called "The Wall" qualifies you as an expert on border control and immigration policy and US-Mexico relations.

I fully expect The Hill to soon run a story headlined "Pink Floyd Singer: Trump's Space Force a Ridiculous Idea" because in 1973 they had a hit with Dark Side of the Moon.

I'm not blaming Beyonce or Brad Pitt or a Pink Floyd bass guitarist for having opinions. They are as entitled to their views as anyone.

The problem is the media who feed us celebrity views, as if they are important, because we lack the sense to realise that success in one area of endeavour does not make one an authority in other areas.

President Obama was a very effective community organiser, but that didn't make him an expert on world religions. Whenever he insisted "Islam is a religion of peace" – which it may or may not be - I used to wonder when Obama had moved from Commander-in-Chief to Theologian-in-Chief.

Similarly, when the-then Australian Opposition Leader Bill Shorten refuted claims that Islam was "incompatible with Western democratic liberal values" I wondered when it was that he had found time to study the Koran and the Hadiths. Shorten was a shrewd unionist. I wasn't aware he was also an expert on comparative religion.

If my child swallows a coin, I am not calling my accountant. Don't get me wrong, my accountant is very good. But just because he can count coins doesn't mean he is qualified to remove them from my child's throat.

If we insist the person fixing our pipes knows something about plumbing, why don't we insist that the people lecturing us through the media know something about that on which they opine?

If only we had more successful people like Liverpool football manager Jurgen Klopp who, when asked in March about Coronavirus, told reporters that he was the last person they should ask about matters of public health.

"It's not important what famous people say," Klopp told them. "We have to speak about things in the right manner. Not people with no knowledge, like me, talking about something.

"Why me? I wear a base (ball) cap and I have a bad shave. My opinion about corona is not important. People with knowledge should talk about it … not football managers."

Indeed.

GRETA TELLS AMERICA HOW TO VOTE

Americans anxious to know who a foreign teenager will endorse for President before deciding how they will vote can relax. Greta Thunberg has made her choice.

The Swedish activist began to tweet yesterday: "I never engage in party politics, *but*," ...which, of course, meant she was about to do the very thing she "never" does.

The world held its collective breath.

Even global warming paused in anticipation, as the environmental doomsdayer continued tweeting ... "...the upcoming US election is above and beyond all that. From a climate perspective it's very far from enough and many of you of course supported other candidates. But, I mean ... you know..."

Yeah, yeah, we get all of that. It's one minute to midnight and so we have only 10 minutes to save the world from going off the edge of a climate emergency crisis cliff.

Whatever.

Tell us who to vote for, pig-tailed Swedish schoolgirl!

" ... Just get organised and get everyone to vote #Biden," she finally wrote.

And there it was.

Greta Thunberg – too young to vote and not a US citizen anyway – is endorsing Joe 'fracking' Biden!

If you're looking for a candidate to prevent bad weather or something, Biden's your man.

No doubt Joe Biden will appreciate Greta's support, as well as the smell of her hair. And if Biden wins, he may well nominate Greta as his 15th pick for the Supreme Court.

But the goblin of doom who once resided in the State of Utopia and now spends her time travelling between the State of Rage and the State of Delusion – where Prince Harry and Meghan Markle also live – is not registered to vote in any US state.

Democrats, though, will find a little-known provision in the US Constitution that provides a right to vote in all 50 States, multiple times, by mail, provided you have skipped school to sail across the ocean.

8

ISLAM AND ITS WOKE ALLIES

A WEARY WEST SHRUGS AND CHANGES THE CHANNEL

I'M amazed at how some news items disappear as quickly as they arrive – and it's rarely by accident.

If you coughed you may have missed news last month that three Brits had been stabbed to death in broad daylight by a Libyan refugee yelling "Allahu Akbar". It later emerged that the dead, killed as they socialised in a Reading park, were all homosexuals.

CNN tweeted: "A UK stabbing incident that left three people dead and several injured is declared a terrorist incident by police".

UK stabbing incident. Kind of like that New York jet plane incident back in September of 2001.

"Stabbing incident" imagines the 13cm knife found at the scene had suddenly become animated and, flaying about, randomly caught three homosexuals on its sharpened tip.

I'm old enough to remember when three Brits slaughtered by an Islamic jihadist as they picnicked in a local park elicited more than a weary shrug of the shoulders before being promptly forgotten.

But forgotten it was.

The world immediately dismissed it – like a virus in a Wuhan wet market – as just one of those things that happens from time to time.

Even the gay media socially distanced themselves from the attack.

Immediately after the slayings, UK gay news website Pink News featured three articles criticising children's author JK Rowling for a thought crime against trans men; but had nothing to say about gays being executed for being gay.

This is one of the reasons I despise identity politics. It cares about individuals only so long as they are useful in leveraging political power. But it was politically inconvenient to talk about an Islamist carving up gays with a kitchen knife. So instead they enthused about the rights of men to go under the knife to become women.

British police issued a public order: "Out of respect for those deceased ... please do not circulate footage (of the dead) on social media".

Without footage of the deceased lying in pools of their own blood on the lawns of Forbury Gardens, politicians and the media could maintain the fiction that it was a 'mostly peaceful' jihad.

LGBT rights charity Stonewall UK told their 200,000 twitter followers: "Our thoughts are with those affected by the attack in Reading on Saturday. It's heartbreaking to hear two of the victims were LGBT. But we can't let Islamophobic, racist and xenophobic rhetoric be used to divide us. We must stand together to make progress."

I was fascinated to read that "the victims were LGBT". I've known Ls and I've known Gs. I've known people who claimed to be B (we all knew they were Gs in denial) and a couple of Ts ... but I've never known anyone who went the full acronym!

But more to the point, you just know it's going to be bad when a tweet about a triple murder has the word "but" in the middle of it.

When gay rights campaigners eulogise you with "killing gays is bad but talking unkindly about Muslims is way, way worse", you really have been bent over.

James Furlong, David Wails and Joseph Ritchie-Bennett were stabbed in the neck by an Islamist and then stabbed in the back by their fellow gays.

Q News reported that "after the men were identified, mourners gathered outside the pub for a minute silence and played Somewhere Over The Rainbow".

Islamists kill and Westerners respond with a fabulous tune from The Wizard of Oz. That'll show 'em.

If the victims had been straight, mourners would have sung "Imagine". But Over the Rainbow seems more apt.

The song was made famous by Judy Garland who, as Dorothy, muses to Toto that there must be a safe space.

"Do you suppose there is such a place, Toto? There must be. It's not a place you can get to by a boat, or a train. It's far, far away. Behind the moon, beyond the rain…"

It's certainly not in Britain. Even the Scarecrow knew that.

Reading Pride co-founder Jamie Wake said, "I wish I could stand here and say I can make sense of the senseless. Sadly today, like many others, I can't."

For every jihadist there are a thousand Jamie Wakes who are so woke as to be unable to make the connection between gays being thrown from buildings in Islamist nations and gays being stabbed to death by an Islamist just up the road.

"Someday I'll wish upon a star," he sang with fellow mourners. "

> Wake up where the clouds are far behind me
> Where trouble melts like lemon drops
> High above the chimney top
> That's where you'll find me, oh."

He told Q News: "We become so used to seeing incidents like this on the television. This time, we cannot change the channel."

But change the channel we must. Because police don't want anyone viewing the carnage and the media have moved on to concerns about Islamophobia before the blood has dried.

Reading Council leader Jason Brock "promised a permanent memorial where people can pay their respects to the victims".

This is the well-rehearsed role of local officials. They won't promise action to ensure you can enjoy a summer's evening in the park without being all jihaded. But they can promise those who survive you will have a place to mourn.

Bishop of Reading Olivia Graham told mourners: "You know, we still can't believe that this has happened. This is the kind of thing that happens in other places …"

By other places one presumes the Bishop meant Streatham, Cambridgeshire, London Bridge, Thornton Heath, Manchester, Westminster, Parsons Green …

The UK's Interior Minister Priti Patel lit a candle at the vigil since that was easier than actual policing to stop Islamists like Khairi Saadallah.

"What we saw here on Saturday evening in Reading was the actions of one lone individual," Ms Patel said. "The security services have records on thousands of people and rightly so,"

Ah yes. Thousands of lone wolves who under no circumstances are to ever constitute a pack.

The stabbings in Reading were "the actions of one lone individual" in the same way that bombs dropped on the UK during the blitz were all dropped by lone individuals.

Neil Basu, the national head of Counter Terrorism Policing told ABC news: "We must be vigilant to the ongoing threat. If you see any suspicious activity, don't hesitate to act - report it."

Except that Khairi Saadallah had been briefly "on MI5's radar" last year before being dismissed as a blip.

Jonathan Hall, the Independent Reviewer of Terrorism Legislation, whose job is to inform UK public debate on security laws (except that no debate is allowed) told the ABC that Khairi Saadallah may have been "suffering from poor mental health".

So you're not allowed to say anything that might imply some people like to kill infidels, since that would unfairly stigmatise an entire group of people, but you are allowed to suggest that people prone to depression are likely to go on a stabbing spree because victimhood pyramid.

The ABC concluded its report by helpfully noting that "the attack was reminiscent of some recent incidents in Britain that authorities also called terrorism".

For the media, every lone wolf attack is vaguely reminiscent of a recent unrelated incident that will not divide us because mental health religion of peace we're all in this together somewhere over the rainbow click change the channel.

CALLING JIHADISTS 'JIHADISTS' MAKES JIHADISTS SEEM LIKE JIHADISTS

Satire (based on a true story): Police are considering dropping the terms "Islamist terrorism" and "jihadis" because such terms give Islamic jihadis a bad name every time they slaughter civilians.

Proposed alternatives include "people abusing the religion of peace" and "so-called" Islamic jihadists.

But activists pointed out that politicians had been using such obfuscations since 2001 without success.

Let's Just Get Along spokeswoman Misty Eyes told journalists: "People still assume that Islamic jihadist attacks are being carried out by Islamists waging jihad, and that's wrong because Islamophobia."

She suggested police replace terms like "Islamist terrorism" with "a certain faith-based terrorism".

"It's a beautifully inclusive term which leaves open the tantalising possibility that the suicide bomber who just blew up your bus could have been the Anglican vicar, or even a nun."

When asked if there were questions that needed to be answered about Islam and its compatibility with Western values, Misty Eyes responded with a moving rendition of John Lennon's Imagine, while BBC journalists provided backing vocals.

Reporters from The Guardian and the ABC in Australia gave a warm round of applause and then asked if they could perform Somewhere Over the Rainbow before the press conference resumed.

Attacks such as the London bombings of 2005 as well as the Westminster, London Bridge and Manchester Arena assaults, all in 2017, have been officially deemed 'Islamist terrorism.'

But UK Diversity Council chair Mustaf bin Jokin argued that this created the impression there might have been a common link between the Islamic attacks ... like Islam.

"Whenever Islamists go around killing infidels the police create a negative perception by saying what happened," he said.

"That the majority of terror attacks around the world are perpetrated by Islamists quoting the Koran doesn't mean the public should believe that the majority of terror attacks around the world are perpetrated by Islamists quoting the Koran."

Mustaf bin Jokin wondered why police couldn't say Islamic terror attacks had been carried out by "adherents of Osama bin Laden's ideology", and simply pretend bin Laden was Presbyterian.

"Or Catholic," he added.

Another suggestion was that police learn from CNN's coverage of the Black Lives Matter riots and start referring to terror attacks as "mostly peaceful jihads".

Instead of reporting that jihadis detonated bombs with screams of "Allahu Akbar", police were encouraged to say witnesses heard shouts of "*Woo-woo*" and, where appropriate, "*Yippee–kai-*yay".

Police Commissioner Max Confusion took time out from recording a new TikTok video in support of International Non-Binary Day to address the issues raised.

"I want to be very clear that being clear is not what we want to be about," he said.

When asked if the public might object to being told half-truths about terrorism, Commission Confusion insisted that "this is why we have to be completely untruthful".

"I'm recommending that we no longer refer to terror attacks at all, but instead say 'the bus spontaneously combusted', or the concert hall, or the underground metro. Whatever."

He said he was not worried that using deliberately vague language to describe Islamic terror attacks would build resentment and distrust toward police.

"The half-witted bigots already resent us," he complained. "I don't know why. We went to a lot of effort installing those LBGT Pride Crosswalks. And if they defund us, they can forget about our float at next year's Mardi Gras."

9

GENDER EQUALITY IN WOKETOPIA

TOWARDS A KINDER, WOKER QUEENSLAND POLICE

Drongo alert:

Based on an actual news report, this piece may contain traces of satire and irony.

Criminals have described a decision to scrap gender quotas designed to get more women into the Queensland Police Force as a major setback for women's rights and thievery.

The criticism comes after a Crime and Corruption Commission Report a found the Queensland Police Service's 50/50 gender recruitment strategy led to the appointment of female officers who were cognitively, physically, and psychologically below standard.

The report, tabled in state parliament on Wednesday, also found that 200 meritorious men were rejected in favour of women who, though unsuited to the police force, were appointed in order to correct a perceived gender imbalance.

The quota policy was abandoned in 2019.

But criminals were yesterday highly critical of the decision to ditch the quota system complaining that it would only serve to reinforce toxic masculinity within the police force.

Crime boss Pasquale Alnerodiseppia told *The Spectator Australia* that criminals were "sick and tired of cisgendered, aggressive, white males in uniform kicking down the doors of our meth labs and wrestling us to the ground".

"We would like to see a kinder, gentler officer on the beat," he said. "And if that means recruiting women who fail the physical exam, then even better."

He said criminals would be wearing white this week to identify with the suffragettes and "to show solidarity with women who, as a result of this decision, will be excluded from the police force for no reason other than their inability to catch bad guys".

He said the "Wear White 2 Steal Cars and Stuff" campaign meant criminals of any race or economic status could afford to dress the part and support the reintroduction of gender targets for policing.

A colleague, Mick "The Brick" Malone, said studies had proved that criminals do better when more women were in positions of law enforcement.

"Our research shows that if you improve your diversity you get better results," he said.

"Having more women patrol the streets can make a huge difference to our productivity and to our bottom line."

He said gender quotas were important because "a police force in which 75% of officers are male does not accurately represent the communities from which my friends and I are thieving".

"Systemic misogyny needs to stop. Our friends in the police need to listen and learn and do better."

Mr Alnerodiseppia rejected suggestions that gender quotas were a form of reverse discrimination.

"Reverse discrimination is just one of those meaningless terms people love to throw around, a bit like 'private property'," he said.

"The real discrimination is insisting that criminals must be caught by men. If the Government truly believe in equality of opportunity they would keep gender quotas in place to ensure we have the chance to escape from women."

Both said they appreciated the irony of a wanted felons lecturing police on rights issues but insisted that structural misogyny was a community-wide problem.

"We all have a role to play in dismantling the patriarchy that prevents women who can't pass a psych test or successfully complete a physical examination from becoming the front-line in the fight against crime," Mr Alnerodiseppia said.

Mr Malone added "Let's regulate quotas and let's implement them properly. Not because it is a magic wand that will cure sexism, but because it will add more diverse people to the police service and, one unsolved crime at a time, that is how we will change the world."

THE UN DECLARES: THE BIGGEST CORONAVIRUS ISSUE IS ... MEN

What do you think has most alarmed United Nations General Secretary Antonia Guterres about the Covid-19 pandemic?

Has he been stunned by the ability of a virus to overwhelm societies, despite our advances in modern medicine?

Has he been shocked at the treachery of the Chinese Communist Party which allowed the virus to spread around the world?

Has he been appalled at the swift surrender of civil liberties, as governments have used the virus as an excuse to bully citizens?

Meh.

Not so much.

What keeps the UN chief awake at night is the real problem revealed by the Coronavirus – men.

The former Vice President of Socialists International told a Town Hall meeting of young women on August 31 that: "The Covid-19 pandemic is demonstrating what we all know: millennia of patriarchy have resulted in a male-dominated world with a male-dominated culture which damages everyone – women, men, girls & boys."

And here we were thinking that the main thing this pandemic demonstrated was that groups like the UN and the WHO are run by a bunch of circus clowns.

Many people expected the comment, which was broadcast via the UN's official twitter feed, to be quickly deleted – not because it was stupid, but because it only detailed two genders.

The UN had, after all, tweeted on March 7 that "Trans women are women. Every woman is a woman. Women are limitless, formless ... women are the world."

But putting aside the UN's perpetuation of cis-normative patriarchal stereotypes (a big issue for the three people who care about such things) the comments show that if you thought a global pandemic couldn't be weaponised for the purposes of identity politics, you'd better think again.

When the globe's chief globalist insists that Covid-19 demonstrates patriarchy, his face mask has well and truly slipped. There is nothing the UN won't manipulate in order to reshape the world in their leftist image. The UN is simply using the virus to push another agenda.

Guterres told the Town Hall meeting: "Beyond the virus itself, the response has had a disproportionate and devastating social and economic impact on women and girls."

That's UN speak for: "Men are the most dead and women are the most affected".

He waves away the fact that Covid-19 kills significantly more men than women – the WHO reported in August that 63 per cent of deaths related to Covid-19 in Europe have been among men — with a dismissive "beyond the virus itself".

Perhaps Guterres believes more men need to die in order for women to feel better, a sentiment echoed by Australia's Clementine Ford who tweeted in May that "CV-19 is not killing men fast enough".

Or maybe the disproportionate number of male deaths is just typical of men – keeping most of the disease for themselves.

Guterres complained: "Between 70 and 90 per cent of healthcare workers are women, but their salaries and conditions often fail to reflect the lifesaving roles they occupy."

On this, he has a point.

It is wrong that women working as nurses saving lives earn significantly less than World Health

Organisation Director-General Tedros Ghebreyesus whose advice in January that there was "no clear evidence" coronavirus could spread between people no doubt cost lives.

"Defund the UN to pay female health workers more!" would find popular support.

Guterres went on to say: "The pandemic has exposed the crisis in unpaid care work, which has increased exponentially as a result of school closures and the needs of older people and falls disproportionately on women."

To be fair, this is true.

Men overwhelmingly die of Covid-19 – more than their female counterparts – leaving women responsible for raising children and working. It is selfish of men to do that. They do it in war as well.

This systemic misogyny has been going on for years.

Women oppressed by the worldwide mandemic must be heartened to know that Guterres is so committed to them.

Aside from turning a Chinese germ into a battle of the sexes, nothing says "I've got you ladies" like running an organisation that puts Saudi Arabia and Somalia on its Commission on the Status of Women.

It's cute when globalists pretend to care about human rights.

TAX CUTS ARE SEXIST!

The Morrison government's planned tax cuts will benefit high-income earners and most high-income earners are men. You know where this is going, don't you.

Yes, tax cuts are sexist!

News.com.au had the headline: "Blokes big winners under tax cut plan but women get screwed."

Samantha Maiden reported that proposed tax cuts, designed to stimulate a flagging economy, would benefit men twice as much as women.

"The reason is based on the simple arithmetic that men tend to earn more than women and are more likely to be high income earners," she wrote.

"That's raised fresh concerns the tax cut plan is unfair to women."

Samantha Maiden quoted an Australia Institute report which said that for every dollar of tax cut that women would receive in the October budget, men would get $2.28.

"In other words, men get more than twice the tax cut that women get," she wrote.

It's almost like the evil misogynist Treasurer Josh Frydenberg sat down and worked out the tax cuts based on taxpayers' genitalia.

Maiden continued: "If the tax cuts were divided between men and women, blokes get 70 per cent of the tax cut cash and women secure only 30 per cent of the tax cut."

And if the amount of tax taken by the government was divided between men and women?

Samantha Maiden forgets to mention that high-income earners pay a higher tax rate and, fair or not but fact, most high-income earners are men.

So are tax cuts really sexism against women? Or are they actually addressing a historical wrong against men?

Or maybe taxes and tax cuts have nothing to do with gender at all.

That last line was, of course, a joke. Everyone understands that everything is about gender in 2020.

Unless it's about race. Or sexuality.

Speaking of which, if it is true that tax cuts overwhelmingly benefit men, then gay male couples will fare much better than heterosexual couples.

Tax cuts are heterophobic!

And these gay male couples will be advantaged even more when compared to lesbian couples.

We await the headline: "Gays big winners under tax cut plan but heterosexual and lesbian couples get screwed."

THORNS AMONG THE ROSES – DAVID SHARMA'S INTERNATIONAL WOMEN'S DAY DEBACLE

Liberal politician Dave Sharma handed out pink flowers on International Women's Day, sending all the petals on Twitter into a meltdown.

If you believe the Twitterati, handing a flower to a woman today – of all days – was "performative virtue", "deeply sexist", "creepy" and "patronising".

A smarter man would have forgotten the anniversary and given flowers a week from now as an apology. That's what the rest of us do.

Instead, Sharma stood outside Edgecliff station in his Wentworth electorate and handed flowers to passers-by who happily received them as they were intended – a perfectly nice act of kindness.

But every rose has its thorns. And the miserable whiners on Twitter, who insist on visiting their misery on the rest of us, were prickly.

"Am I the only one to find this offensive?" Tweeted one woman.

Looking for offended people on Twitter is like looking for a haystack in a pin cushion so, of course, the woman did not lack for company.

Sharma's twitter feed was bombarded with brickbats, not bouquets.

One self-described feminist screeched: "Nothing screams misogyny, like handing out flowers to keep the little women happy."

Was it Shakespeare who wrote: "Of all the flowers, me thinks a rose is best for screaming misogyny"?

Another tweeted: "I am appalled and insulted that you deem such a patronising and gender stereotyping image appropriate … you should apologise for the deeply sexist gesture."

I wondered if men should also apologise for the patronising and deeply sexist diamonds. Or maybe I was missing her point. But like all men, I want to understand women and so will commit to giving the matter serious contemplating during commercial breaks while watching the football at the weekend.

Therese Raine took time out from raging against the evil Murdoch empire to rage against men giving flowers.

"How about equal representation in parliament, in Cabinet, on boards, as CEOs and generally in the C-suite … Not little purple flowers that droop at the end of the day and fade to nothing like promises," she wrote.

The tweet, with its admission that Therese only knows "flowers that droop at the end of the day", tells us less about women's rights than it does about where hubby Kevin must be buying his blooms.

(Handy hint: Women always know when their flowers were bought at a service station. It's one of their innate skills)

And, according to ABC fact-checkers, only 30 per cent of Kevin's Cabinet was comprised of the fairer sex (one of whom fairly knifed him in the back).

So you have to feel sorry for Kevin when February 14 rolls around every year.

"Happy Valentine's Day Therese."

"If you think giving me roses today makes up for not being able to give me better than six sisters in

Cabinet back in 2013 you're sadly mistaken, Kev."

Ouch.

It wasn't just women on Twitter who didn't receive flowers who were upset that women in Wentworth did. A woke of men took to Twitter to denounce Sharma's chivalry.

One man, who described himself in his bio as "just a fellow traveller on stolen land", messaged Sharma saying: "So thrilled you got the chance to grandstand."

What fool Sharma. Flowers are an expensive way to grandstand when a wokey Twitter bio will just as easily do the job!

The most blistering reply was: "We don't need your flowers Dave, we need long-term structural reform on the system that discriminates against women. Give us equal pay, equal representation, law reform, increased funding for DV & sexual assaults. Oh a decent Minister for WOMEN & a new Govt."

And so on International Women's Day poor old Dave Sharma experienced the frustration of every man — giving flowers when what she really wanted was something else. Like chocolates. Or dinner.

Or the patriarchy on a pike.

Reasonable people understand Sharma was not suggesting that handing out flowers solves problems. And sure, there was some photo-op politicking to go with it. But giving flowers was simply a nice, harmless gesture.

That which we call a rose by any other name would smell as sweet. Except on Twitter, of course.

READING, WRITING – AND GENDER STUDIES

Let's play a game of spot the odd one out and see how you go.

New South Wales Greens Senator Mehreen Faruqi, lamenting university funding cuts, yesterday tweeted:

"Yet more devastating uni cuts. This time to valuable courses like maths, IT, gender studies and science."

One of these things is not like the others.

If you picked "gender studies" as not belonging in a sentence about "valuable courses" like mathematics, IT and science, you'd be right.

This is not to say that a Bachelor (or is it a Bachelorette?) in Arts majoring in gender studies is not valuable. People with ambitions to serve hamburgers – or to join the Greens – would no doubt find such a course helpful.

But for people hoping university will provide them with actual skills that could lead to an actual job that makes an actual contribution to society, a degree majoring in gender studies is slightly less helpful than a Certificate IV in advanced puppetry.

University of Melbourne associate professor Fran Martin – speaking in a promotional video on the university's website – says that gender studies helps students answer "what seem like simple questions about complex fields".

"How do we know if we are male or female might seem like an obvious kind of question," she tells prospective students, "but we would suggest answers are more complex than you might initially think.

"We try to offer really innovative and challenging approaches to thinking and researching about these urgent questions for us in the world today."

It is difficult to imagine how a young adult might need a few years at university to determine whether they are male or female.

There are two genders. You are biologically one or the other. It's easy to tell. If you have a penis you are a male. If you have a vagina you are a female.

Congratulations. You have now not only completed a major in gender studies, but have also avoided $100,000 in student debt.

Now, for the love of God, please invest your time and money in something helpful like mathematics or science.

But while the Chinese are pouring concrete on coral reefs in our backyard, Greens politicians are worrying that our young people won't get the chance to spend years learning the difference between boys and girls.

That, in the middle of a catastrophic economic downturn, the Greens see gender studies as a funding priority tells you everything you need to know about their fitness to ever govern.

And that Senator Faruqi – whom we presume is a woman but, without a major in gender studies, who can be sure – thinks she can smuggle gender studies in amongst math, IT and science, without anyone noticing tells you everything you need to know about the tiny bubble Greens politicians inhabit.

One can only hope that if Senator Faruqi ever embarks on a major in gender studies, she includes a side of science.

THE LIBERAL PARTY – CAUGHT IN THE GENDER TRAP?

While Australians are worried about actual problems like rising unemployment, the Liberal Party is worried about gender imbalance among its MPs.

It's hard to believe that Australia's conservative party would allow itself to be defined by progressive values, especially when progressives cannot even define the word "woman".

But Liberals are allowing themselves to become convinced that anything less than 50 per cent of their MPs being women is inherently bad.

Nobody ever gives cogent reasons as to why there should be an equal number of men and women in parliament. That women comprise half the population is a statistical fact, but not an argument for the composition of parliament.

And the argument that "we need more representation of women" is a misuse of language since every member of parliament represents men and women equally.

The sexist idea that only a woman can truly represent the interests of women was well and truly dismantled this earlier week when it was revealed Australia's foreign minister Marise Payne was yet to speak to her Qatar counterpart about the alleged strip search of 13 Australian woman at Doha airport more than three weeks ago.

Imagine if a male foreign minister said he was waiting for an official report before raising the subject with Qatar's foreign minister.

Meanwhile, the possibility that men dominate parliaments because most women are far too intelligent to pursue a career in branch stacking, faction dealing, fundraising and functions at all hours that interfere with family life is not allowed to be considered.

Anything less than male-female parity is now prima facie evidence of the Liberal Party's "problem with women". Only when parity is achieved can Liberals say they are inclusive and hold their heads high.

But if the Liberals were serious about a parliament that mirrored the general population, they would worry less about gender and instead focus on pre-selecting people with backgrounds other than in law.

Or they would insist that half of all MPs were professing Christians.

Or they would insist on pre-selecting candidates who were actually conservatives, regardless of gender, rather than people who were a pale shade of green.

A report released this week by Liberal think tank the Menzies Research Centre warned that the Liberal Party was taking only "incremental steps" towards gender balance.

Currently, 25 per cent of Liberal MPs across Australia are women. This is well short of the 50 per cent mark the party was hoping to achieve by 2025.

By contrast, 46 per cent of Labor MPs are women.

And how's that working out for them? The ALP lost the last federal election and received around 300,000 fewer votes from women than did the Liberal Party.

No wonder the MRC report says that a significant number of Liberals deny that gender imbalance matters.

But like I said, it is now an article of faith that anything less than equal numbers of men and women is evidence of a problem.

So the MRC report insisted that "the first step in addressing the representation of women in the Liberal Party is to acknowledge that the Party does in fact have a problem". In other words, if you think that gender imbalance is not a problem, you are the problem.

The report rejected the idea of "quotas", as used by the Labor Party, but demanded "targeted intervention" which was a fancy way of saying quotas without using the word.

Each Liberal Party division, it said, should set targets for female representation that were measured and reported every year.

So the Liberals may not be using quotas, but their fixation on social engineering shows that they are taking Australia down the same woke cul-de-sac as Labor, only more slowly.

The Liberals will betray their conservative base who believe in meritocracy and they will disappoint progressives for not doing woke as well or as quickly as the ALP and Greens.

Whatever diversity candidates they do get into parliament will bring with them their baggage of imagined grievance, which they will then project onto the party and onto society at large.

Nothing good can ever come from prioritising the right genitalia over the right resume.

CANDY CRUSH QUOTAS

THE United Nations – having eradicated the evils of sex slavery and child marriage – has turned its attention to gender equality in the computer gaming industry.

Wait. Females continue to be sold as slaves? And the UN's own data reveals around 12 million underage girls are forced into marriage every year?

Oh well, those girls will have to wait. Right now the UN's entity for promoting women's welfare is focused on the pressing issue of female representation in gaming.

UN Women complained via its official twitter account last week that: "Women make up almost half (46%) of gamers, but you wouldn't know it by looking at the people running the gaming industry".

We can only imagine the surprise when geniuses at the UN realise women comprise 50% of people using toilets. Afterall, you'd never know it by looking at the people running around as plumbers.

That women comprise 46% of gamers is based on gamers being defined as anyone who has ever played any kind of computer game, including on their mobile phone.

It's tempting to tell the social justice worriers at the UN to get back to us after they have removed Bejeweled and Candy Crush players from their statistics. Oh, and playing Farmville while waiting for the bus doesn't make you a gamer either.

But even if we accept that my mother's occasional game of Words with Friends makes her a gamer, it does not follow that she therefore wants to work in the gaming industry. Liking videogames doesn't necessarily translate into a desire to do a math and tech-oriented job.

It would be as silly as screaming "misogyny" because the percentage of women who drive automobiles is far greater than the percentage of women who manufacture them. My wife wants to drive the car. The only thing stopping her from looking under the bonnet is her complete lack of desire to do so. And just because you consume something does not mean you should create it.

Recent studies have shown that 99.9% of cat food eaters are cats. But you wouldn't know it by looking at the people running the cat food industry. (The remaining 0.1% allows for people like my cousin Eddy who once tasted cat food while drunk).

What kind of correlation would one expect to find between those who consume a product and those involved in its manufacture?

If 100% of tampon users are female (a statistic that until recently was universally agreed), does that mean 100% of those involved in making women's hygiene products should be women? If the answer is no, then what percentage would be acceptable to the hand-wringers at the UN?

The figures used to argue for diversity in the gaming industry actually prove diversity is not required. If 46% of gamers are women, as the UN boasts, then women are clearly interested in the games that are being produced, regardless of who produces them.

The UN gender quotas are a solution in search of a problem. Of course, the real question is why the UN cares about gaming at all.

But we do hope they convince the industry to adopt gender quotas soon so that Uygher women in China can produce video games, just as soon as they stop being interned and killed.

JOE BIDEN: WHAT I DON'T KNOW ABOUT WOMEN

Biology is no match for ideology in Joe Biden's America, where the President this week insisted "there's not a single thing a man can do that a woman can't do as well or better".

A quick-witted journalist would have asked: "Do you mean like walking up stairs?"

But the media were too busy enjoying the virtue bubbles Biden was blowing their way to exercise quick wit, let alone independent thought.

In the fairy tale of Joe Biden's imagination, where science turns into chocolate drops that melt on the tongue, women are identical to men, only superior.

Now it's quite possible that Joe Biden's wife is physically stronger than him and forced him to say it.

It's also possible that bumbling Joe meant to say "there's not a single thing I can do that Kamala Harris can't do as well or better. Not a single thing. I'm going to bed now".

And, of course, it is very possible that Joe Biden wasn't actually aware of what he was saying or where he was or who he is.

But it is certainly not true that there's not a single thing a man can do that a woman can't do as well, or better.

Men are better at peeing while standing up. Men are better at assembling IKEA furniture. And men are better at killing spiders.

According to my wife, men are better at taking out the trash. So, there's also that.

Men can walk into Kmart and walk out again in under five minutes.

And when was the last time the ladies managed to oppress another gender for millennia?

Well?

See what I mean!

I would have added that men are better at growing a moustache, but that would not be true since women can be just as good, though they typically start much later in life.

But I digress.

The point is that I think we all understand it is good to want to empower women. And no one has done more to empower women than Joe Biden who repeatedly refers to the long, foreboding shadow of Kamala as "President Harris".

But Biden's statement on women is sexist and it is wrong.

Imagine the uproar if Donald Trump had said there's nothing a woman can do that a man can't do as well or better.

Of course, when Joe Biden says that, he is talking about trans women. And so everyone cheers, including Glamour Magazine's 2015 Woman of the Year, the 1976 men's Olympic decathlon champion Caitlyn Jenner.

But Biden's latest foray into the gender wars is an example of a man who is now so woke that he has progressed beyond any need of science or even basic understanding of human nature.

The truth is that women can do whatever men can do, apart from just about every physical activity.

The trouble is that progressives, who prefer the term chestfeeding to breastfeeding, reject the very notion of physical difference (except, of course, when playing race politics in which case they reject the very notion of anything other than physical difference)

So the Democrats will nod approvingly as the Marine corps lower physical fitness requirements in order to make it possible for women to enlist, all the while insisting – straight-faced – that anyone who says there are some things women can't do is a misogynist who must be cancelled.

And let's not mention the fact that no woman has yet broken the 4-minute-mile, a feat that thousands of men have achieved since the first man in 1954.

If my daughter says she wants to one day slam dunk from the free-throw line, I will have to crush those dreams. Go ahead and call me a woman-hater.

Why does the left insist on denying the obvious unique strengths and weaknesses present in men and in women?

There are things men can do that women cannot and there are things women can do that men just can't. Acknowledging this does not mean that we do not treat each other with dignity and respect.

Far from it.

Recognising difference in acknowledgement of complementarity leads to an appreciation of the sexes. Without it, we are left only with competition between the sexes. And we all know who wins that – the physically stronger sex.

Equality and difference are not mutually exclusive. This should be obvious.

What should also seem obvious is that there surely must be more important and pressing issues for the Biden administration to be concerned with other than how quickly they get pregnant women parachuting into battle.

10

WOKE GOES THE ENVIRONMENT

LOCUSTS FOR LUNCH? THE CSIRO RECOMMENDS THEM

Australia's peak science body says we should eat insects to save the planet.

"Follow the science," they say.

Like hell.

Insects require less feed, use less land, consume less water and emit less gas than cows, pigs or chickens, our taxpayer-funded boffins have reported.

Therefore, the science goes, if people eat bugs instead of stepping on them, the Greta Thunberg sponsored climate crisis will be averted and we will all be saved.

Hallelujah!

Prime minister Billy Hughes could never have imagined, back in 1916 when he established what is now known as the CSIRO, that it would come down to this – men in lab coats declaring that if we make grubs our grub we ant going to die from global worming.

Predictably, our friends at the ABC loved the idea.

ABC Breakfast host Lisa Millar, sipping a green ant flavoured beverage, opined: "In 100 years we will be surprised that we didn't eat insects. It's such an easy solution to the food issue."

Yeah right. Just like walking is such an easy solution to the transport issue.

ABC staff should get back to us when the canteen lady at their Ultimo headquarters replaces the beef pie with worm pie and asks every Chicken-Little lefty customer "do you want flies with that?"

But for those of us who don't want to end up looking like Gollum, we're not chowing down on crickets any time soon.

CSIRO entomologist Dr Brian Lessard, whose surname – said quickly – sounds like Lizard which is entirely appropriate given his enthusiasm for eating bugs, told ABC Breakfast that indigenous people "have been eating insects for tens of thousands of years".

And?

Indigenous people have been chasing emus with sticks for tens of thousands of years too. But that's not an argument for the rest of us to follow suit.

Lessard said that one of the reasons for the "drive" to get Aussies crunching on creepy crawlies was "to engage the expertise of Aboriginal Australians but to make sure they reap the financial benefit from their intellectual copyright".

That a particular group of people have an intellectual copyright on digesting insects would be news to most people, for whom digesting insects is as simple as sleeping with their mouth open. But I digress.

The report Lessard co-authored for the CSIRO, entitled Edible Insects Industry Roadmap, says: "By becoming braver in our food choices and incorporating insects into our diet, we can lower our environmental footprint, improve our health and be more connected to our land and culture."

Lessard might like to consider that most Australians don't want to be Bear Grylls. Our idea of a 'brave food choice' is a kebab at 3.00 am, not a beetle.

And most Australians don't eat to "be more connected to our land", whatever that means. If eating ants makes one more connected to our land, then perhaps it is possible to be too connected to our land.

And one more thing: "Chuck another cockroach on the barbie" is hardly going to help the tourism industry recover if international borders ever reopen.

Lessard told the ABC: "By 2050 we are going to have to feed 9.7 billion people using the same limited resources we have today. Insects are a really sustainable way of producing high-quality protein to meet that challenge."

If the CSIRO cannot imagine any scientific advances in the next 30 years such that their best advice to Australians is 'eat moths', then one wonders why we should continue to fund them.

HOW GLOBAL WUHANING LED TO GRETA'S GOODBYE

World leaders stole her childhood and now coronavirus has stolen her crisis. So there's nothing left for activist Greta Thunberg but to go back to school.

The teen campaigner, dubbed the Goblin of Doom for her incessant warnings that carbon emissions are about to destroy the earth, has spent the past year circling the globe lecturing world leaders and organising protests.

But the same country that was exhaling a good portion of those emissions suddenly coughed up a flu bug that really did change the environment.

The Chinese flu has now made travel all but impossible. World leaders are suddenly preoccupied with an actual problem. And mass gatherings to protest a naturally occurring gas are banned for fear of contracting an unnaturally occurring virus.

Moreover, the great Covid-19 lockdown of 2020 has given the world a glimpse of "the new normal" should Greta realise her net-zero emissions dream. And no one likes it.

So last year's Time Magazine Person of the Year suddenly has a lot of free time on her sanitized hands.

She tweeted Monday: "My gap year from school is over, and it feels so great to finally be back in school again!"

We can all say amen to that. Though, sadly for the Left, it leaves them looking for a new child to take their cues from.

Eleven months ago, Greta was skipping class to scold world leaders at the UN: "You have stolen my dreams and my childhood ... how dare you!"

Watching world leaders grovel as the pigtailed Swedish school girl staged a hissy fit from the UN assembly podium was cringeworthy and yet morbidly fascinating.

For all her faults, she at least got to sneer "How dare you!" at UN leaders. What I wouldn't give to do that! Along with about nine million Israelis, I suspect. But I digress.

Nothing better highlighted the hysteria and hypocrisy of warmists than world leaders inviting a kid to hector them about public policy and "saving the planet".

The same people who dismissed anyone expressing doubt about climate change with shouts of "but you're not a climate scientist" suddenly changed their retort to "but you're not a climate scientist, or a Swedish school girl with fiery visions".

The only thing more absurd than Greta being put front and centre on the world stage was the amount of media coverage her every utterance on the weather was given.

"I shouldn't be up here," Greta complained at the UN last September. "I should be back in school on the other side of the ocean!"

Indeed.

And now, thanks not to global warming but to global Wuhaning, she is.

THE ABC WANTS TO KNOW IF YOU'RE SUFFERING FROM 'CLIMATE GRIEF'

"Climate grief" is overwhelming many Australians who now suffer from "eco-despair" because of global warming, the ABC has warned.

The national purveyor of climate doom published an article today warning that constant reporting of doom was creating a sense of doom that could leave many Australians feeling doomed.

ABC health reporter Paige Cockburn wrote: "Feeling miserable, anxious, helpless and just generally terrible because the world is becoming less habitable? You're not alone.

"Climate grief – or eco anxiety/despair – is a strong psychological response to the current and future loss of habitats, species and ecosystems.

"It's recognised by the Australian Psychological Society (APS) and sufferers may feel emotions like fear, anger, guilt, shame, grief, loss and helplessness."

Returned veterans suffering from PTSD will be heartened to learn that a bunch of activists now know just how they feel because of CO2.

Of course, the best remedy for climate grief would be a strong dose of empirical scientific evidence.

Failing that, teachers and politicians could stop trying to create an environment of hysteria. Or we could simply defund the ABC.

But since those options are about as likely as a Tim Flannery climate prediction coming true, what to do with the growing number of traumatized people racked with guilt and shame every time they switch on a light?

How do we help good people who can't even start their car engine in the morning without hearing in the back of their mind an angry Swedish teenager chiding them "How dare you"?

Fear not, The Australian Psychology Society has devoted much of its website to helping people "cope with climate change distress".

The Society warns that failure to process feelings of grief or guilt about climate change could lead to people being overwhelmed and unable to function in their everyday lives.

This could explain why Greens like Adam Bandt and Sarah Hanson-Young make so little sense. Emotional wrecks are unsuitable for involvement in public debate.

The website recommends climate change worriers consider "having a day job that is separate to your activist work" in order to avoid sinking into a fully-fledged eco-funk.

If getting a job sounds a bit extreme, another coping strategy for those burdened by "the existential threats to civilisation as we know it" is to take what the Australian Psychology Society calls "a doona day". Because, you know, sometimes you just need to lay in bed while the planet burns and, besides, it beats going to work.

Other coping strategies are to "watch a fire, gaze at a waterfall, or pick flowers without exerting attentional effort".

If this fails to take your mind off polar bears stranded on ice blocks then the website encourages you to "let yourself have a cry from time to time".

"Some people find that expressing their sadness by crying can be a relief. It is sad that our planet is struggling to cope with overpopulation and overconsumption. These feelings are real, so let them out" it advises.

Dr Tristan Snell, a counselling psychologist and researcher in environmental psychology at Deakin University told the ABC that "there's no ritual around loss of environment".

"When you lose someone, there's a funeral and all sorts of ways people connect and this helps process that loss. That's just not the case for loss of environment," he said.

Someone might like to advise Dr Snell that the Earth is still very much alive. When you want to hold a funeral before the patient has even died, you really are in a bad way!

The ABC article laments the fact that "no research on climate grief among Australian Indigenous people exists".

No doubt it will be done, because everything – even eco grief – must be viewed through the prism of race. Black Climate Grief Matters.

But it will probably not be done until research on climate grief among the two-spirited genderqueer trans women is first completed.

While it's all very well for the ABC to publish articles to assist snowflakes afflicted by climate torment, what about the acute sense of grief and loss the rest of us feel, knowing our taxes are used to pay someone to write this stuff?

THE LEFT WANT TO KEEP US LOCKED DOWN TO SERVE THEIR GREEN AGENDA

Leftists have turned to alchemy to try to transform the Covid-19 pandemic into their fabled climate emergency.

Former ABC journalist Quentin Dempster tweeted on Thursday: "Australia's National Cabinet should stay on to coordinate decarbonising of energy/transport/manufacture to urgently mitigate climate change."

Well no, Quentin. If I wanted Daniel Andrews to run my life I would move to Victoria, lock myself in my home and vote for him.

The National Cabinet, formed by the PM to help steer Australia through the pandemic by determining such things as whether or not we may see our mums on Mother's Day, should be disbanded the moment the lockdown ends. And the lockdown should end yesterday.

But gloomy environmental doomsdayers – who practice social distancing when they meet, not by shaking hands but by shaking heads – are insisting on the old adage that one should "never let a crisis go to waste".

They imagine current restrictions on our freedom continuing after Covid-19, but this time in service of their grand green agenda.

Wednesday's Sydney Morning Herald editorial was headed: "Scientific approach for Covid-19 must be applied to climate change".

Of course, our "scientific approach to Covid-19" has been no more scientific than the approach to the great plague of 1666 – social distancing, face masks and an emphasis on personal hygiene – except that we have an app.

But I digress.

The SMH went on to say: "Our response to the coronavirus provides important lessons for how we should respond. It is time the federal government accepted the warnings from scientists about climate change just as seriously and took a similarly proactive approach."

It's not difficult to guess the lessons environmental activists might have learned over the past two months:

* Say that our computer modelling – which is another way to say "our guessing" but it sounds scientific when you use the word "computer" – indicates we are on the verge of the apocalypse. And don't just say it; have someone sign it for the deaf, like in an actual emergency.

* Insist that millions upon zillions of people will die. And don't be afraid of using outrageous numbers. The more unlikely the number, the more enthusiastic the media will be to report it and the more inclined people will be to believe it.

* No more of these "we have three years to act" warnings that environmentalists have been using for the past decade. The threat must be immediate. "A gazillion people will die every day starting next Tuesday if we don't act now," is much better.

* Hold up a graph and use a catchy, memorable phrase to tell people what they must do. "Flatten the Curve" has already been used so another slogan would need to be thought up, but this should easy enough since the public love to rally around pithy slogans that are quite meaningless -- Free Tibet; Love is Love; Hugs Not Drugs. A Fair Go for All. Something along those lines.

* Tell people we must "flatten the curve", or whatever, by locking ourselves in our homes until enough solar panels have been built or until a reduction in global temperatures has been achieved – whichever comes last.

* Keep people in lockdown by constantly moving the green goal posts. "We started with 0.5 degree average reductions, but now computer models say death and destruction

unless we double that. So no-one is going back to work anytime soon. And no, you can't play golf."

The past two months have taught us that people will nod in agreement before calling the police to report a neighbour who shows any sign of dissent.

* Churches can remain closed, as they were during the pandemic, to prevent pastors speaking faith to people's fears.

* Declare people not working with the wind or the sun (peace be upon Gaia) to be "non-environmental workers" who must lose their livelihoods. A nice touch would be to have them stand on their front lawns and clap appreciation for environmentalists at 8pm every Thursday.

* Require people to stay home and watch Netflix (YouTube will be blocked so that no-one can view Michael Moore's Planet of the Humans) until the climate emergency is over and the earth is healed which will be whenever Adam Bandt says so. And all of this can be done without ever going through the hassle of giving annoying people, by which we mean the public, a vote.

* Anyone who complains should be accused of literally hating the planet and of wanting people to die. "How dare you question the climate lockdowns?" they should be told. "Your Facebook posts are actually polluting the Earth."

French philosopher Bruno Latour, quoted in The Guardian last month, said: "We have learned that it is possible in a matter of weeks to slow the economy, which until now had been considered inconceivable.

"The incredible discovery is that there was in fact in the world economic system, hidden from all eyes, a bright red alarm signal, next to a large steel lever that each head of state could pull at once to stop 'the progress train' with a shrill screech of the brakes."

As the threat of Covid-19 recedes and governments look to ease restrictions, watch as the environmentalists try to wrestle control of the lever for their beloved climate emergency.

WHY WE MUSTN'T FLY OVERSEAS – EVEN IF WE COULD

Australians must stop flying overseas, turn off their air conditioners and drive more slowly if the world is to achieve net zero greenhouse gas emissions by 2050, according to killjoys at the International Energy Agency.

Imagine telling Aussies, who currently are not permitted to fly anywhere, that they must fly less.

Or demanding that Sydney motorists must drive more slowly – which, if they did, would be called parking.

Where do a bunch of faceless European clima-crats get off insisting there must be laws about when North Queenslanders can or cannot use their air-con?

And yet that is exactly what the Paris based agency has done in its newly released "Net Zero by 2050 – a Roadmap for the Global Energy Sector" report.

IEA boss Dr Fatih Birol insists that if we don't reach zero emissions by 2050 then the coming apocalypse – by which we mean Greta Thunberg going from yelling "How dare you" to screaming "I told you so" as her childhood dreams go up in flames with the planet – will be unavoidable.

Also, a rise of 1.5 degrees Celsius means the earth would hit what the World Meteorological Organization last week called the "temperature limit".

This, of course, is a totally artificial limit set by a treaty that was drawn up by unelected, unrepresentative, unaccountable technocrats with a penchant for drama.

It has zero natural significance other than to give climate weenies something to harp over endlessly.

But back to Mr Birol, who was recognised by the Financial Times in 2017 as Energy Personality of the Year.

The Turkish born engineer wants first world countries to give up their use of fossil fuels, which essentially means becoming third world countries.

He also wants governments to mandate green fetishes like solar panels and electric cars which most of us don't want – hence the need to mandate them.

But, according to the IEA report, the above measures would drive us only 92% of the way toward the utopian zero emissions target.

To appreciate what 92% of the way means, think of driving your Tesla on one charge from Sydney to Thredbo – because the IEA have prevented you from flying to Davos where all the accommodation has been reserved for the World Economic Forum's next climate bedwetting session – and you come to a grinding halt in Bunyan. It's that bad.

Anyway, the final push to get to global net-zero emissions would require "behavioural changes driven by the active and willing participation of citizens" – which is what technocrats say when they mean "draconian laws – such as don't fly overseas, don't drive so fast and don't turn on your air-conditioning unit – imposed upon browbeaten and unwilling citizens"

That Mr Birol, who is about as much fun as a vacation in Chernobyl during the late 80s, was named Energy Personality of the Year does not say much about the competition.

The IEA said people in wealthier nations had higher levels of energy use, which meant their behavioural changes were especially important in "reducing excessive or wasteful energy consumption".

That, of course, is a long-winded way of saying, "We need Westerners to do this because we dare not ask the Chinese."

Finally, and most worryingly, the IEA report warned that if these behavioural changes were not adopted global carbon emissions would reach 1.7 billion tonnes in 2030 and 2.6 billion tonnes in 2050.

And then there would be nothing left for our political class to do but send everyone to their rooms for time out. A disciplinary measure they have spent the past 18 months perfecting.

THE WORLD ECONOMIC FORUM: LOCKDOWNS ARE IMPROVING CITIES

The World Economic Forum — an economic think tank that thinks it's great that everything is closed — announced today that "lockdowns are quietly improving cities around the world".

"Lockdowns significantly reduced human activity ... leading to Earth's quietest period in decades," the WEF enthused in an article accompanied by a dystopian video showing cities without people.

"Urban ambient noise fell by up to 50% at some measuring stations during the tightest lockdown weeks, as buses and train services were reduced, aircraft grounded and factories shuttered."

It sounds like paradise doesn't it?

Don't worry that lockdowns have led to job loses, suicides, drug overdoses, isolation, mental health issues, domestic abuse, bankruptcies and homelessness.

And never mind that every minutiae of life is now dictated by health officers.

How's the serenity? So much serenity. It's so quiet you can almost hear the devastation!

Imagine how excited those sociopaths at the WEF will be when they realise that cemeteries are dead quiet. Oh, the possibilities!

The WEF boasted that a massive reduction in noise had made it easier for scientists to monitor earthquake activity. Well if that doesn't cheer non-essential workers while they are trying to figure out how to pay their rent, nothing will.

I'm all for viewing the glass half-full. But cheering a pandemic because it creates an opportunity to reset the world with less humans and even less human activity is something else entirely.

To imagine that cities are improved by closing them down is like imagining that marriage is improved by divorce.

And to think you can enhance human life by cutting humans off from each other is akin to recommending decapitation as the cure for a headache.

It's not innovative. And it's certainly not progressive. At best it is creepy. But more likely, it is sinister.

The totalitarians at the WEF, who last year promised us that in the future "you will own nothing and you will be happy", now insist that removing our freedoms in order to protect us from a virus with a fatality rate of about two per cent – all the while destroying our lives – is an improvement.

By improvement, they can only mean that clearing the streets and closing businesses has made it easier to find bugs to eat.

Silent streetscapes devoid of people who are all imprisoned in their homes as technocrats regulate every aspect of life is an incredibly twisted vision of "improving" things.

Cities are supposed to be busy and noisy and bustling with activity. What is a city without people? There is nothing to celebrate about a beehive without any bees.

But while the WEF glories in the silence, anyone with ears to hear will have noticed an other phenomena – as the seismic noise subsides, the incessant nannying noise from non-elected globalists increases in inverse proportion.

That WEF boss Klaus Schwab and his globalist friends are so desperate to convince us that lockdowns – something they only have in prisons – are in fact a public good, only serves to make us wonder if restrictions in pursuit of zero covid cases are really just the training wheels for a new normal in pursuit of zero carbon emissions.

If you listen carefully you can hear Guns 'N Roses performing the WEF anthem ...

> *Take me down to the paradise city*
> *Where the grass is green*
> *And the streets are empty*
> *Ooh, ooh, take me down.*

Singing quietly, of course. From their bedrooms. Via Zoom.

WTF WEF?

THE GREENS: THE SEASONS ARE NOW AUTUMN, WINTER, SPRING AND CLIMATE CHANGE

The Greens are blaming their political opponents for summer.

Of course, summer happens around this time in Australia every year. But Greens Senator Mehreen Faruqi says that summer shouldn't be occurring and that the Liberals need to make it stop.

Noting that the Harbour City was hot over the weekend, Senator Faruqi tweeted: "36 degrees today.

39 degrees tomorrow. Stay hydrated, Sydney. And don't forget to remind your local Liberal MP that this shouldn't be happening in November. #climatecrisis".

The Senator, who seems to have had a bit too much sun, did not say when she believes that summer should be happening. It officially starts tomorrow.

Nor did she say what she believes local Liberal MPs can do about summer.

Presumably, Senator Faruqi thinks MPs should take more of people's money while promising to change the weather by flying to conferences in Europe where they will agree to take even more of people's money while continuing to promise better weather for everyone.

This junket can be repeated *ad nauseum*, by simply yelling 'climate crisis' on hot days. It's the best Marxist plan yet devised to accumulate money and power.

But a couple of hot days at the end of an Australian Spring do not constitute a climate crisis.

Discrete weather events are not indicative of broader climate patterns, as we are reminded by the Greens whenever there are below-average temperatures. But politics, right?

So Senator Faruqi, who seems genuinely surprised to be living in Australia, jumps like a cat on a hot tin roof, demanding the Liberals turn down the sun because hot.

That Sydney had temperatures at this same time of year of 39 degrees in 1878 and in 1941, of 40 degrees in 1946, of 41 degrees in 1982, and of 39 degrees in 1988 was of no relevance.

And don't worry that Dorothy Mackellar wrote about a "sunburnt country" in 1908, long before Senator Faruqi or any other Chicken Little ever thought to run around screeching "climate crisis".

According to the Greens, the seasons are now Autumn, Winter, Spring and Climate Change.

Senator Faruqi aims to channel Sydneysiders' momentary discomfort because of the heat into permanent anger at her political opponents because, we are supposed to believe, they could stop Summer if they really wanted to; or at least move it to a better spot in the calendar.

But after a hot weekend, the Sydney temperature today is slightly lower than average and the overcast skies have ruined my planned beach day. So who do I call to complain?

ENVIRONMENTALISTS BARRACKING FOR THE VIRUS

In the fight against coronavirus, it is disconcerting to have people barracking for the virus.

The latest cheer-leader for the epidemic is Australian model Elyse Knowles who this week described Coronavirus as "a gift" given to the planet.

"Mother Nature has proven to us all that by minimising the collective human footprint, our world can take a breath and re-set," she told online magazine *A Conscious Collection.*

As at the time of writing, 188,437 people had died of Coronavirus. Ms Knowles didn't say how many of her fellow citizens would need to be 'minimised' before Mother Nature, behaving more like a wicked stepmother, had made her point.

But presumably close to 200,000 deaths was good progress since "beaches and rivers are glistening with crystal blue water", Ms Knowles enthused.

Who knows, if the virus offers up 300,000 human lives, Mother Nature may see her way clear to clean up the Great Barrier Reef. And imagine what Gaia might do for half a million lives! The possibilities really do become quite exciting!

Ms Knowles, a Myer ambassador when the store is not in lockdown to allow Mother Nature to take a breath, received support online including one person who wrote: "Humans are the plague of the earth and in lockdown the world is starting to slowly heal itself before we start destroying it again."

Did you get that? The plague is not the plague. Humans are the plague. And so that's why they're cheering for COVID-19.

Ms Knowles, a Byron Bay resident, continues a tradition of Australian celebrities cheering for anyone but the humans.

I remember the fuss in 2007 when singer Deni Hines learned that the marching band she was to tour Australia with would be wearing bear-skin hats.

The "passionate vegetarian" told The Weekend Australian: "Someone was trying to tell me they have to cull the bears, and there are too many. You know what? As a vegetarian, there are too many humans and I'd love to cull them but I am not out doing it."

I read Hines' comments and wondered which humans she would "love to cull".

I'm betting she didn't have herself in mind. Presumably, that is why she chose to comment "as a vegetarian" rather than as a human. Those who complain that the world is over-populated never volunteer to be part of the solution.

An article in the environmental magazine Wild Earth went beyond calling for a human cull and actually promoted "voluntary human extinction", a "phasing out of the human race" that would solve the planet's problems.

The magazine article, published back in 1991, said: "If you haven't given voluntary human extinction much thought before, the idea of a world with no people in it may seem strange. But, if you give it a chance, I think you might agree that the extinction of Homo Sapiens would mean survival for millions, if not billions, of Earth-dwelling species ... phasing out the human race will solve every problem on earth, social and environmental."

I love the cheerful exhortation to give voluntary extinction "a chance". If you close your eyes and listen you can see the editorial staff holding hands and swaying together as they sing their anthem: 'All we are saying, is give death a chance!'

Well, why not? It would be wrong to knock extinction without having at least tried it! Death is something everyone should give a go, at least once during their lifetime.

Curiously, Wild Earth continued to be published for another 13 years. When the magazine did disappear from the planet, in 2004, it wasn't because staff had kindly phased themselves out of existence for the betterment of the planet. Evidently, they wanted other people to give voluntary extinction a chance.

COVID-19 is only a gift to the planet if you and your loved ones don't have it. Enthusing about the environmental pay-off of 183,000 deaths is not enlightened; it's sick.

11

POLITICIANS BEHAVING WOKELY

THE GREENS: IF YOU DON'T GO COMMANDO, A CHILD IN AFRICA WILL DIE. OR SOMETHING

My parents used to encourage me to eat my vegetables because "there are children starving in Africa", as if my table manners and the plight of African orphans were inextricably linked.

It worked because I was young and stupid.

Speaking of which, NSW Greens MP David Shoebridge is upset that "the 30 wealthiest schools in NSW have a combined income greater than some of our South Pacific neighbours like Tonga and Samoa".

Does Mr Shoebridge really believe the people of Tonga would have more if private schools in NSW had less?

Is he seriously suggesting some sort of perverse, inverse relationship between prosperity at Knox Grammar and poverty in Samoa?

Could it be that spoilt Scott's College boys in Bellevue Hill are the cause of lower than expected economic activity in Fiji and Vanuatu?

Of course not.

But it sounds about right if you are young and stupid. Or a Greens voter. But I repeat myself.

The NSW Greens spokesman for Justice and Police tweeted today: "The 30 richest schools in the state had a total income of more than $1.7 billion – exceeding the GDP of small Pacific Island nations like

Tonga and Samoa."

And?

Well?

Imagine the horror when Mr Shoebridge learns that Australians spend $1.8m on underwear every year. Will he urge Greens supporters to go commando style in order to support sagging Pacific Island economies?

The sad truth is that if he did, they probably would.

"These schools should be ashamed!" replied one of Mr Shoebridge's simpletons when he revealed the sinister relationship between NSW private school funding and the Gross Domestic Product of Samoa.

"It's greed pure and simple!" said another.

A third tweeted: "No more funding privaledge!"

Indeed, the money is clearly needed to fund literasee.

The federal government spent $35 billion on indigenous affairs last year, but I don't see Mr Shoebridge suggesting that this negatively impacted the productivity of workers in New Caledonia.

No. It is only the private school kids on Sydney's north shore who adversely affect the living standards of our neighbours in the South Pacific.

And if you believe that, you'll eat all your greens tonight because if you don't, a child in Africa will starve.

"YOU GET THE POLITICIANS YOU DESERVE" HAS NEVER BEEN MORE INSULTING

Hundreds of New South Wales families are being evacuated from flooded homes. Meanwhile, our political advisors are busy jerking off on MPs desks.

Government imposed lockdowns have devastated businesses across the nation and, with Job Keeper ending next week, thousands of Australians do not know how they will pay their bills. Not to worry; our politicians are occupied having sex in the Parliament House prayer room.

The Covid vaccine, which we are told is key to beating the pandemic and to opening up the country, is being rolled out at a snail's space.

Whatever. Our politicians and journalists are focused on weaponizing allegations of rape in order to score cheap political points against ideological opponents.

The old adage "you get the politicians you deserve" has never been more insulting.

And the truism that politics is downstream from culture has never been more depressing.

Violence against women is a real problem in our country, demanding real action. But those who protest most passionately about women's safety rejected an invitation to discuss solutions with the Prime Minister because it did not provide them with the photo op they were after.

And it's not like the Prime Minister doesn't have time to meet with people since he abdicated responsibility for running the country to state premiers who can't wait for the next sneeze to give them an excuse for emergency powers and regular television spots.

But the pressing issue right now is women's rights.

Not the rights of women stuck overseas, unable to return to their own country because of arbitrary border closures. And certainly not the rights of females in utero who are more likely to be aborted than males. Feminists have banned any negative discussion on abortion because, well, it's healthcare, right?

And not the rights of female athletes whose livelihood is threatened by the insistence that biological males, identifying as women, should be allowed to participate.

No. Our sports administrators insist we are much too polite to raise any objections. And certainly not the rights of Indigenous women who are 32 times more likely to be hospitalised as a result of family violence than are non-indigenous women.

That issue will be studiously ignored because our political elites are far too sensitive to make a scene about anything other than Australia Day.

And so here we are – saddled with serious problems being handled by fundamentally unserious people.

Meanwhile, our universities won't defend free speech because they are afraid of the students.

Our Christian ministers won't defend Christianity because they are afraid of their increasingly woke congregations.

Our conservative politicians won't defend conservatism because they are afraid of the ABC and of Twitter, but I repeat myself.

And our young adults won't defend Western civilisation because they have been taught to be afraid of it and, worse, to hate it.

Other than that, things are going well. And China says hello.

> *I come from a land down under*
> *Where women rage and men blunder*
> *Can you hear can you hear the thunder*
> *You better run, you better take cover.*

HOW THE LEFT CAN'T LET TRUMP DIE – WHILE WISHING DEATH UPON HIM

US media continues to be gripped by Trump derangement syndrome with Thursday's New York Times breathlessly reporting a non-story about the non-President which was really just an excuse to rue the fact that Trump hadn't died of Covid; a story lovingly republished by *The Sydney Morning Herald* and *The Age*.

In an article that took four reporters to write, the former newspaper quoted "people familiar with his condition" saying Trump was "sicker than acknowledged with Covid-19".

Two anonymous sources said Trump came perilously close to requiring a ventilator. They might as well have said "gloriously close".

You could almost hear the collective sighs from the four reporters as they madly scribbled in their notebooks "we were so close", and asked again to be told just how near they were to being able to report Trump's death, rather than his recovery.

Readers of the *New York Times* joined the reporters' lament.

"Too bad COVID lost that one," wrote one reader.

"We were so close," wrote another.

"If only ..." wrote a third.

We could go on, and on, but I think you've got the general idea.

Joe Biden's call for "healing and unity" was clearly resonating with progressives as they united in their grief at Trump's healing.

Buried in the New York Time's "if only this were an obituary" piece was this: "A person close to the former president denied that he had been seriously ill, echoing comments Mr. Trump himself made after he was sick."

So Trump probably did not almost die after all. But the New York Times decided to go with "imagine if he had!"

Of course, Trump supporters will love the story since, if true, it simply proves that Trump really is a badass who was functioning at a level his haters never expected.

He looked death in the eye and stared it down. He is either Superman or kissed by God.

The wonderful irony is that even as the New York Times and their readers bemoan the fact that Trump did not die of Covid, they must keep him alive for the same reason that the Democrats were set on re-impeaching the already once-impeached former President.

They cannot let Trump die since without Trump the Left are left with nothing but "you know, the thing", as Joe Biden famously put it.

THE GREAT KIWI KOWTOW

New Zealand has offered to teach Australia its special brand of bend-over diplomacy in order to get back into China's good books.

The generous offer came from Kiwi Trade Minister Damien O'Connor who went as far as offering to mediate a trade settlement (by which he meant a capitulation) on our behalf.

It comes a month after his kowtowing colleague, New Zealand Foreign Minister Nanaia Mahuta, offered to negotiate a truce (by which she meant a surrender) with China.

But more significantly, it comes just two days after China agreed to give New Zealand more of their money, in part to further punish Australia for having the temerity to ask questions about coronavirus.

As they say, those Kiwis are bought and paid for.

Mr O'Conner said Australia needed to "show more respect" (by which he meant ignore China's appalling human rights record) and "be more careful with wording" (by which he meant be more liberal with flattery) if we wanted a good relationship with China (by which he meant become China's bitch).

"We have a mature and honest relationship with China, and we've always been able to raise issues of concern," said Mr O'Conner, whose brown-nosing diplomatic triumphs include persuading the Chinese to come clean about Covid, to stop persecuting the Uighurs and to recognise the sovereignty of Taiwan (by which I mean none of those things).

Clearly, Mr O'Conner's lecture (by which I mean slap with a feather) was part and parcel of New Zealand's trade deal with China, wherein they are required to speak on behalf of China against those refusing to be subjugated.

Every bully has his minions and they enjoy a special protected status. Of course, part of their role as is to fulfil certain needs of the bully.

Understanding this, the Australian Government did not take New Zealand's advice as seriously as if New Zealand government ministers had been talking about something they actually understood (by which I mean rugby union or sheep).

Australian Trade Minister Dan Tehan said our nation's trade policy would "be guided by three Ps: proactivity, principle and patience" (by which Mr O'Conner heard "placate from the prostrate position").

Australia is big enough to overlook the immaturity and disrespect shown by New Zealand's Trade Minister (by whom I mean Comrade O'Conner) in 'advising' his closest ally on how to show maturity and respect to a Communist foe.

But Australia would be ill-advised to ignore the naivety (by which I mean lack of experience, wisdom and judgement) demonstrated by our cousins across the Ditch.

New Zealand pulled out of ANZUS yet still expects Australia and the US to protect them. Now they insist on flirting with China at the very time Australia and the US are trying to keep China out.

In the event that China ever tries to invade New Zealand they will no doubt put up a spirited defence (by which I mean scream for

Australia's help).

Right now, however, New Zealand's woke, socialist progressives (by which I mean those who will shake hands with the Devil if the price is right; and become the Devil for a dollar more) are snubbing their allies and preferring to dance with the bear.

Australia doesn't actually have an issue with China over trade. It is China that has a problem with Australia, not over trade, but over our determination not to allow them to continue buying us piece by piece.

Our previous trade with them has become their weapon of choice to try to force us to accept their demands.

New Zealand (by which I mean a lamb that loves the abattoirs) is about to sell its soul to China for easy money, and its effort to have us sit down with China is just another ploy by China to have us acquiesce to their demands.

ANTHONY ALBANESE WARNS THE TSAR

Some people have something to say and other people just have to say something. Anthony Albanese is firmly in the latter category.

The Labor leader, who is clearly struggling with an acute case of relevancy deprivation syndrome, yesterday called a special press conference to showcase his growing irrelevance.

Having failed miserably to assert himself in any meaningful way in domestic affairs, the would-be prime minister who is preferred by just 26% of voters, decided it was time to insert himself into the presidential election.

Albanese's big announcement was that Prime Minister Scott Morrison should pull President Trump into line with a lecture on being a good sport.

Whoever is advising the opposition leader must want him gone soon. You could almost hear the collective eye-roll from the press gallery.

After waxing lyrical on the origins of our alliance with the US and the general importance of democracy, Albo came to his point.

"Scott Morrison has a close relationship with President Trump," he said, in what was clearly intended to be the most backhanded of compliments.

"He should be contacting President Trump and conveying Australia's strong view that democratic processes must be respected. I will now take questions."

There was an awkward silence. A silence long enough for us to feel sorry for the invisible man of Australian politics.

Coronavirus, which is being handled by state premiers, has consigned Albanese to the national sidelines. Unless he wants to pull Victoria Labor leader Daniel Andrews into line – and we all know that is not going to happen – he is merely spectating from a Covid-safe distance, like the rest of us.

The federal Government's October budget boasted a deficit that a Labor leader like Albanese could only dream of running up. He was reduced to complaining that the financials were sexist. Yawn.

As if all of that was not bad enough, the ghost of former ALP leader Kevin Rudd has been attracting attention almost every day, albeit with an ill-conceived campaign against Rupert Murdoch. But at he's in the news.

Heck, even Rudd's cheesy handball videos get more attention than anything Albo says.

If there's any truth to Oscar Wilde's axiom that the only thing worse than people talking about you is people not talking about you, then Albanese is very much in the 'things are worse' category.

So there stood yesterday's man, blinking awkwardly, hoping like hell that someone would ask a question in response to his insistence that the government give the US President a stern talking to.

"What possible good could come from your intervention when Republicans can't even bring the President to heel?" a reporter eventually asked.

It was a polite way of saying, "What the heck are you going on about Albo?!"

So granted, it wasn't the question Albanese had hoped for. But he bravely soldiered on.

"Well I would have thought that Scott Morrison says he has a strong relationship with

President Trump," Albo repeated, clearly grateful for the chance to again point out that the PM was friends with Evil Orange Man Bad.

One suspects this smear by association (Trump is a goose, the PM gets on well with Trump, therefore the PM is a goose) was the entire point of Albanese's press conference.

But having made that point twice, he now had to push on as though he really believed intervening in the US election was sensible, let alone possible.

"The fact is that pressure needs to be brought by people who believe in democratic processes," he said, as if the US was about to descend into tyrannical rule because the US President was asking the US courts to ensure US laws had not been broken during the US election. "These [democratic processes] are values which are universal," Albanese warned.

Putting aside the fact that democracy is hardly a universal value, what sort of "pressure" could Australia really bring to bear on a supposedly petulant Trump?

Albanese, shrinking in front of the cameras with every word that he spoke, replied straight-faced: "We saw on Saturday night, with both

Anastacia Palaszczuk's acceptance speech and Deb Frecklington's gracious acceptance of her non-election, her concession speech I think brought credit to our democracy."

So there you have it.

In the middle of a global pandemic, and with the nation facing soaring unemployment, the Labor leader's contribution to the national discourse was to suggest Scott Morrison phones Trump and saves the world superpower from impending doom by recounting how nice a couple of Queensland women were to each other last Saturday.

Can you imagine how Anthony Albanese would react if British Prime Minister Boris Johnson called to tell him to respect our federal election results?

It is safe to say that if Albanese lasts long enough to see the next federal election, there will be no argument about whether or not his heavy defeat will have been legitimate.

LABOR: THE PARTY OF THE WORKERS - OR THE WOKE?

Labor might need to split into two separate parties if it is to represent workers as well as inner-city poodle pulling latte sippers, according to veteran parliamentarian Joel Fitzgibbon.

Admittedly, Fitzgibbon didn't quite put it like that.

But he was clear that Labor would struggle to represent both workers and the privileged, tertiary educated, public sector employed elites who sneer at them while riding on their backs.

Okay, the shadow minister for agriculture and resources didn't exactly frame it in those terms.

But he was alluding to how difficult it was for Labor to win the hearts of workers while spending all their time smooching the migrant, green and welfare vote.

What I think he meant to say was that his party was having a hard time appealing to both workers and to wokesters.

Here's what Fitzgibbon actually said: "I just don't know how we reconcile the difficulty of being all things to people in Melbourne, and another thing to a group of people living in central Queensland.

He told the Blenheim Partners podcast: "I am very fearful about how the Labor Party will manage ... (to) juggle these two electoral bases and I do fear that, it won't be in my time, but the party might end up splitting."

The national Right faction convenor of the Party sounds like he fears that Labor has become so progressive they have left their constituents behind. And one can't help but think he is right.

Moreover, it is increasingly clear that there is no pathway onto the treasury benches from the woke left of politics. The failure of the Greens to grow their brand makes this abundantly clear.

The working class – most of whom prefer continuity over rapid change, patriotism over national self-loathing, the nuclear family over an LBGTIQ+ alphabet soup and local attachments over contrived diversity – could not be blamed for feeling as if the Labor Party is more likely to preach at them than to represent them.

It is now clear that working class Australians sit at the bottom of the identity politics hierarchy. The constituency the Labor Party was founded on is these days derided as ignorant, racist and patriarchal by the very people trusted to represent their interests. Oil and water.

Fitzgibbon's warning comes as opposition Treasury spokesman Jim Chalmers prepares to visit the Queensland town of Warwick where he will reportedly argue that climate change "isn't some inner-city preoccupation".

No doubt the people of Warwick will be excited to hear that it's a United Nations preoccupation as well. But I digress.

It will be interesting to see how Labor's plan to win back regional

Queensland with a speech from someone with a PhD on the prime ministership of Paul Keating, representing a city electorate, and with a working life spent entirely in politics actually goes.

If Chalmers can convince workers that it is possible to leave their mining jobs for a career in renewables without being worse off – all while saving the planet – he might then explain that Father Christmas is real. And the Tooth Fairy.

But back to Fitzgibbon. What is hilarious about dividing the ALP so as to offer voters a choice between Labor and Labour is that the ALP already has a branch that panders to progressives – the Greens.

The Greens will never preference the Liberal Party so why Labor continues to push left in a bid to out-Green the Greens while alienating their traditional base makes no sense. But then, leftism never did make any sense.

Fitzgibbon's observation that workers and wokesters are mutually exclusive predictably led to many on Twitter insisting that he was unfit to remain in the Labor Party – not for promoting fossil fuels but for espousing too much common sense.

NOBODY HATES LIKE LEFTISTS

President Trump has contracted coronavirus and, in response, the world hs held a competition to determine who was the most awful person. Competition has been fierce.

Many of the same people who had spent the week demanding President Trump condemn hate immediately wished him dead when it was revealed he had COVID-19.

New York Times film critic Simon Abrams made a strong play for most awful person when he tweeted: "For once I am rooting for the virus"

Former Liberal Party leader John Hewson was an early entry from Australia.

Hewson, who is best known for losing an unlosable election, didn't offer any well wishes to the man who is famous for winning an unwinnable election.

He simply tweeted: "Question to Donald – Can you really get ill from a 'Hoax'?"

It was a fair effort at awful. But Hewson was no match for journalist Jane Caro.

"Does Trump really have COVID? Is this bullshit? Or what?" she tweeted.

And then she added: "For the record, I will be delighted to have my doubts about Trump's COVID diagnosis proved wrong."

Charming.

She later deleted the tweet but not before hundreds of her followers had liked her ability to put their awful into a pithy sentence they had the good sense not to write.

She was joined by hosts of Network Ten's The Project who boast that the program is "news delivered differently" when "news distorted regularly" would be a more accurate description.

Like Caro, they speculated that Trump might have been lying about having coronavirus. After all, he lies about everything else, right?

Journalism teacher and Sydney Morning Herald columnist Jenna Price developed the theme.

"Does anyone believe him? Or is he trying for the sympathy vote?" she tweeted.

There was zero sympathy from Ten News political editor Peter van Onselen who tweeted: "I'm surprised Melania gave the Donald COVID-19 because she's done such a good job socially distancing from him."

Hilarious.

It was almost – but not quite – as funny as one of his 'balanced' newspaper columns in *The Australian*.

Van Onselen, who regularly co-hosts The Project, is no longer sure if he is an entertainer or a serious political commentator and so has become neither.

ABC broadcaster and producer James Findlay reacted to news that President Trump had a potentially life-threatening illness by tweeting: "There's a bottle of champagne in the fridge and it's getting opened right now."

And that's how he tweets about people contracting a disease before he drinks!

The tweet was later deleted.

Occasional Sky News guest Dee Madigan had no such regrets about her awful tweet.

"2020 has slightly redeemed itself," she wrote upon hearing the President and the First Lady had tested positive for Covid-19.

Imagine being so ghoulish that you believe your year gets better when someone you only know from television contracts a potentially life threatening illness.

When one of her 49,000 twitter followers chided her for being glad someone got become sick because politics, Madigan doubled down.

"idgaf," she wrote, which is apparently how the cool kids write "I don't give a f–k".

Telstra hoped the most awful person award might be given to a corporation.

Good luck getting Australia's largest telco to provide fast internet, but they sure can deliver high speeds when pandering to woke Trump haters.

While Telstra staff took hours to sort out my last billing inquiry they needed hardly any time to mock President Donald Trump for contracting coronavirus.

Telstra's official twitter account posted the message "Don't even try and blame 5G for this" in response to Trump's tweet, 45 minutes earlier, advising that he and his wife had Covid-19.

If only Telstra's customer service was as fast.

But not even Telstra could out awful Queensland Deputy Premier and Health Minister Stephen

Miles.

The senior *Australian* politician, tweeting to the leader of Australia's key ally, wrote: "Have you considered intravenous disinfectant?"

Stephen Miles doesn't like Donald Trump. We get it. But surely puerile responses like this are unbecoming of a man within 1.5m of the Premier's chair.

Donald Trump's odds of recovering from Covid-19 are much better than the odds of Trump haters recovering from Trump Derangement Syndrome.

DEMOCRATS PREFER WISHES AND FEELINGS TO CONSTITUTION AND LAW

THE Democrats – in opposing the nomination of a new Supreme Court judge until after the November 3 election – want to turn the United States Senate into the Make-a-Wish Foundation.

"Democrats are united in fighting to honor Ruth Bader Ginsburg's last wish," tweeted Senate Democratic Leader Chuck Schumer.

Joe Biden's running mate Kamala Harris said: "We must honour that wish and fight for her legacy."

Elizabeth Warren spelt it out: "With voting already underway for the 2020 elections, Ruthie's 'most fervent wish' was for her replacement not to be named 'until a new president is installed.' We must honor her wish."

Well sure.

And Abraham Lincoln's death bed wish was for the Senate to confirm Amy Coney Barrett as a Supreme Court justice. Several anonymous sources have confirmed it.

And I read somewhere that George Washington's last words were "Build that wall!"

But unfortunately, there is no "most fervent wish" clause in the United States Constitution.

The death of Justice Ruth Bader Ginsburg, 87, on Friday sent the Democrats into a terrible panic.

President Trump now has the opportunity to nominate a pro-life judge to replace the pro-abortion, left-lurching Ginsburg. This would tilt the court's balance 6-3 in favour of conservative judges.

"If they even TRY to replace RBG we burn the entire fucking thing down," tweeted left wing writer Reza Aslan.

Alsan also claims to be a "scholar of religions" – having converted from Islam to Christianity and back to Islam again. It seems that in all that chopping and changing, he missed the "love your enemies" part. But I digress.

Another leftist, with more than 15k followers, tweeted: "Fuck you Ruth Bader Ginsburg fuck you for not retiring under Obama fuck you for dying under Trump fuck you fuck you."

Punctuation is difficult when you're so worked up.

And I could quote the reaction of other prominent leftists to RBG's death, but you get the idea.

Once the temper tantrum was exhausted and the leftist tears had dried, the Democrats had to find an argument as to why Donald Trump should not be allowed to nominate a replacement, as the Constitution empowers him to do.

Unable to find any reason in law – a common but never insurmountable problem for the Left – progressives did what they always do; they urged people to think with their feelings and to reason with their emotions.

Afterall, who would not be deeply moved by an NPR story telling how "just days before her death, as her strength waned, Ginsburg dictated this statement to her granddaughter Clara Spera: 'My most fervent wish is that I will not be replaced until a new president is installed.'"

The revelation was followed by a parade of caring, compassionate Democrats solemnly insisting that the only decent thing – the only humane thing – to do was to honor Ginsburg's dying wish.

Actor Kumail Nanjiani said: "No matter where we go from here, this is a remarkably selfless statement to make on your deathbed."

Nanjiani – who would be better advised to stick to reading a script rather than writing his own material – did not say whether Ginsburg's "remarkably selfless" wish would have been the same had Obama been president.

Nor did he explain how using one's dying breath to engage in political plotting rather than to farewell family was "remarkably selfless".

But don't think. Only feel.

Author and feminist activist Gloria Steinem wrote: "We each can honor Ruth Bader Ginsburg by asking ourselves, 'What would Ruth do?'"

And don't think what Ruth would do. Feel it.

The danger of thought is that you might recall that Ruth was asked, just months before the 2016 election, if the Senate had an obligation to consider Obama's nominee to the Supreme Court to replace the deceased Antonin Scalia.

Ruth Ginsburg told The New York Times: "That's their job. There's nothing in the Constitution that says the President stops being the president in his last year."

But who wants to believe verified quotes advocating the law when you can instead choose to believe dramatic last gasp words and wishes based on hearsay? Remember, truth is felt.

The Founding Fathers had wishes. They wrote them down. We call it the Constitution.

And the Constitution of the United States doesn't play second fiddle to Ruth Ginsburg's last wish because the Supreme Court seat didn't belong to her.

But if you practice feeling rather than thinking, you can so cloud your judgement that it is possible to imagine Trump is a dictator for wanting to do what the Constitution says, while a Supreme Court justice is supreme leader who gets to decide who replaces her.

In a bid to safeguard abortion, the Democrats would taint the legacy of a revered Supreme Court justice by propagating a story that the judge's dying wish was for people to ignore the Constitution. Let that sink in.

And if we want to talk about dying wishes, we might consider that every aborted child's "dying wish" is for the Supreme Court of the United States to stop facilitating their painful, gruesome murders.

Meanwhile, given Joe Biden's condition, voters have a right to know his most fervent wish and which grandchild he has dictated it to since that is now the basis by which Democrats want to govern.

DONALD TRUMP IS ROBERT MUGABE?

I'm old enough to remember when journalists gave us the news and we added our own prejudice.

These days journalists report everything through the sieve of their own personal bias, so that what we ought to think about events is baked into the news.

Just ask ABC 7.30 host Leigh Sales. She'll tell you.

With US President Donald Trump refusing to concede election defeat, Sales tweeted: "Robert Mugabe keeps coming to mind."

The most obvious problem with Sale's in-depth, non-partisan analysisis that the Zimbabwean dictator, unlike Trump, never cried about rigged elections. That's because Mugabe was the one rigging the elections.

Mugabe won his nation's 2013 election after reportedly receiving more than 350,000 votes from people aged over 85 and 109,000 votes from people aged over 100 – in a nation where life expectancy at the time was 51.

Anyway, Joe Biden keeps coming to mind.

Another problem for Sales is that Mugabe didn't attempt to stay in power by challenging the validity of votes through legal channels open to him, as Trump is now doing. Mugabe instead used violent militia to silence his political opponents and to retain power.

I don't know why, but ANTIFA keeps coming to mind!

Zimbabwe's leader Robert Mugabe, unlike Trump, was a Marxist which is why the murdering, cheating thug was, at least in the beginning, a hero of the left.

And speaking of Marxists, the Democrats do come to mind. Actually, so does the ABC commentariat.

Donald Trump has always said he would accept the result of a ballot in which legal votes were counted. Robert Mugabe famously said that "only God" could remove him from office.

Hillary Clinton urging Joe Biden, before to the election, not to "concede under any circumstances" comes readily to mind.

Finally, what are the odds that the Leigh Sales and former US ambassador to the UN Samantha Power would both post tweets, within hours of each other, comparing Trump to Mugabe?

Sales tweeted "Mugabe comes to mind" soon after which Power tweeted "He's going full Robert Mugabe".

It's fun how the Twitterati sit in their tax-payer funded echo chamber, gleefully acknowledging one another's left-wing woke tweets.

I'm not for a second suggesting that one plagiarised the other. Not at all. But now that we've mentioned plagiarism, Joe Biden comes to mind.

But to say that Donald Trump reminds you of Robert Mugabe? Seriously? The left are losing their minds.

TONY ABBOTT: SKILLS AND EXPERIENCE STILL COUNT FOR SOMETHING – JUST

Wanted: Envoy to advise Government on trade and to promote opportunities for the United Kingdom in emerging markets post-Brexit.

The successful applicant will have voted 'yes' to gay marriage and preferably marched at a recent Gay and Lesbian Mardi Gras.

He or she (or they, in the case of a gender-neutral applicant) will be pro-abortion, with special consideration given to applicants who have actually had one.

Experience trading in climate doom and gloom is essential.

The successful candidate must be able to endure a prolonged political squeal from a woman, without looking at his watch.

A dislike of blue ties and of Donald Trump is highly desirable.

Actual skills would be a bonus but are not necessary.

Silly Tony Abbott – assuming a role representing the UK in trade required him to be an expert in trade, rather than an expert on diversity and inclusion.

Didn't the former Australian Prime Minister know, when applying for a job advising on trade, that how he voted on gay marriage was far more relevant than his experience in trade?

He really is a dinosaur.

Only a knuckle-dragging neanderthal would imagine qualifications meant more than views. In 2020, correct views (by which we mean Leftist views) are the qualification.

How will Mr Abbott negotiate fabulous trade deals if he is not an LGBTQ ally? The simple answer is that he cannot.

Conservative UK politician Caroline Nokes told reporters: "He's got very poor views on LGBTQ rights and I just don't think this is a man who should be anywhere near our Board of Trade."

If that's the standard then the Queen is not fit to advise herself. The Church of England, of which she is the head, still insists marriage is between a man and a woman.

Labour trade spokeswoman Emily Thornberry said: "I am disgusted that Boris Johnson thinks this offensive, leering, cantankerous, climate change denying, Trump-worshipping misogynist is the right person to represent our country overseas."

What I think she meant, but was unable to say for choking on woke, was: "I am disgusted that Boris Johnson thinks this Oxford-educated Rhodes scholar who, as Prime Minister of Australia, successfully negotiated free-trade deals with China, Japan and South Korea is the right person to represent our country overseas."

Her Labour Leader, Sir Keir Starmer, told Sky News: "I don't think he's the right person for the job and if I was the Prime Minister I wouldn't appoint him."

Then again, Sir Keir had no concerns about Jeremy Corbyn, so as a judge of character he makes a very fine Opposition leader – and likely will for many years to come.

First Minister of Scotland, Nicola Sturgeon, told Sky News: "If I had anything to do with that decision he wouldn't be a trade envoy" by which she meant "As First Minister of Scotland I don't get to do much."

Actor Sir Ian McKellen, of Lord of the Rings fame, said Mr Abbott ought not advise the government on trade because of his views on "abortion, climate change, gay people and women".

He forgot to mention Mr Abbott's views on Black Lives Matter, plastic straws, border control, the

Brisbane Broncos coaching vacancy and strawberry flavoured gelato – all of which likely disqualify

Mr Abbott from having insights on international trade.

Sir McKellen signed a letter that began: "As committed equality and environmental activists, we urge the government to reconsider its proposed appointment of Tony Abbott as a trade envoy to the UK Board of Trade".

Well who better to judge a trade envoy based on LGBTQ views than an environmental activist! Sorry, I mean a "committed" environmental activist.

You'd think Gandalf would have the last word on the issue. But you'd be forgetting a bitter character who failed to grasp his "precious" international role after leaving Kirribilli.

Kevin Rudd tweeted: "Just what you want as your pin-up boy for a modern, globalising, post-Brexit Britain: a rolled-gold misogynistic, climate change denialist, pioneer of 21st century knighthoods for the Antipodes. What on earth were the British Government thinking..."

The answer, of course, is that they weren't thinking of Mr Rudd.

Last night Downing Street confirmed Mr Abbott's appointment as trade advisor. It seems actual skills and experience still count for something. Just.

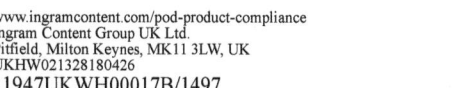

www.ingramcontent.com/pod-product-compliance
Ingram Content Group UK Ltd.
Pitfield, Milton Keynes, MK11 3LW, UK
UKHW021328180426
11947UKWH00017B/1497